Designmuseum

Book of 20TH Century

design

Dedicated to Elizabeth,

her sister Lucy and her two brothers Tom and Matthew

First published in 1998 by
The Overlook Press, Peter Mayer Publishers, Inc
Lewis Hollow Road
Woodstock, New York 12498

A CIP Cataloging-in-Publication Data for this book
is available from The Library of Congress.

Printed and bound in Italy

ISBN 0-87951-852-9

9 8 7 6 5 4 3 2 1

Managing Editor: Julian Flanders
Project Editor: Sarah Larter
Senior Art Editor: Zoë Maggs
Editor: Susie Duke
Page Layout: Jill Bennett
Picture co-ordination: Lorna Ainger
Production: Garry Lewis

Designmuseum

Book of 20TH Century

design

Catherine McDermott

THE OVERLOOK PRESS
WOODSTOCK & NEW YORK

contents

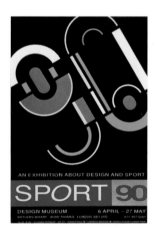

foreword

THE DESIGN MUSEUM seeks to create a new awareness of design and architecture among the general public. Through publications like this, it aims to demonstrate in a stimulating and accessible manner, how design and the built environment impact on the social, cultural and economic wellbeing of society. Unlike a traditional museum of the decorative arts, the Design Museum is a museum solely of the twentieth and twenty-first centuries, concerned exclusively with the products, technologies and buildings of the industrial and post-industrial world.

The Design Museum Book of Twentieth-Century Design introduces some of the seminal buildings, products and graphic designs of the twentieth century, reflecting the vast social and technological changes of the past hundred years. Divided into thirteen sections, it contains three hundred and sixty-two entries, illustrating those designs that have helped to shape our visual culture and built environment. The book presents the achievements of the great masters: architects and designers such as Marianne Brandt, Le Corbusier or Raymond Loewy, and explains clearly why these figures are regarded as important. But the book also focuses on humbler works by unknown designers. Throughout, the selection has been steered by the need to include alongside the great icons, certain products or buildings which may not be accustomed to the glare of the limelight but which have, nonetheless, served as useful barometers of twentieth-century thought and attitudes, be they a housing squat in Amsterdam or a disposable package for a breakfast cereal.

As we approach the end of the century, this publication is intended to serve as an introduction to some of the important design movements of a century, which like no other, has had difficulty in defining and evaluating its achievements. A century that has experienced great bursts of Utopianism, and yet has wrestled with a deep sense of disquiet over the destruction of the natural landscape and the experiences of two world wars. Despite such seeming contradictions, one thing, however, is certain: the twentieth century will be remembered as *the* century of mass communication, mass consumption, mass production – and mass design.

Paul W Thompson.

DIRECTOR, DESIGN MUSEUM

fashion

EDWARDIAN ERA

JAEGER

THE BEATLES

FASHION AT THE BEGINNING of the twentieth century reflected the old order, with formal clothes for men and tight-corsetted silhouettes for women still the prevailing taste. There were, however, signs of change in the taste for artistic dress that was made popular by the reforming spirit of the Arts and Crafts Movement and the even more dramatic impact of World War One. Women called on to do traditional men's work were required to wear functional clothing as a patriotic duty and that experience was to change attitudes to clothing forever. At the same time the ideas of Modernism ushered in a demand for simpler, streamlined ideas which suited the new spirit of the times. In Russia, for example, the artistic avant-garde designed clothes that would reflect the goals of the revolution: minimalist designs using bold geometric fabrics which were modern, practical and functional. These changes came together in the fashion mainstream in the form of the century's most influential designer, Coco Chanel. Inspired by English menswear, she combined this tradition with clothes that were simple, easy to wear, sporty and relaxed. Her clothes cut all ties with the past, broke away from a fussy outline and created a look for the modern woman that remains inspirational to this day. Hollywood also played a key role in popularizing these ideas, and at the same time focused on the traditional elements of glamour and couture that never disappeared. After the constraints of the World War Two this theme reappeared with a vengeance in the "New Look" of Christian Dior. His full skirts and tight bodices were a revelation to a generation used to rationing and coupons and inspired not only affluent women but a new and powerful consumer group, the teenager. Now for the first time teenagers created an original style of dressing that broke the dominance of fashion designers, who had hitherto set the pace. That revolution was to have important repercussions in the 1960s when young people rebelled against the conservative and oppressive ideas of their parents and liberal reform movements throughout the world questioned all aspects of the status quo and demanded immediate change. The movement for civil liberties, the anti-Vietnam War demonstrations, the 1968 revolution in Paris and the Prague Spring produced a generation of people committed to challenging social norms and conventions. Young people experimented with sex, drugs and their personal appearance. These experiments had a profound effect on fashion. The mini skirt was the most popular expression of the new, more relaxed attitude to the body. However, some fashion designers like Paco Rabanne went further, producing topless and transparent outfits. During the same period the Gay Liberation and feminist movements demanded a public space for alternative attitudes to sexuality and lifestyles. By the 1970s themes of androgyny and cross dressing moved from the worlds of subcultures and pop music into the mainstream.

The economic recession of the 1970s meant that many design areas moved toward the classic, the safe and the conventional, and fashion was no exception. However dramatic change was about to come. Japanese designers, such as Issey Miyake and Yohji Yamamoto, were exploring alternatives to the tight silhouette, popularized in the mainstream by such television series as *Dallas*. At the same time Italian designers such as Giorgio Armani reworked the formal tailored jacket in soft unconventional fabrics. One undeniable influence came, however, from a more surprising source. The Punk revolution in Britain was not only about music and anti-establishment lifestyles, it also produced a new attitude to clothes. In 1971 Vivienne Westwood and Malcolm McLaren opened the first of a series of shops in London's Kings Road. Selling ripped and torn t-shirts, and clothes with references to bondage, they delighted in anarchy, irony and the Punk principle of "Do-It-Yourself". London led the way in new style directions and if you wanted to know what was directional and important in fashion you read two style magazines: *The Face* and *i-D*. London set the pace and in the early 1980s Vivienne Westwood took these ideas and placed them in the international arena of Paris couture with a series of seminal catwalk shows that would change the fashion map forever. Widely dismissed as unwearable and outrageous, she nonetheless introduced a series of original fashion ideas, including underwear as outerwear, fall-down socks, uniforms, pattern and the mini-crini that were

GIORGIO ARMANI

imitated by designers all over the world. The rest of the fashion world took note and produced variants of these themes that produced inspirational clothes by leading designers such as Christian Lacroix and Romeo Gigli. The decade of the 1980s became the decade of serious devotion to designer clothes.

Other important fashion themes at the end of the 1990s include the quest for wearability in clothes, stylish clothes that are both comfortable and relaxed. At the same time there is also a desire for individual character in fashion, but what often appears to be the idiosyncratic expression of the wearer is actually a designer look. Interestingly the consumer still wants an individual look, for example the recent trend for secondhand recycled clothing, but it often appears to be less the work of a designer and more that of a stylist. In the 1990s the arrival of new synthetic materials and information technology is also changing the fashion industry. These new materials include paper with felted and bonded fabrics and new innovations to Lycra. Also important are a new generation of fibres and fabric finishes, which include a Teflon finish for wool that provides a fully breathable membrane, making it possible to produce a waterproof cashmere raincoat and offering the consumer and the designer new possibilities for fashion.

PRINTED FABRIC

NEW FABRIC

The Edwardian Era

DATE: 1901–10

Toward the end of the 1860s, the fashion for huge crinolines disappeared. The fashion for restrictive women's clothing did not, however, disappear but enjoyed a final flourish in the fashions of the Edwardian era. In the years leading up to World War One, women identified the dramatic curves of the hourglass with luxury, status and class and it therefore remained the style of the rich and aristocratic, inevitably filtering down to the middle classes. These outfits state clearly that the wearer leads a life of formal leisure supported by money and staff, bypassing any practical or functional demands of her clothing.

The level of applied decoration on these two dresses also places them within the tradition of late nineteenth-century and early twentieth-century decoration. Naturalistic flowers, ruffles, elaborate pleating, embroidery and lace contribute to a sumptuously layered effect that reflect the domestic interiors – also the preserve of women's taste – of the period.

Aesthetic Dress

DATE: 1900S

From the 1860s, a dress reform movement for women argued that the traditional restrictive corset and crinoline clothing of the period was unhealthy and cumbersome. Women started to demand clothing that could comfortably be worn for sports, cycling and other outdoor activities. Although this movement was generally viewed as extreme and eccentric, some of their ideas filtered through into mainstream fashion.

The artistic movements of the late nineteenth century encouraged women to adopt the loose flowing garments inspired by the medieval period from which they drew so much inspiration in their art and architecture. In the 1860s, Jane Morris – the wife of William – was famously photographed in dresses which, although conventional by twentieth-century standards, used flowing fabrics and ignored the fashion for tightly defined waists.

Aesthetic dress became a combination of the practical and the artistic, which aimed at establishing for the wearer an association with the new and the daring. By the turn of the century this fashion had been reproduced by many commercial outlets including Liberty's, the famous London department store, which produced a whole range of dresses in this style, such as the 1905 design pictured here, bringing the avant-garde into the mainstream.

Savile Row Tailoring

British tailored clothes of the nineteenth century, particularly those designed for sporting activities, were widely admired for their quality and functionality. Tailoring as a profession emerged in the late seventeenth century when it was required for formal attire and horse riding. Stiff fabrics, such as tweeds and worsted, were sewn together using seams and darts to produce jackets reinforced with a firm structure of padding and interfacing. By the twentieth century this tradition had developed a reputation for producing some of the world's finest tailored suits, an industry centred in London and more particularly in Savile Row.
This famous street in the city's West End is still the home of traditional tailors including Welsh and Jeffries, Maurice Sewell and Norton and Sons.

The classic Savile Row suit is designed to fit each individual client and is cut and constructed by hand. It takes up to eighty hours to create the template needed to create a master pattern for the client and to finish the suit by hand. There are three categories of tailoring: those made exclusively by hand; semi-bespoke, which is a combination of manufacture by hand and machine; and ready-to-wear, which is made by machine to fit a standard size.

The classic fabric for tailoring is wool cloth; other fabrics simply don't possess the durability and versatility needed for fine tailoring, although tweed, flannel and gaberdine also have the strength and body which enable them to hold a shape. The Savile Row suit has come to represent a quality and elegance that has less to do with fashion than tradition. The Duke of Windsor, seen here in 1938, epitomized this style of dress.

Coco Chanel

DATE: 1920s

DESIGNER: Coco Chanel (1883–1971)

Gabrielle "Coco" Chanel is quite simply the most famous fashion designer of the twentieth century. She was the embodiment of the modern woman. Her clothes were based on the simple idea of producing comfortable and streamlined garments that broke away from the prevailing taste for the fussy and the elaborate. In this sense she is the fashion equivalent to the great designers of the Modern movement in the 1920s.

Her lifestyle is part of the same legend. She was brought up in an orphanage and used her many affairs with influential men to advance both her career and her financial position. Easy wearability was the key to her success. Her clothes were sporty, relaxed and well-suited to the new outdoor life promoted as a vital ingredient of modern living in the twentieth century. Significantly, Chanel is also credited with having turned the suntan into a vital fashion accessory.

Many of her ideas were adapted from men's clothing and the tradition of English tailoring, which she learnt at first hand from raiding the wardrobe of her English lover, the Duke of Westminster. Her classic suit represents this new approach. It looks simple with a geometric, box-like cardigan jacket worn over a short skirt, but she also introduced to this aesthetic the principle of couture: her clothing may have been simple, but cut, finish and fabric were always of the highest quality. Chanel also reduced her colour range to a palette of greys, black and cream with the occasional use of red.

Burberry

DATE: 1920S

The British Burberry is now
synonymous with the waterproof
mackintosh. Styled like an army
overcoat, it became one of the most
familiar fashion accessories of the
twentieth century. Its origins go
back to the 1860s when Thomas
Burberry, the founder of Burberrys,
started his own draper's business
and developed a waterproof cloth
that was hard-wearing, impenetrable
to rain, yet cool and light to wear.
The story has it that although
Burberry called the cloth gaberdine,
the name was changed to Burberry
by one of its most famous
customers, Edward VII, who on rainy
days simply called for his
"Burberry".

By the early twentieth century
Burberry raincoats had become
standard outdoor clothing as well as
offering specialist protection for
sportsmen and explorers. The
explorer Scott and his team, for
example, wore specially designed
Burberry windproof suits on their ill-
fated Antarctic trip. Other versions
of the coat were designed as school
uniforms. The coats appealed both
to men and women: belted and with
the collar upturned, the Burberry
became a cliché of the sexy,
debonair film hero and heroine. The
private detective, the lone hero of
Hollywood movies, had to wear the
obligatory rainwear. Its role as a
contemporary classic, however, has
been somewhat superseded by
waterproof rivals such as the
Barbour jacket.

BURBERRY
BOOK,
patterns and
prices, post
free on men-
tion of the
"Queen."

Jaeger

DATE: 1920S

A movement emerged during the twentieth century that espoused the view that clothes were not just about fashion but should be part of a rational healthy lifestyle. These ideas had their roots in the work of nineteenth-century dress reformers, in much the same spirit as English writer Edward Carpenter, for example, had promoted the open-toed leather sandal for men. These clothes became an important statement of social belief and attracted a great deal of sympathy from individuals who felt fashion was a distraction from life's more important issues.

Using the same rationale, the German-born Dr Jaeger developed a new open-weave fabric for undergarments which were advertised with an emphasis on healthy living. A wider range of clothing, which went under the same name, was commercially successful in establishing a reputation for practical, well-made and durable outdoor wear. Inevitably Jaeger looked to the wider tradition of such garments; thus the tweed suit, such as the 1929 version seen here, using woven Scottish cloth, recommended itself as a hard-wearing and practical accessory for outdoor life. Jaeger continues to be a successful brand today.

Tailored Coat
R950
(Half lined)

West of England,
Scotch & Yorkshire
Tweeds
Fawn, Brown,
Mauve, & Grey

94/6

Costume
D105
(Coat lined)

Fawn, Mauve, Grey,
Brown, & Tan
Tweeds

79/6

14

Coat
P532
(Half lined)
Belt from side fastening
with slide

West of England,
Scotch & Yorkshire
Tweeds
Fawn, Brown,
Mauve, & Grey

63/-

Sheath Dress

DATE: 1920S–30S

The sheath dress of the 1920s and 1930s still retains the power to shock. Made from skin-tight fabric cut on the bias, the dress clings to the body outline and gives the impression of near nudity. Every contour of the female form can be seen and this sleek streamlined image is reinforced by the use of shiny reflective fabrics such as satin. The sheath dress is the fashion equivalent of the Modernist tubular steel chair. They are both about minimalism and purity of form, creating effects that have the technical precision of the machine. With her white hair – the effect of science not nature – cut in a geometric bob, Jean Harlow epitomizes the look of the new *femme fatale* of the twentieth century.

Trouser Suit

Coco Chanel was the first designer to adopt men's tailoring when she wore the breeches and tweed shooting jackets of her lover, the Duke of Westminster. She adapted many of the lessons she learnt from wearing these clothes for her own couture range of the 1920s and was thus responsible for drawing a direct line from the English tailored man's suit to Paris couture and then Hollywood.

By the 1930s, trousers had crossed over to the female wardrobe and the trouser suit had been adopted by some of Hollywood's most famous film stars, including Marlene Dietrich, Katharine Hepburn and Greta Garbo. In their films and press photographs they created a fashionable sexual ambiguity, reworking an old device of using men's clothes to enhance femininity, in the same way that actresses often wore oversized male pyjamas in the movies.

Katharine Hepburn in particular used the trouser suit to project the modern image of the new American woman as an independent person who could operate on her own terms in the male professional world.

The new trouser suits needed some adaptation for the female form. The trousers needed the fly piece removed and tailored waistline darts introduced. In the jacket, the stiffened men's interfacing was replaced by two layers of fabrics.

Leather Jacket

Fashion has a long tradition of appropriating items of functional clothing for more general usage. The brown leather flying jacket, shown here, was worn as regulation issue by the British Royal Air Force crew of a Hampden bomber in 1941. Such jackets are among the most popular and widespread garments of the postwar period. Designed to protect the early flyers from the cold temperatures of the cockpit, the jackets were fur-lined and zipped to the neck and came to be worn by flying crews all over the world. The durability of leather also protected the wearer from injury, making the jackets a popular choice for early motorcyclists. More than this, however, leather was masculine and sexy and could be worn functionally or informally with jeans and T-shirts. More recently the leather flying jacket has become a unisex garment worn by men and women.

One of the most important challenges to the restraints and conventions of nineteenth-century dress was not fashion-led but came about through the historical circumstances of two world wars. The women's movement and other dress reformers may have argued for changes to women's clothes but it was the onset of war that rapidly advanced their cause. Quite simply, women were now needed for jobs that had traditionally been the preserve of men – and they needed functional work clothes to do this work, as demonstrated in this photograph of women working for the Land Army in 1943. Not only did it become acceptable for women to wear these clothes, it was seen as a patriotic duty. In the years after the war women were inevitably reluctant to return to the conventions of formal dress and the way was opened for women to introduce items such as men's jackets and trousers into their everyday lives.

Workwear

DATE: 1940S

The New Look

DATE: 1947

DESIGNER: Christian Dior
(1905–57)

On February 2, 1947, Christian Dior's collection was dubbed the "New Look" by American fashion editor Carmel Snow. It was more than a new direction in style, it was one of the truly original moments in twentieth-century fashion. Dior's designs cut straight across the social feelings and the fashion of the time. In 1947, the general mood was still towards austerity and the need to sacrifice personal needs. Much of Europe lay in ruins and the slow process of rebuilding was a daunting programme. Many felt that during such a period Dior's look was inappropriate.

When Dior's extravagant dresses were shown on the catwalk, riots ensued: women wearing the clothes were attacked in the streets, while the American ambassador declared the style "unpatriotic". Nonetheless, Dior had struck deep feelings – after the trauma of the war, women wanted a moment of extravagance.

Interestingly, Dior chose not to look into the future for his radical collection but to the *belle époque* tradition of the 1880s, a style which saw the female body incarcerated in steel corsets and swathed in metres of material. It was ironic that Dior, from the rarefied world of Paris couture, produced the first postwar rebel look – a look which later found its way into the high streets via the rock and roll skirts worn by teenagers of the 1950s.

Teenage Consumer

DATE: 1950S

In 1959, the London Press Exchange – then one of Britain's largest advertising agencies – commissioned Mark Abrams to write a seminal study of key shifts in the consumer market. Called *The Teenage Consumer*, Abrams' research highlighted the new postwar phenomenon of teenage taste and style. Abrams, who had studied the social attitudes of working-class groups before and during the war, came to an important conclusion: that the new teenage market of the 1950s was dominated by the style aspirations of young, working-class people.

One of the most visible new aspects of teenage culture were the Teddy Boys. Wearing American-inspired "DA" haircuts, long drape jackets, crepe-soled shoes and tight trousers, they represented something totally new in British fashion. Such clothes in the 1950s were highly individual and even confrontational for a society that viewed young people's independence as a social problem. A Teddy Boy outfit also required serious commitment: the average cost of the outfit was around £20 – roughly £700 at today's prices. It is a look which has gone down in history as a classic heroic style for working-class teenagers.

1950s Casual Wear

DATE: 1950S

The rise of a new and affluent culture in postwar America encouraged informality and a more relaxed way of life. An obvious manifestation of this was the development of the first youth culture to seek new ways of dressing, independent of adult fashion. The first items to capture the imagination of this new market were sportswear – items like the sneaker, which developed from the athletic running shoe – and practical, easy-to-wear work clothes, such as denim jeans and the T-shirt vest seen here worn by James Dean, whose style of dress typified the 1950s casual look.

Worn by manual workers for their cheapness, comfort and durability, these associations were also attractive to American bohemians and artists looking for a dress code that would reinforce their image as creative radicals in what still remained a deeply conservative society. It was unsurprising, then, that in the artistic communities of New York, white T-shirts, sneakers and jeans were worn by artists such as Jackson Pollock. Jeans – which had been produced by companies such as Levi's for over one hundred years – and T-shirts were both authentically American dress.

Jackie Kennedy

DATE: 1950S–60S

DESIGNER: Oleg Cassini (born 1913)

When Jackie Kennedy became America's First Lady she immediately became one of the most influential fashion leaders in the world. Both young and beautiful, she stepped onto the world's centre stage and influenced the look of a whole generation of women. Initially criticized for wearing the clothes of leading French couturiers, Jackie Kennedy looked for an American replacement and chose Oleg Cassini as the official dressmaker to the White House.

Cassini was brought up in Florence where his mother ran an exclusive dress shop. The family emigrated to America in 1938 where Cassini worked as a costume designer in Hollywood, creating many of the clothes worn by his wife, the actress Gene Tierney. Cassini's clothes for Jackie Kennedy were chic and stylish, most notably his trademark suit and pillbox hat which gave her a formal but modern image for the early 1960s. She is seen here arriving in London in 1962 wearing the characteristic hat and an ice-cream pink wool bouclé suit.

Mini-Skirt

DATE: 1960S

Whether it was actually invented in London is not clear, but what is certain is that the mini-skirt came to represent the image of London's Swinging Sixties and became the most popular expression of a new relaxed attitude to the body.

Jean Shrimpton, shown here at the Melbourne Cup in 1965, caused a sensation when she appeared to present the fashion prize to the best-dressed lady attending the race meeting. In contrast to the prevalent dress codes, the "Shrimp" came hatless, gloveless and minus stockings, as well as wearing a mini.

The mini also represented some fundamental changes in fashion retailing. When America's *Time* magazine published its famous map of London in 1964 it did not illustrate the historical sites of interest but the new boutiques of Carnaby Street and Kings Road. These independent fashion outlets, including *Granny Takes A Trip*, *Hung On You* and *Lord John*, challenged the dominance of the larger department stores and more traditional fashion retailers. The most famous of these shops was *Bazaar*, opened by Mary Quant in 1957. More than any other designer, Quant popularized the mini-skirt in Britain and led the way in designing clothes specifically for young people. Although the mini-skirt gained wider acceptance – by the end of the decade even the Queen wore shorter skirt lengths – it always looked better on skinny, young and trendy models such as Jean Shrimpton and Twiggy.

As teenagers during the 1950s, the Beatles were part of the same revolution in style and culture that was, albeit slowly, affecting British life. As a port, their home town of Liverpool was always more open to outside influences than other English provincial cities. Deeply taken with American music and style, they first adopted the leather jackets and slicked back hair worn by 1950s cult heroes such as Marlon Brando and Elvis Presley.

For John Lennon, his seminal experience of the period was listening to Elvis sing *Heartbreak Hotel* in 1956 on Radio Luxembourg. There was the further influence of Liverpool Art College, which Lennon attended, where he met another early band member, the painter Stuart Sutcliffe. It was Sutcliffe's German girlfriend, Astrid Kirchherr, a Berlin art student, who introduced the Beatles to the famous "mop-top" haircut, a variant of the "Beatnik" style then popular among young students.

In 1962, manager Brian Epstein proposed a new image for the Beatles. They were to wear sharp grey wool suits, cropped collarless jackets, tight trousers and Chelsea boots. The Beatles swapped the uniform of American working-class teenagers for a new, confident and uniquely British style.

The Beatles

DATE: 1960s

Hippie Culture

DATE: 1960s

Towards the end of the 1960s the social revolution of the decade began to take a different direction. The consumer culture of Pop, with its emphasis on the throwaway and the instant, suddenly found itself challenged in a number of significant ways. Things changed fundamentally in Britain with the massive expansion of higher education places and the availability of grants. These new students became part of a widespread movement seeking alternative lifestyles and attitudes, in which clothing and image were fundamental. The search for spiritual priorities was closely linked to the widespread experimentation with drugs and a sympathy with the religions and culture of the East. Ethnic and Indian clothing became fashionable and, to reinforce the power of the individual, an eclectic mix incorporating quirky secondhand items became part of the new hippie culture.

The Chinese Revolution

DATE: 1940s

Mao Tse Tung (1893–1976) has been described as the most influential fashion designer of the twentieth century, because it was his revolution that made the uniform of the single-breasted collared jacket, loose trousers and soft-peaked hat obligatory clothing for literally millions of Chinese men and women. These clothes became one of the most powerfully iconic outfits of the twentieth century. In the 1960s they were worn by Western political radicals, and items such as the hat became a popular fashion accessory among young liberals in the 1960s. The suit in soft, cotton fabric has since become a fashion perennial and inspired designers including Issey Miyake and Comme des Garçons.

Mao was the great non-European Marxist who stressed the role of the peasantry in the Revolution rather than the industrial worker – whom traditional Marxists believed would engineer social change. Mao ran China as a totalitarian dictatorship and the idea of a uniform for the people, with its underlying message of order and discipline and, more importantly, the suppression of the individual, reflected the regime's ideology.

Although the idea of loose soft cotton trousers and jacket had some links with traditional Chinese peasant clothing, the outfit owed much more to the clothing adopted by the early Russian revolutionaries, including the "Lenin"-style hat.

Punk

DATE: 1970S

In 1971, Malcolm McLaren and Vivienne Westwood opened the first of a series of shops on the same site at 436 Kings Road, London. Believing that culture and style in London had reached a dead end, they went in search of a different direction. In 1975 they opened Sex, a shop that sold provocative soft-porn rubber clothes and accessories. Two years later this was followed by Seditionaries, London's first authentic Punk shop. McLaren and Westwood acted as a catalyst for a revolution in British music, fashion, design and culture – Punk.

   McLaren had always encouraged like-minded young people to hang out at the shop and on Saturdays it acted as a kind of club for those also searching for an alternative identity. Punk sought a focus away from the tail end of the despised hippie movement: McLaren provided one. He had always loved the antics and slogans of the Dadaists and direct confrontation with the mainstream. The Punk band, the Sex Pistols, which included John Lyndon, show here in 1976, gave him the direction to develop a new attitude. An anti-fashion style quickly followed: ripped and torn clothes fastened with safety pins, aggressive tribal make-up, black lipstick and brightly coloured hair. Westwood elaborated on these themes in her own designs for the Sex Pistols which included bondage trousers, "Destroy" T-shirts and workmen's boots for both sexes.

This 1987 image shows the New York hip-hop–rap bands The Beastie Boys and Run DMC, whose distinct identity highlights a youth culture which requires specific dress codes. In this context trainers have become especially significant, the key accessory which marks the tribe to which you belong.

They have their origin in the development of footwear for sport. From the 1940s sport shoes such as the sneaker and then the trainer were worn as leisure wear, reflecting the new relaxed lifestyle of postwar America. This began a key shift in the way people used clothing: the cross-over of footwear and other sportswear from one activity to another and the idea that you didn't have to pursue a sport to wear the clothing. Now the styling and association of the trainer was more important than its original intended use. Today what was originally designed as a high-tech and specialized sporting shoe has become a key item in the development of street style, street gangs, music fans and surfers, each selecting a particular brand as a tribal sign and wearing the appropriate sports clothing to complete the image. Major manufacturers such as Nike and Adidas quickly responded to this "street style" by developing new versions of trainers which are deliberately targeted at the youth market through their sponsorship of youth icons like Michael Jordan, Magic Johnson, and Prince Naseem.

The main players in this industry have now built up a billion dollar industry exploiting the nuances of styling and design that are so crucial in this market.

Sportswear

DATE: 1980s

Japanese Design

DATE: 1986

DESIGNER: Yohji Yamamoto
(born 1943)

Until the beginning of the 1980s, the concept of Japanese fashion design in the context of the international market simply did not exist. Integral to the increasing awareness of Japanese fashion designers has been Yohji Yamamoto.

Yamamoto studied fashion in Tokyo under Chie Koike, who, having studied with Yves Saint Laurent, provided a link with the world of Paris couture. Yamamoto was, therefore, able to combine a knowledge of the European market and the growing internationalization of his home country to produce clothes that were radically new and yet nonetheless essentially Japanese. He developed a unique style which broke away from the predominance of closely fitted, tailored fashion, introducing a looser feel to the cut of clothes by draping and layering. Yamamoto's simple, minimalist effects relied on the quality and the feel of fabrics, which also made his clothes extremely difficult to copy. He viewed clothes as sculptural pieces, their pleats and folds producing eye-catching forms which shaped the body in a way which was reminiscent of the traditional Japanese kimono but which was nonetheless relevant to a contemporary lifestyle.

New and innovative fabrics have always been the touchstone of Yamamoto's work. Recent designs have included a series of garments that are difficult to recognize as conventional clothes until worn, when they fall around the body to produce sculptural effects that have been widely imitated by other designers but never matched. Along with fellow Japanese designers, Issey Miyake and Rei Kawabuko of Comme des Garçons, Yamamoto has revolutionized fashion design.

Giorgio Armani

DATE: 1989

DESIGNER: Giorgio Armani
(born 1935)

In the postwar period, Italian design attracted international attention for its creativity and originality: fashion design was no exception. During the 1970s, Giorgio Armani ensured that Italian fashion design would continue to occupy centre stage. Armani revolutionized women's and men's tailoring by removing the traditional stuffing from jackets and by making suits in lightweight fabrics, such as wool and viscose mixes, to create a softer and more relaxed style.

Soft fabrics for tailoring require extra care in the cutting, pattern construction and stitching so they don't stretch out of shape. Armani concentrated on the signatures of bespoke tailoring – the careful construction, the hand-made buttons, hand-stitched edges and interesting linings – but created a new, casual look by using velvet and soft fabrics for tailoring. These new tailored jackets were almost more like shirts and worked best when worn with simple T-shirts or fitted knitwear, such as the ubiquitous black polo neck. Armani epitomized the classic 1980s style and, more than anyone else, he broke down the dividing line between daywear and evening wear, and between the formal and the casual, fusing these elements into a single style.

Androgyny

DATE: 1980s

For decades, androgyny – the merging of traditional gender appearances – had remained a subcultural trend, marginalized to the private world of members' bars and clubs. By the late 1960s, however, it began to enter the mainstream. Transvestism and androgyny were made fashionable by Andy Warhol and his coterie of "superstars" who featured in films such as *Chelsea Girls* and *Trash*. Many rock musicians began to question concepts of masculinity through their dress and use of make-up over the coming decade. David Bowie and other figures of the Glam Rock movement helped to make bisexuality chic and influenced many fields of design including fashion and graphics. In the early 1980s these themes found expression once again with the emergence of the New Romantics focused on the clubs of London. An important figure in this context was Boy George who, with his friend Marilyn, turned a lifestyle of dressing up in women's clothes into a public career as a pop star. Boy George wore make-up, adapted items of ethnic dress, such as deadlocks, and converted the whole package into a trend in which androgyny became a fashion statement.

Costume for Madonna

DATE: 1990

DESIGNER: Jean-Paul Gaultier
(born 1952)

During the 1980s, a number of openly gay figures became highly influential through their pop videos, fashion designs, theatre and dance presentations. The pop singer Boy George, the dancer and choreographer Michael Clark, the performance artist Leigh Bowery and the film-maker John Maybury have been particularly important in pushing a gay sensibility toward the mainstream.

But the most important figure to appropriate gay culture has undoubtedly been Madonna. Through her enormous fame, she has been able to borrow ideas from the periphery and place them at the centre of contemporary culture. Her use of imagery, drawn from sadomasochistic and fetishistic sexual practice, has entered the mainstream discourse through her videos and most notoriously through her *Sex* book.

In 1990 Madonna commissioned Jean-Paul Gaultier to design the costumes for her *Blonde Ambition* tour. Gaultier has redefined notions of gender and sexuality through his clothing. He has designed skirts for men and pinstripe suits for women. His longstanding fascination with underwear has produced outfits which are little more than bras, corsets and suspenders, a look which was worn to great effect by Madonna. Gaultier has always looked to street-style and nightlife culture for inspiration. He has transformed fetish clothing into items of high fashion, combining, for example, traditional suits with rubber opera gloves and cod-pieces.

Slogan T-Shirt

DATE: 1984

DESIGNER: Katherine Hamnett (born 1948)

This image of Katherine Hamnett meeting Prime Minister Margaret Thatcher was taken in 1984 at a Downing Street reception to celebrate British Fashion Week. In her regal velvet robes, Thatcher, who was effecting her own political and economic revolution, makes an interesting contrast to Katherine Hamnett, who staged something of a publicity coup by wearing sneakers and one of her trademark slogan T-shirts, and by cross-questioning the Prime Minister on the effects of acid rain. Hamnett had worked on a number of slogan T-shirts inspired by the anti-nuclear women's protests at the Greenham Common airbase in England. Although Hamnett was deeply committed to ecological and peace movements, the meeting may have been less of a culture clash than it first appeared. Throughout the 1980s, Hamnett's fashion company proved hugely successful in selling a range of crumpled jumpsuits and casual suits to the new affluent professionals who were doing so well in Thatcher's Britain.

Printed Fabric

DATE: 1989

DESIGNER: Paul Smith
(born 1946)

Paul Smith brought about a significant shift in attitude to British menswear during the 1980s. Traditionally an extremely conservative market, Paul Smith introduced a range of classic men's clothes with a twist that gave his designs a freshness and edge that quickly attracted sales both in his home market and abroad, particularly in Japan. Paul Smith took the standard office uniform – the suit, the shirt and the tie – and introduced new fabrics and choices of colour that gradually won over his customers.

Smith had identified an important gap in the market – the new affluent professional men of the 1980s who wanted to look serious for business and the office but did not want to dress in the obligatory drab dark suit. With this design strategy as his mainstay he was able to develop more adventurous lines including his trademark patterned shirts of this period. Often printed in "Day-Glo" colours with 3D versions of fruit, flowers and vegetables, these shirts echoed the tradition of the 1960s and the 1980s fashion for colour, pattern and decoration. Now the young city highflyer could wear a suggestion of radical chic but remain perfectly safe in the knowledge that to wear Paul Smith was a mark of excellent taste.

John Galliano

DATE: 1997

DESIGNER: John Galliano
(born 1960)

John Galliano was part of the British fashion new wave of the 1980s. A graduate of St Martin's School of Art in London, he was an extremist who saw the potential for turning clothing into subversion. Although such experimentation continues to inform his work, Galliano has since moved on to become a designer of international stature – so much so, in fact, that in 1996 he was appointed chief designer to Dior, one of the world's most prestigious fashion houses and one of the most coveted design jobs in the world. Galliano has been chosen to revitalize the rather stuffy world of French couture with his extraordinarily original talent. Like other British contemporaries, his ideas derive from stories, from a narrative of cultural fragments that inspire him, including the late eighteenth century and the French Revolution.

Vivienne Westwood

DATE: 1996

DESIGNER: Vivienne Westwood (born 1941)

Vivienne Westwood is one of the world's fashion superstars. She has come to embody those elements of British creativity – the cultural export of ideas, style, anarchy, history, irony and multi-layers of culture – that have inspired new international directions. However, this was not always the case. When, in 1990, John Fairchild, editor of the tough trade paper, *Women's Wear Daily*, named her as one of the six most important fashion designers in the world, it marked a change in her reputation – Westwood's contribution to fashion design was at last taken seriously.

There is an exploratory edge to Westwood's work, a risk element that has influenced clothes from the most expensive of couture to the high street. Her genius includes a new approach to the cut of clothes and the impact of her influential ideas such as underwear as outerwear, tights under jackets, the "mini-crini" skirt and the boned corset using eighteenth-century baroque prints.

Westwood's approach is rooted in history and this preoccupation reflects the strengths and obsessions of the most creative forms of British design. Her research is in the great museums of London, such as the Victoria and Albert and the Wallace Collection.

For Westwood, fashion is a way of reappraising history: she embodies the idea that the British creative tradition is literary rather than visual. Indeed Westwood's starting points are words not pictures. Her clothes are quintessentially British and more than any single individual, she has helped place London as the world's centre for leading-edge fashion.

Synthetic Materials

DATE: 1990s

The invention of synthetic materials has offered the consumer new levels of comfort and functionality. This ongoing process of technological innovation since the beginning of the twentieth century has become an important fashion theme. Two companies producing new synthetic fabrics are Dupont and Courtaulds. Their development of high-tech fibres has helped to shift fashion emphasis from innovative cut to innovative cloth. Dupont, famous for discovering nylon in 1938, introduced Lycra as the stretch fabric of the 1980s and the company continues to develop improved versions. Courtaulds launched Tencel, produced from cellulose of harvested, managed trees. It is a soft, supple fabric with a lustre finish, offers the qualities of silk or cotton, can breathe like natural fabrics, but is more durable and easy to wash.

Other new fabrics include Berghaus's outdoor fabric, Polartec, made from recycled plastic bottles; W.L. Gore's Gore-Tex, a thin membrane applied to any cloth, which prevents water penetration but, through its micro pores, allows moisture to escape; and a material with microscopic holes, launched by the swimwear manufacturer Speedo, which allows all-over tanning. In addition to new fibre sources, Scientists are working on genetic modification of natural fibres. In the garment shown here, the British designer Hussein Chalayan has used Tyvek paper, originally used for envelopes. He has compensated for the non-stretch element of paper by reinforcing it with special cutting and stretching techniques.

Alexander McQueen

DATE: 1997

DESIGNER: Alexander McQueen (born 1969)

One of the 1990s generation of radical young British fashion designers, Alexander McQueen started as an apprentice to Gieves and Hawkes, one of Savile Row's famous tailors. He then borrowed money to complete a postgraduate fashion course at St Martin's School of Art in London, where his work caught the eye of Isabella Blow, a well-known patron of young fashion designers. She bought his collection and ensured that his work, with its themes concentrating on the body and sabotage of tradition, attracted media attention. Blow recognized in the young McQueen the raw energy of style that provided a new look for the 1990s. His designs provided stunning images for the press – most notably his bumster trousers, cut to reveal the cleavage of the buttocks. In 1997 McQueen was appointed head of design at Givenchy in Paris. It was a shock move: Hubert de Givenchy represented the highest echelons of Paris couture, but it was felt to have lost its way, to be conservative and staid. McQueen brought radical anti-fashion into the mainstream, and did nothing to ease the transition, deliberately playing on his working-class origins. Asked to comment on Givenchy talent, he famously replied "What talent?" Nonetheless, his work revived interest in Givenchy, where he works closely with a small team of British collaborators, including stylist Katy Englander, art director Simon Costin, who has produced jewellery made from animal body parts, and hat maker Philip Treacey, who transformed the hat into an art form. The influence of Costin and Treacey can be seen here.

architecture

THE FORSTER HOUSE

GLASGOW SCHOOL OF ART

CASTLE DROGO

ARCHITECTURE IS GENERALLY REGARDED as the mother of the arts, fostered in antiquity and traditionally considered to be the most prestigious artistic profession, free from the lowly trade associations design may have. Architecture has always carried with it more educational and professional possibilities, a tradition that still continues in Italy where most designers start from the base of an architectural training. At the beginning of the twentieth century architects played a key role in the move to establish a Modern Movement. They were part of a much wider artistic and intellectual vision, which incorporated, for example, the influence of new forms of painting that emerged before 1914. Cubism, for instance, offered a new conception of space that was fragmented and infinite, while abstract art offered a move away from the problem of representation and tradition, towards purity and universality. Themes centering around the cleansing and redemptive power of art were to inspire architecture in the years following World War One.

In the early years of the twentieth century there was a desire to express the new age with a new society that would live and work in the new cities of the future. Nowhere was this better expressed than in New York City, where during the 1920s the Manhattan skyline was developing into one of the most familiar in the world. Industry and the machine provided the blueprint for the new society, and buildings began to be modelled on the way machinery was designed. Architecture was concerned, not solely with outward appearances and display, but with function and efficiency. This was to be a total vision, not simply about designing buildings but what went into them and the space around them – the street, the town, city and country were all to form part of a totally reformed environment. Modernism provided a universal language for architecture. It signalled an end to traditional hierarchies of building; for example, the nineteenth-century tradition that the more important a building, the more ornate its decoration and ornament. Buildings would now share the same vocabulary and not only this, architects believed that if you reformed architecture you could reform society by making people healthier and society more stable.

Even within this context there were many different visions of the new architecture, from the hard line of the Soviet Constructivists to the more spiritual work of Walter Gropius, seen in the abstraction of form and sculptural composition of buildings such as the Bauhaus school, and the modern classicism of Le Corbusier and the International Style. There was also a place within the Modern Movement for a more gentle approach to form and materials, which was encapsulated in the work of the American Frank Lloyd Wright and the Scandinavians Alvar Aalto and Gunnar Asplund. Here architecture used traditional and local building materials and types and introduced organic curves and form, offering a softening effect, which was to have a deeply influential impact on the century as a whole.

In the 1920s and 1930s the new architects across Europe focused their energies on the city and new building forms. The Futurist Sant'Elia wrote, for example, about the need to reinvent and rebuild the city and the values of the nineteenth century, such as concerns for decoration, were swept away. Architects all over the industrial world looked to the city as the model for the future and nowhere was this more forcibly expressed than by Le Corbusier. In his book *Towards a New Architecture*, he illustrated grain silos and ocean liners as the models for architecture. Architects began to plan grand visions – visions of tearing down the industrial slums and the "dead museums" of the past and building new cities that would liberate people and set out the possibilities for a Utopian life. For hard-line Modernists this meant using the new materials of reinforced concrete, it meant the skyscraper and it meant the use of geometric form for buildings. It was a totalitarian vision that in the years leading up to World War Two produced ever more daring plans. After the war, however, architects began a process of reworking Modernism in an attempt to engage with the important postwar issues of the new consumer society, science, technology and the space age. Modernism was to become only one of many possible architectures now needed to fulfil the desire and needs of a much more complex technological and economic world. From the 1950s there had been attacks on the Modernism ideal and a demand for architecture to be seen as more communicative and relevant. Examples of this can be seen in the science-

fiction fantasies of the Archigram group, which demanded an adaptable architecture for the throwaway society. Other visionaries such as Buckminster Fuller argued for a high-tech approach while at the same time architects including Luis Barragán in Mexico were re-exploring a more traditional vernacular approach to buildings. In this postwar context the American response is interesting. Dominated in the 1950s by the minimalist buildings of European architects such as Mies van der Rohe, there was a search for a more American and a more democratic tradition of building. One famous attack in the 1960s came from Robert Venturi. In his book *Complexity and Contradiction in Architecture*, he called for a more complex use of space and for a reinstatement of architecture as language, as a cultural signifier. "Less", Venturi wrote, "is a bore". A decade later, these now widespread reactions against Modernism were reflected in a book by Charles Jencks called *The Language of Post-Modern Architecture*. Postmodernism was the term most people used to describe the new architecture that no longer offered one style, but the development of highly radical and different forms of building. It led to a desire to create an architecture to which people could relate and that offered identity and memory to the user and passer-by alike. Firmly back on the architectural agenda were decoration, historicism, playfulness, wit and irony.

EMPIRE STATE BUILDING

CHRYSLER BUILDING

SEAGRAM BUILDING

The Forster House

DATE: 1891

London, England

ARCHITECT: Charles Francis Annesley Voysey (1857–1941)

During the 1890s, British architecture was the most creative modern architecture to be found anywhere in the world. Voysey was part of a group of distinguished architects and designers which falls under the general heading of the Arts and Crafts Movement. Within this group, however, Voysey was one of the most talented and influential practitioners. For his informality of planning and simplicity of form, Voysey has been hailed as one of the fathers of twentieth-century Modernism, although Voysey himself found little to admire in the new architecture of the 1920s.

The Forster House was built in Bedford Park in London and pioneered another important British contribution to town planning – the garden suburb, which combined convenient town access with the pleasures and freedom of the country. It was in sharp contrast to the red-brick houses of the earlier development from the 1870s and this strikingly original house effectively launched Voysey's career. The exterior was simple; Voysey was not interested in reworking past styles, creating instead a generic vernacular of white roughcast walls, stone dressings and iron brackets that held a deeply pitched roof. The interior space was interesting because it attempted to create a modern way of living: a large living room with no separate parlour or dining room, with the staircase set to the side of the house to free up the living space. The interior was more conventional, using oak furniture and vernacular detailing.

Glasgow School of Art

DATE: 1897–1909

Glasgow, Scotland

ARCHITECT: Charles Rennie Mackintosh (1868-1928)

Although Mackintosh is now one of the world's most famous architects, his work was not always highly rated. He died in 1928 a neglected figure, and the postwar period saw some of his most famous buildings threatened with demolition. It was not until the 1960s that his work was reassessed, and his importance as a key transitional figure from the historicism of the nineteenth century to the abstraction of the early twentieth century, acknowledged.

Mackintosh was part of an artistic renaissance in Glasgow at the turn of the century. He worked closely with his wife Margaret Macdonald, with whom he had trained at the Glasgow School of Art. Their original style, seen in their architectural drawings, interiors and furniture for private clients, very quickly attracted interest from all over the world, but particularly enthusiastic were the Vienna Secessionists.

Mackintosh's most famous building was the Glasgow School of Art. The first phase, including the entrance shown here, was completed between 1898 and 1899. Huge windows dominate the entrance and the front can be read as an abstracted form of traditional Scottish castle architecture. It still functions as an art school, attracting many visitors drawn to Mackintosh's distinctive detailing seen here in the railings and window brackets. The second phase of building, including a library, was completed in 1909.

Casa Battló Apartments

DATE: 1905–07

Barcelona, Spain

ARCHITECT: Antoni Gaudí
(1852–1926)

Gaudí is not only one of the great individualists of Spanish architectural history but his impact internationally has made him a key twentieth-century figure. He worked almost exclusively in and around his native city of Barcelona, then as now the artistic capital of a fiercely independent region, proud of its traditions and history. Gaudí merged his native Catalan style with Moorish features and natural forms, to produce some of the most novel architecture of the late nineteenth and early twentieth century.

Perhaps his most famous work is the still uncompleted Sagrada Familia church, begun in 1883. However, his most original version of Catalan Art Nouveau, known as "Modernismo", can be seen in the remodelling of an apartment building into a residence for the Battló family, with offices on the ground floor and apartments for rent. Here Gaudí's distinctive language of ornament is no longer simply applied to a building but constitutes the essential structural elements. The facade is covered with highly coloured mosaics,

constructed with broken glass, while the roof outline resembles the form of an exotic reptile. Gaudí's highly original use of sculptural form established him as one of the great artist-architects of the twentieth century. However, it should be said that this does not mark the start of something new, rather the culmination of the previous century's obsession with revivalism and natural forms. Nonetheless, Gaudí became an inspirational figure for many Postmodernist architects in the postwar period.

Castle Drogo

DATE: 1910–30

Devon, England

ARCHITECT: Edwin Lutyens
(1869–1944)

In the context of British architectural history, Edwin Lutyens remains a complex figure. He worked within the tradition of nineteenth-century British Arts and Crafts yet he is arguably the most influential British architect of the twentieth century. However, his vision of architecture was not part of the quest for new forms of Modernism. Lutyens was the British establishment's chosen architect, commissioned to design war memorials, government buildings for the Empire and work for major banks. None of this endeared him to the architectural avant-garde, who saw him as a reactionary figure holding back progress. Recently a more sympathetic reappraisal of Lutyens' work has viewed his handling of form and space, his use of traditional materials and his reinterpretation of the vernacular as qualities that seem more sympathetic than they did forty years ago. In addition to his work for the establishment he was also the last great country house architect. Castle Drogo, built for a wealthy tea merchant, is an example of this work. It is a romantic vision of a castle. Constructed of granite, it is built on a rocky outcrop on the edge of Dartmoor. The interior of the building opens into a series of dramatic spaces; particularly notable is the library and the basement kitchen which is lit from above by a glazed rotunda.

Chrysler Building

DATE: 1928–30

New York City, USA

ARCHITECT: William Van Alen
(1883–1954)

The Chrysler building is probably one of the most familiar buildings in the world. Indeed for many its opulent and dramatic profile has come to symbolize the Manhattan skyline. It was one of a number of high-rise buildings planned in the 1920s that established New York as the modern city of the twentieth century.

The building has a slightly curious history. It was designed for the Chrysler motorcar company – its foyer was planned as a showroom for new models, and the exterior metal sculptural decoration evokes car grilles and emblems. In fact, the building was never used by Chrysler. Also, during the construction of the building, Van Alen was accused of financial impropriety and, whatever the truth, he never recovered his reputation.

Standing at 320 metres (1,048 feet), the Chrysler Building remains the most flamboyant example of Art Deco in New York's midtown district that saw so many corporations vying for attention, including the Woolworth building across the street and the Chenin Insurance headquarters on the opposite block.

Empire State Building

DATE: 1931

New York City, USA

ARCHITECTS: Richmond H. Shreve (1877–1946), William Lamb (1883–1952) and Arthur Loomis Harmon (1878–1958)

In one of the most enduring images of popular culture, the giant gorilla "King Kong" hangs from the mooring mast at the top of the most famous skyscraper – New York's own "eighth wonder of the world" – the Empire State Building. Standing on Manhattan's 34th street and 5th Avenue, for forty years after its completion this 381-metre (1,250-foot) marvel was the world's tallest building. Designed by architects Richmond H. Shreve, William Lamb, and Arthur Loomis Harmon, the exterior's vertical thrust and simple, yet powerful, limestone and granite form was the very definition of a modern skyscraper. Although less exotic than its rival Chrysler building, the sleek marble lobby artfully highlighted with polished metal epitomized the Art Deco style. Widely acclaimed, the Empire State Building was not an immediate success: the Depression left much of its office space unfilled. But in postwar prosperity it flourished, becoming one of America's greatest tourist attractions. Since its opening in 1931, nearly 120 million people have visited the observatories from which, on a clear day, one can see for up to fifty miles.

Schröder House

DATE: 1924

Utrecht, The Netherlands

ARCHITECTS: Gerrit Rietveld
(1888–1964) and Truss
Schröder-Schräder
(1889–1985)

The Schröder house has become a
metaphor for Modernism and a key
building of Dutch De Stijl, one of
the most coherent groups within
the Modern Movement. The house
was the first open-plan home. Its
internal organization reflected the
new way of life that Modernism
advocated – unencumbered,
unostentatious, flexible,
dramatically different to the
constraints of the nineteenth
century. It opened up light and
space, with a view originally
overlooking meadows. The windows
opened out to ninety degrees,
creating the impression that the
house merged with the landscape.
It is also interesting because it was
one of the few Modernist homes
partly designed by a woman: Truss
Schröder-Schräder collaborated with
Rietveld on the design of her own
home. She seems to have been
responsible for the internal
planning and saw herself and the
house as models for the new life of
the twentieth century. The Schröder
House was distinctive in that, apart
from the fixed staircase and
bathroom, the spaces could be
opened up using a system of
flexible screens which you could
simply draw across if you wanted
privacy. The downstairs area is
more fixed, with four or five rooms
but a gap at the top of a screen
wall to give a sense of space.
Another key feature was the
functional fitted furniture, fold-down
ledges and cupboards.

Le Corbusier is the most influential architect of the twentieth century, yet surprisingly few of his designs were actually built. However, it is his vision of the future, revealed in his drawings and published writings, that has dominated Modern architecture. As a Modernist, Corbusier was dedicated to the creation of a new aesthetic for a new way of life and his chief source of inspiration was the machine. He wanted to create architecture that functioned with the same slick efficiency and economy of design as a car or an aeroplane.

Corbusier's philosophy is reflected in his famous aphorism "the house as a machine for living in". In the 1920s these ideas were put into practice in a series of modern villas for wealthy clients in the Paris suburbs, the exteriors of which evoked the machine, with interiors which were largely free in plan. Placed in the interiors of houses such as the Villa Savoye was specially designed furniture, discrete sculpture within the free-flowing interior space, which rendered the house a totally designed entity. This house has become one of the best-known expressions of twentieth-century International Style; sixty years later its design continues to influence architectural practice.

Villa Savoye

DATE: 1929–31

Poissy, France

ARCHITECT: Le Corbusier (1887–1965)

Seagram Building

DATE: 1954–58

New York City, USA

DESIGNER: Ludwig Mies van der Rohe (1886–1969)

Mies van der Rohe is one of the most influential architects of the twentieth century. His buildings became the blueprint for a modern industrial society. As an architect, Mies is famous for his ability to derive maximum effect from a minimum use of form, reflecting his legendary axiom "less is more".

Largely self taught as an architect, his formative years were spent in the German office of Peter Behrens where he supervised the construction of many important projects. After World War One he placed himself at the centre of the New Modern Movement, designing astonishingly original buildings. Between 1919 and 1929 his important works included the Wolf House at Guben and the German Pavilion at the 1929 International Exhibition in Barcelona – one of the most important buildings of the twentieth century.

After a short period as Director of the Bauhaus, political pressure forced him to leave Germany and move to the USA where, in 1938, he accepted a teaching post at the Illinois Institute of Technology, Chicago. Here he began to establish his distinctive architecture principles, using exposed metal frame structures to exploit bold rectangular forms. In the immediate postwar years his career acquired superstar status. Two of his skyscrapers – Lake Shore Drive Apartments, Chicago (1950) and the Seagram Office Building in New York (1954–58) – came to express the ambitions and spirit of the most powerful nation in the world. Mies' work symbolized the power structure of American executive life, inspiring the shape of hundreds of commercial quarters throughout the world.

From 1919 to 1928, Walter Gropius was the director of the most famous design school of the twentieth century – the Bauhaus. It was no coincidence that when the opportunity arose to build a new school Gropius designed it himself, to show what the new architecture should and could be. The School remains one of the seminal buildings of the Modern Movement. As its director, Gropius was responsible for establishing a new approach to design education, an approach that still influences the way design is taught. While design education in the rest of Europe remained largely dominated by outdated nineteenth-century attitudes, the Bauhaus developed a syllabus on a pattern clearly recognizable in most design colleges today. It set out a common foundation year from which students moved on to specialize in the design area of their choice, for example furniture, product design or graphics.

Within the building itself, the different elements of the course were expressed in a series of distinct areas connected by single-storey blocks. Gropius aimed to make the effect functional but spiritually pleasing, and so different activities were expressed by a different treatment of the façade. For example, the workshop block, which Gropius considered to be the heart of the school's activity and identity, used a reinforced concrete frame, hence the curtain wall, which wraps around the corner to reveal what goes on inside. Designed by Gropius and his students, the interior was equally important, most notably his office and the lecture theatre, which featured folded canvas and steel chairs by Marcel Breuer.

Bauhaus School Building

DATE: 1926

Dessau, Germany

ARCHITECT: Walter Gropius (1883–1969)

Maison de Verre

DATE: 1927–32

Paris, France

DESIGNER: Pierre Chareau
(1883–1950)

Maison de Verre was designed by the architect Pierre Chareau who embraced the Modernist aesthetic with enthusiasm. For many architects and designers this private house, built for a gynaecologist and his wife, is one of the most poetic and beautiful expressions of Modern-Movement architecture and it enjoys an iconic status.

What made it so distinctive was the use of glass bricks in the main external walls. Glass bricks had been used in the past, mainly for industrial buildings, but never before had they been featured so extensively in a domestic context. Up to the present day, the use of glass bricks has come to signify modernity. In 1927, they created a sort of membrane, which gave the house a tremendous feeling of transparency and light. Inside, the complex spatiality of the design – walls which are nearly transparent, interior spaces defined with the use of screens and built-in furniture – have inspired subsequent generations of architects.

Also significant for contemporary designers was the fact that the project was a conversion of an existing building and, as such, has offered a blueprint for architects working in the same way. Maison de Verre remained Chareau's most important building. In 1940 he emigrated to America and worked on a number of private commissions, including a house for the painter Robert Motherwell.

When Eileen Gray died in Paris, aged 97, she was virtually unknown. Two decades later she is now widely recognized as one of the twentieth century's most talented and individualistic designers. Although she designed buildings, she was not strictly speaking a practising architect, nor had she any formal architectural training. Her work concentrated on a select group of interiors for a small but influential group of clients, and custom-made furniture, lamps, mirrors and hand-woven carpets. In the 1920s and 1930s Gray was unique as a designer, a women practising within a predominately male world. She was fortunate: Gray came from an affluent Irish family which supported her

decision to train at the Slade painting school – circumstances that, after the death of her father, allowed her to lead an independent life in Paris.

During the 1920s Gray's work attracted much attention. Those who found her work interesting included the Dutch De Stijl architect J. J. P. Oud. While in France she became friendly with many leading architects and designers, including Le Corbusier. This encouraged her to go beyond interior decoration and experiment with architecture. In 1927 she not only designed a house – the Villa E.1027 in the south of France – but every aspect of the furnishings and interior. The floor coverings, murals, furniture and light fittings were all made in her Paris

workshops. It was a brilliant tour de force. Le Corbusier admired the results so much he visited the house often. It was from here in 1965, in fact, that he swam to his death. Gray only completed two houses but produced plans for many other projects, including a scheme for a vacation centre which incorporated offices, de-mountable cabins, a restaurant and sports centre.

Gray's work required wealthy clients and remained exclusive. She did not share the machine-age preoccupations of many of her contemporaries in the European Modern Movement. The fact that her work did not translate into a wider commercial context helps to explain her low postwar public profile.

Villa E.1027

DATE: 1927–29

Roquebrune, Cap Martin, France

DESIGNER: Eileen Gray (1878–1976)

Casa del Fascio

DATE: 1932–36

Como, Italy

ARCHITECT: Giuseppe Terragni
(1904–41)

Fascist Italy, under the leadership of Benito Mussolini, promoted the new imagery and technology of Modernism to express the ambitions of the nation. The Casa del Fascio, built for Fascist mass rallies, remains Terragni's masterpiece and one of the key projects of the Italian Rationalist Movement. Mussolini, a great admirer of new inventions and industrial advances, admired the simplicity of form of Modernism but also wanted to combine this with the monumentality of the great Italian classical tradition. For Mussolini, identification with Ancient Rome was a way of reinforcing the new power of both the state and the people. The building was to be Como's headquarters of the Fascist party and includes a meeting hall, offices and a gallery. Terragni's design for the Casa is a cube by a double cube, a model classical proportion using white marble. The site was placed on an axis leading across Como's Piazza del Imperio to the east end of the city's Cathedral, thereby suggesting a link and an equal status with another symbol of Italian power.

Terragni was part of Gruppo 7, a collective made up from graduates of the famous architectural course at Milan's Polytechnic. They disliked the stripped classicism that informed much Italian Fascist architecture. The Casa del Fascio expressed their version of Modernity with its famous framed glass roof which top-lights the central hall. Technology was a feature of the main glass doors, which were electronically controlled so they could be opened simultaneously. In this way the crowds inside could flood into the square demonstrating the dynamic power of Fascism. In the 1970s, Terragni's work was rediscovered and inspired a number of New York architects.

As a young student, Mendelsohn's friends included Paul Klee and Wassily Kandinsky, and his early drawings were inspired by these Expressionist artists. This influence can be seen in the Einstein Tower, one of his most famous buildings. It was commissioned by the Einstein Foundation as an observatory and laboratory to prove Einstein's theory of relativity, and research work began in 1924. In design terms this was one of the most important examples of German Expressionist architecture. Mendelsohn used cement stucco not to express the pure geometry of Modernism, but the dynamic, sculptural form of curves and domes.

Other commissions quickly followed, buildings which placed Mendelsohn at the centre of new German architecture. He visited the USA the Soviet Union, and brought back the new ideas he had seen. Tragically, his career in Germany was cut short: as a Jew, his position became untenable. In 1933 he emigrated to England where he worked with Sergei Chermayeff. Their most famous collaboration was the De La Warr Pavilion in Bexhill-on-Sea. At the same time Mendelsohn worked on buildings in Palestine, including the Hebrew University in Jerusalem. His last years were spent in San Francisco working for the Jewish community.

Einstein Tower

DATE: 1921

Potsdam, Germany

ARCHITECT: Eric Mendelsohn (1887–1953)

Paimio Tuberculosis Sanatorium

DATE: 1929–33

Paimio, Finland

ARCHITECT: Alvar Aalto (1898–1976)

Alvar Aalto's ability to fuse the functional with the humane has ensured his position as one of the twentieth century's great architects. More than any other designer, his work has helped to define what is now described as Scandinavian Modernism.

When Aalto joined the CIAM, an international group dedicated to Modernist ideals, he came into direct contact with mainstream Europe. Interestingly, however, he became more friendly with an art circle which included Constantin Brancusi, Fernand Léger, László Moholy-Nagy and Alexander Calder, than with other architects. During the same period he completed one of his most famous projects, the Tuberculosis Sanatorium in Paimio. It revealed Aalto's unique contribution to architecture, for here he was not only concerned with new architectural forms, but with the human and psychological needs of the user. The building was designed and orientated to allow patients optimum access to light and air. They recuperated on balconies reclining on his famous plywood armchair, which formed part of the treatment programme. The pitch of the seat was calculated to be at such an angle to help patients' breathing and open up their bodies to the recuperative rays of the sun. Inside the building Aalto's use of natural materials reflected his interest in the need for both a human and humane aesthetic.

Restaurant Building, Stockholm Exhibition

DATE: 1930

Stockholm, Sweden

ARCHITECT: Gunnar Asplund
(1885–1940)

Before 1930 Asplund had worked on a series of Swedish buildings that were well designed, but safe and traditional. However, his work for the Stockholm Exhibition in 1930, marked a new direction. Using steel and glass Asplund created a series of startling Modernist buildings, flooded with light. These buildings not only established Asplund's reputation, but helped to place Sweden on the international design map.

Most distinctive was the Paradise Restaurant with its use of glass walls, the large glass tower, large coloured sunblinds and slender columns. These details came to express a Scandinavian approach to architecture referred to as Swedish Grace. In 1930 the Swedish Exhibition attracted international visitors who were in the main full of admiration for what they saw. Asplund's influence became widespread and after 1945 he inspired a young generation of European architects engaged in the postwar rebuilding programme.

Falling Water

DATE: 1935–37

Bear Run, Pennsylvania, USA

DESIGNER: Frank Lloyd Wright
(1869–1959)

Frank Lloyd Wright was one of the great American individualists in architecture. He is important not only because of the quality of his ideas and buildings, but because almost single-handedly he created the idea of the architect as superstar. His architectural style changed throughout his career from decade to decade, almost from project to project. A common thread running through his work, however, is his attempt to create an organic architecture, which has a dialogue with nature. This reflects his readings of the nineteenth-century critics Ruskin and Viollet-le-Duc, whose romantic ideas had a tremendous influence on him.

Falling Water exemplifies these ideas and remains one of his most startling and original works. It was built for the Kaufmann family as a weekend retreat, on a site overlooking the Bear Run stream that the family wanted to be incorporated into the final design. The house is a mix of natural and man-made forms. Frank Lloyd Wright had observed that a high rock ledge beside the stream could be used to cantilever the house, so that it stood above the stream and at the same time could become almost part of it. Each cantilever has a balcony which overlooks the stream, bringing inhabitants into contact with water and nature: the whole house seems to merge with the landscape, its layers becoming the strata of the terrain.

Notre-Dame de Haut

Associated with the purity of Modern-Movement architecture, the expressive forms of the chapel at Ronchamp come as something of a surprise. Situated on the top of a hillside, the building's organic form dominates the site. Le Corbusier claimed that the dramatic roof-line's anthropomorphic form was inspired by a "*réaction poétique*" to a crab's shell he had originally picked up on a Long Island beach in the 1940s.

For others it resembled the symbolic enclosure of a nun's veil.

Ronchamp was a project on which Le Corbusier lavished a great deal of personal attention. He wanted to create a place of peace and tranquillity, a religious and spiritual sanctuary. In this way Ronchamp exemplified a move away from his prewar work, which simulated the sleek lines of the machine by the use of pure form and white concrete.

This building became one of the most accessible and popular examples of Le Corbusier's architecture. In some ways the techniques he used in the design of Ronchamp indicate a return to his very early work. This can be seen in his use of natural forms for the concave and convex walls and in the materials, which included the rubble of the destroyed church, which the chapel replaced, and reinforced concrete.

DATE: 1955

Ronchamp, France

ARCHITECT: Le Corbusier (1887–1965)

Eames House

DATE: 1949

Pacific Palisades,
California, USA

ARCHITECT: Charles Eames
(1907–1978)

The name Eames is synonymous with furniture, but he preferred to describe himself as an architect: "I prefer the word 'architect' and what it implies. It implies structure, a kind of analysis as well as a kind of tradition behind it." He trained as an architect in the 1930s, producing largely conventional work, but in 1937 an important meeting changed his career and placed him at the very centre of new design experiments in America: Eames was invited by Eero Saarinen to teach at the Cranbrook Academy of Art, then a small and unknown school, but with ambitions of becoming an American Bauhaus. Here Eames worked alongside the influential sculptor–designer Harry Bertoia, and met key figures such as Florence Knoll. This shaped his attitudes to both design and architecture and marked the beginning of his fascination with new technology.

Eames never ran an architectural practice, but Eames House provided the prototype for a few private commissions. It consisted of two steel-frame prefabricated units, bought from an industrial catalogue, divided by a patio space. These frames were painted grey with infill panels, some of which are constructed from opaque materials while others are painted in bright yellows, reds and blues.

Charles and his wife Ray were true polymaths, working on children's toys, films and exhibition designs. In this respect the architecture and furniture are interchangeable – their approach and aesthetic remained a unified and single one.

During the 1950s, Eero Saarinen helped to establish an original American architectural style that combined the European tradition with sculptural organic forms. Saarinen was responsible for some of America's best-known buildings, including the TWA terminal at John F. Kennedy Airport, with its dramatic roofline designed between 1956 and 1962. Through a daring use of concrete, Saarinen wanted to restore to architecture a new expression of form and excitement that would contrast with the anonymity of the high-rise building.

Saarinen was originally born in Kirkkonummi, the son of Eliel, a leading Finnish architect. Although the family emigrated to America in 1923, Eero returned to Europe to study sculpture – a training that was to have an important influence on his later work. When his father became Director of Architecture at the famous Cranbrook Academy, near Detroit, Eero came into contact with America's most progressive designers, including Florence Shust – who later married Hans Knoll and established one of America's most important furniture companies – and Charles Eames. From 1937, Eames and Saarinen collaborated on a series of furniture projects using plywood, one of which took first prize at the Low-Cost Furniture Competition organized by New York's Museum of Modern Art in 1948.

From 1950, Saarinen's work with his partner Cesar Pelli developed a more inventive style. These buildings include the TWA terminal, with its distinctive parabolic arches that evoke wing forms, and Dulles Airport, Washington D.C. In London's Grosvenor Square, a late Saarinen collaboration with Yorke, Rosenberg and Mardall can be seen in the United States Embassy building.

TWA Terminal Building

DATE: 1956–62

John F. Kennedy Airport, New York City, USA

ARCHITECT: Eero Saarinen (1910–1961)

Sydney Opera House

DATE: 1956–73

Sydney, Australia

DESIGNER: Jorn Utzon
(born 1918)

The Sydney Opera House has become one of the most famous buildings in the world. It is such a potent image that it has now come to symbolize the city of Sydney and the country of Australia.

Jorn Utzon, a Danish architect, won the competition to design a new opera house for Sydney in 1957. Previously he had worked for Alvar Aalto from whom he learnt an organic approach to architecture. His other inspiration was the work of the American architect Frank Lloyd Wright. Utzon's winning design was both functional and symbolic, housing two concert halls and public spaces. Its form evoked both the sea, which provides the dramatic backdrop for the building, and the graceful flight and form of sea birds. In this way the design marks a transition in twentieth-century architecture away from the geometry of early Modernism to a more expressive and sculptural approach to building.

Between 1956 and 1966, Utzon was responsible for the main structure of the building, but it was the engineer Ove Arup who enabled him to realize the ambitious form of the roof. Utzon chose to make the roof the focal point of the design because it was the feature most people would see – it was sited on a point projecting into the bay of Sydney Harbour. In this way, the concert hall, covered by the famous "prow-like" roof, became a sculpture – a fifth facade to the building.

Pompidou Centre

DATE: 1971–76

Paris, France

ARCHITECTS: Richard Rogers
(born 1933) and Renzo Piano
(born 1937)

The Centre National de l'Art et de la
Culture Georges Pompidou is an arts
complex that has become one of the
most famous and best-loved buildings
in Paris. The architects left a large
piazza at the front of the city centre
site, an extension of the building
which has created a wonderful
atmosphere of life and activity. To
increase the internal space, all the
services, air-conditioning pipes and
ducting of the building were placed on
the exterior. The most dramatic feature
is the escalator with its transparent
covering dominating the main facade,
which takes people into the building
and becomes an extension of the
street. The effect of the brightly
coloured blues, reds and greens
resembles, in Rogers' own words,
"a giant Meccano set".

The Centre proved a brilliant
solution to the brief, which
demanded a library, galleries, a
museum of modern art and research
centre. The internal spaces are
completely free of supports,
permitting maximum flexibility. This
was the first "museum" not to be
designed as an imposing monument
in the nineteenth-century tradition,
but as a flexible framework for
cultural activity.

Hong Kong and Shanghai Banking Corporation

DATE: 1985

Central District, Hong Kong

ARCHITECT: Sir Norman Foster (born 1935)

Designed in 1979, this was Norman Foster's first skyscraper and it established the practice as one of the most prestigious in the world. The bank combined many of Foster's architectural preoccupations: his attempt to redefine the faceless office blocks associated with the Modern Movement; a concern with structure; the use of new materials and technology; and his introduction of natural light into the building. It occupies one of the most spectacular sites on the island, leading to the waterfront while the granite rock formations of Victoria Peak rise in the background.

The building is suspended from pairs of spectacular steel masts arranged in three bays, connected at key points by two-storey trusses from which the floor clusters are suspended. This staggered profile created interior spaces of varying width and depth, allowing garden terraces and dramatic east and west elevations. In addition, the combination of solid structure and transparent panels reveals the rich mixture of spaces within. These include a 12-metre (40-feet) -high public concourse from which a pair of escalators rise to the main banking hall and its ten-storey atrium.

Lloyds Building

DATE: 1978–86

London, England

ARCHITECT: Richard Rogers
(born 1933)

Richard Rogers is one of Britain's foremost contemporary architects. His work represents the "High-Tech" phase of Modernism. It emphasizes the structure and working parts of the building, often placing them on the exterior, and argues that since they are the first elements that need replacing, it is more straightforward if they are easily accessible.

As a young architect, Rogers was influenced by the new avant-garde, particularly the work of the Archigram group, elements of which appeared in his collaboration with Renzo Piano on the Pompidou Centre in Paris. The Lloyds commission was the result of a competition to design the headquarters for one of the most important financial institutions in the world located in the heart of the City of London. Again, his approach was to free the internal space by placing lifts and staircases outside the building and cranes on the roof to enable repairs and cleaning. Lloyds' requirement was for a vast underwriting room – the nerve centre of their insurance operation – which offered the flexibility of space so important for their business. Although ten years later the building is overcrowded, Richard Rogers & Partners nonetheless succeeded in creating a building of international prestige. The result was strikingly High-Tech, using steel, polished concrete, and making maximum use of the cramped site by layering the height of the building. Although Lloyds reflects the Modernist concern with technology, most details rely on a one-off customizing approach, rendering it a kind of Arts and Crafts High Tech.

Vitra Design Museum

DATE: 1989

Weil-am-Rhein, Germany

ARCHITECT: Frank Gehry
(born 1929)

Frank Gehry belongs to the great tradition of American individualist architects which includes Frank Lloyd Wright. His idiosyncratic, fun approach has made him America's best-known "fringe" architect. Almost single-handedly, Gehry made this fringe not only mainstream but popular, with clients as diverse as the Disney Corporation and American universities. The public has found this work much more accessible than the rival East Coast aesthetic centred on the New York 5 led by Peter Eisenman.

Gehry invited the viewer or user to reassess their ideas and preconceptions about conventional objects. He used non-traditional materials, such as corrugated iron, chain-link fencing and pieces of wood, placed in surprising contexts. Gehry's own house of 1977, sited alongside traditional Santa Monica bungalows, is an early example of his approach which helped to establish the meaning of the new Postmodernism. Sculptural qualities help to define the effect of his buildings; they sometimes

look as though someone has carved a deep curve into the wall, contrasting with a concave wall place alongside it. Gehry enjoyed close connections with the Pop Art movement, including his collaboration with Claes Oldenburg on the Santa Monica binocular building. These distinctive visual qualities made Gehry's work particularly appropriate for the design of art galleries, such as the Vitra Design Museum, the remarkable Guggenheim Museum in Bilbao, and the American Centre in Paris.

Rem Koolhaas is not only one of Holland's best-known architects but a man who enjoys an international reputation for his buildings and writings on architectural and urban theory. Always a radical with an avowed passion for science fiction, a fascination for public space and architectural wit, he has been described as the "surrealist of the city" and cites Salvador Dali as a bigger influence than Le Corbusier. Attacking Le Corbusier's ideas of city planning as restrictive, Koolhaas believes architecture should explore and represent the full range of human emotions including sensual pleasure, memory and guilt. Like many cities in the late twentieth century, Rotterdam is reinventing itself as a cultural metropolis. It is famous for its regeneration projects, including the reclamation of the dockland area, and the KunstHal, a gallery and arts venue, a quirky take on the traditional values of public building. Koolhaas's approach to what he identifies as the random, messy qualities of urban life can be seen in the KunstHal. The entrance is not obvious, located on a lower level at the "rear" of the building, and instead of the rich and expensive materials one might expect in a major public building, Koolhaas has used throwaway materials such as corrugated plastic, old planking and exposed steel girders.

KunstHal

DATE: 1992

Rotterdam, The Netherlands

ARCHITECT: Rem Koolhaas (born 1944)

Karaza Theatre

DATE: 1987

Tokyo, Japan

DESIGNER: Tadao Ando
(born 1941)

The Karaza Theatre in Tokyo is a modern building that immediately evokes contemporary and traditional aspects of Japanese culture. In doing so it reflects one of the key themes in Tadao Ando's architecture, merging the Western Modern Movement with traditional Japanese sensibilities. What is particularly important to Ando is the Japanese sense of space as the main component of architecture and also the links he sees between these two approaches. For Ando the simplicity and monumentalism of Japanese architecture ties in very well with many Modernist buildings. Ando also uses traditional Japanese form and materials to turn away from what he identifies as the horror of modern city life. For Ando the solution is to use architecture to build haven-like interiors that offer people a spiritual refuge from the pressure of contemporary life. The Karaza Theatre provides this with a sculptural modern building that acknowledges the past.

Museum of Contemporary Art

DATE: 1986

Los Angeles, California, USA

ARCHITECT: Arata Isozaki
(born 1931)

Like so many architects of his generation, Arata Isosaki has been widely commissioned outside his homeland, with the result that he is, perhaps, the best-known postwar Japanese architect. Unlike many of his contemporaries, however, Isosaki has been less concerned with Japanese than Western traditions. So much so, that his work seems more related to the West than to Japan. The Museum of Contemporary Art in downtown Los Angeles (MOCA) is a good example of his mature style. It forms part of a mixed development site and the famous Plaza, shown here, is surrounded by offices, apartments and shops. However, MOCA offers an oasis of culture away from commerciality, housing gallery space, a library and a bookstore. These have been grouped into two buildings on either side of the entrance, which combines a sculpture court and the bookstore. Reflecting Isozaki's interest in classicism, the buildings are Platonic in form: cubic offices, a cylindrical library with barrel vault, and cubic galleries, top-lit by pyramidic roofs. In true Postmodernist style, Isozaki plays with the seriousness of form using colour. Dark green aluminium covers part of the offices, the library vault is clad in copper, while the main cladding material is red sandstone interspersing the large blocks of hewn sandstone. The visitor enters the museum through the library, leaving the world of Postmodernism behind to enter a resolutely minimalist interior of white galleries.

Law Firm

DATE 1984–89

Falkestraße, Vienna, Austria

ARCHITECT: Coop Himmelblau, Vienna, Austria

Coop Himmelblau are a radical group of architects founded in Vienna by Wolf D. Prix, Helmut Swiczinsky and Rainer Michael Holzer. The group developed a theory of architecture that was confrontational, even aggressive. Their outlook was reflected in a series of projects undertaken in Vienna, one of the best-known of which was this roof conversion for a law firm in the city. This extraordinary structure, built from glass and steel, has been attached to the top of a conventional nineteenth-century building. This exterior view of the middle construction houses the conference room, in which curved glass spans the distance between the trusses of the steel construction. The main truss bears the weight of the glass and the folded roof, the underside of which is visible here.

Coop Himmelblau seek to express and reinforce the tensions they have identified in contemporary architecture. The design of their work continues the tradition of experimental 1960s ideas that were meant to challenge the viewer and to introduce an element of dissonance, as can be seen here. For example, no wall is at right angles to the next.

Calatrava trained as an architect in Spain and then as an engineer in Switzerland. He combines a knowledge of the structural possibilities of materials with an architect's eye to create breathtakingly original effects, most notably in this bridge for the 1992 Seville Exposition, but also in bridges in Valencia, Barcelona and the railway station in Lyon, France.

His inspiration is derived from natural forms, for example animal and human skeletons, and he uses this starting point to resolve engineering problems such as tension and stress of materials. Calatrava makes extensive use of reinforced concrete, which he exploits for its plastic qualities, and the curve is a dominant motif in his work, giving technical and engineering inventions a more expressive and human dimension. Calatrava's use of form suggests meanings and shapes that go beyond structure, and also intimate that technology need not be harsh and brutal, but can be expressive and gentle.

Alamillo Bridge

DATE: 1987–92

Seville, Spain

ARCHITECT: Santiago Calatrava (born 1951)

Paul Getty Center

DATE: 1997

Los Angeles, California, USA

ARCHITECT: Richard Meier
(born 1934)

Richard Meier is not only one of America's most famous architects but during the last decade he has attracted frequent European commissions, many of them for art galleries and museums, including the Museum für Kunsthandwerke in Frankfurt. Meier is famous for his white architecture and his intellectual roots lie in his membership of the New York Five, a group who, in the 1960s, sought to revitalize architecture in the USA, by developing an approach to form and theory based on the work of the inter-war Modernists. Each chose a different architect as a model: Meier took Le Corbusier's purist period and evolved, extremely successfully, a white shiny architecture, based on Platonic forms.

Critics have accused his style as being too conservative and commercial but his prestigious commission for the Getty Center confirmed his status as the museum architect *par exellence*. Paul Getty is part of the Getty family, whose tradition of arts sponsorship is legendary and includes the Getty Museum in Los Angeles, a reconstruction of a Pompeian villa.

This new building is a hugely ambitious project to establish the centre as a research institute of international importance. It employs the latest technology for conservation, storage, and the retrieval of books. More a campus than a single building, it is constructed on a desert ridge just outside Los Angeles, on the San Diego freeway. The project includes a gallery, conservation centre, administration buildings and a library. Visitors to the centre will access the site either by foot or a purpose-built tram. Getty stipulated that the building should not be "white" and so Meier has had to abandon one of his trademarks, although the design of the building retains his attachment to basic geometry. In keeping with the defensive positioning of the site, Meier has created a massive and monumental architecture, one that lacks his usual "pristine sheen" due to the use of heavily fossilized marble as the main cladding material. This is informally laid across the ridge, creating what some critics have described as an effect similar to the Great Wall of China.

Temporary Dwelling

DATE: 1996

Wandsworth, London, England

ARCHITECT: The Eco Village Project

Not all buildings are created by architects. In the summer of 1996 a design graduate, Maria Russell, documented a project on a disused piece of land by the River Thames in London. The land was occupied by a group of people concerned about the environment. They named the project the Eco Village. The inhabitants built temporary homes using recycled materials and their political message was a plea for alternative lifestyles. The house is built from materials that have been discarded and often found in roadside skips in the area. Tree trunks recovered from forest demolition caused by another controversial ecological protest, against the construction of the Newbury bypass in Berkshire, England, were used as the structure base. The structure evolved through adaptation and improvisation of the various sheet materials and windows and doors. Inside the dwelling, four columns made from the tree trunks not only support the roof but also a bed, just below the window in the centre of the roof. The builder had no previous experience in the design of buildings. In 1997 the site was closed by the Guinness Company, which owned the land, and the Eco Village was destroyed. The site was left empty while awaiting planning permission to build a supermarket.

PART 3

interiors

JOHNSON WAX BUILDING

MR FREEDOM

IMAGINATION OFFICES

INTERIOR DESIGN IN THE EARLY twentieth century rested largely in the hands of three groups: architects, professional decorators and homemakers. Only in the last thirty years has interior design emerged as a profession in its own right. In the 1990s, alongside these traditional practitioners, there are now a number of leading design practices that specialize exclusively in this field.

During the nineteenth century, the development of the home as a place of domestic leisure and entertainment was one important factor in interior decoration. Almost exclusively in the hands of women, intimacy and coziness signalled a new trend in domestic display, grouping specific pieces of furniture and objects to assert the values of family, status and social position. However, the Arts and Crafts movement in Britain and America sought to simplify interior design by the creation of total environments that aimed to harmonize furniture, applied decoration and wall surfaces to create the ideal of the beautiful house. Simplicity became essential and in these new interiors design began to replace decoration. Architects such as Charles Rennie Mackintosh opened up the traditional rooms of the home – the parlour and the living room – into larger spaces. Clutter was stripped away with the use of built-in furniture, and wall surfaces were painted white to introduce light into the home. For a growing band of middle-class patrons an appreciation of vernacular, craft objects influenced taste in the arrangement of the home.

The important concerns of simplicity and comfort were ultimately to lead to the new Modernist interior of the 1920s and 1930s. One of the revolutionary ideas of the Modern Movement interior was a new attitude to space. Modernist space was unencumbered, flexible and free-flowing with colour used to break up the wall surfaces. In 1925, Le Corbusier built his Pavilion de l'Esprit Nouveau at the Paris exhibition to demonstrate how these radical ideas were not simply futurist fantasies but provided real solutions to the way people would live in the modern machine age. In pioneer projects like this, designers demonstrated how new furniture, made from the "new" materials of tubular steel and plywood, could be used to serve particular functions and to divide space. In this way social and technological changes brought about real changes to interior design. Living spaces now began to be used for a variety of functions that reflected the requirements of their owner. This can be clearly seen in the pioneer house built by Gerrit Rietveld for Truss Schröder-Schräder, which used screen panels that could open and close interior spaces, new forms of lighting and large expanses of window to let in light and relate the interior to the outdoors – a key theme in the new modern home. At the same time, however, the tradition of rich opulent interiors continued, at first with the Art Nouveau movement and then after World War One with the work of French decorators such as Emile-Jacques Ruhlmann

BARNEY'S

whose glamorous interiors, using precious materials and surfaces, were widely imitated throughout the world. Throughout the 1920s and 1930s the introduction of modern conveniences in the bathroom and the kitchen as standard introduced a level of uniformity into interior design. However, it should be remembered that the individual was always the arbiter of interior decoration, deciding the degree to which each room should be designed.

After 1945 new materials and technology again brought changes into interior design. A growing industry of books and magazines offered advice for the design of the home and a sense of growing internationalism prevailed. One of the most important examples

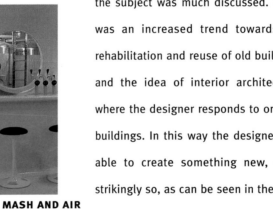

MASH AND AIR

was the dominance in the 1950s of Scandinavian design. This aesthetic, which stressed natural materials and texture, wooden furniture in modern organic forms, and woven fabrics, dominated taste until the 1960s. But the same period witnessed a new eclecticism, which permitted a variety of styles and choices to compete.

The 1960s witnessed another important shift with the rise of Pop design targeting young consumers anxious to create environments that were unique, temporary, witty and fun. Young interior designers were inspired by popular culture, including theme parks, the USA and Pop art. The design of boutiques reflected this new mood. In London Biba evoked the glamour of 1920s

Hollywood, while Mr Freedom used inflatable sculptures based on those of Claes Oldenburg. Interior design was now an expression of individuality and by the 1970s embraced various themes, including recycling, revivalism and the continuation of Modernist approaches. During the 1970s interior design became more of an academic discipline with formal theories, and the subject was much discussed. There was an increased trend towards the rehabilitation and reuse of old buildings and the idea of interior architecture, where the designer responds to original buildings. In this way the designer was able to create something new, often strikingly so, as can be seen in the work of the the Italian designer Carlo Scarpa or Ron Herron's Imagination building, which responded to the old structure in a new way: for example, opening a surface that had been hidden to light or basing certain design features on the old building. In this way interior design ties in with one of the principles of Postmodernism – the reclamation of memory and identity.

In the 1990s people have expectations about the quality of interior design both in the public and private spaces they inhabit. Visual awareness about the past and the present has become much more sophisticated and for this reason interior design is seen as a service they have come to expect.

CHIAT-DAY OFFICES

78 Southpark Avenue

DATE: 1906, reconstructed by the Hunterian Museum, Glasgow, Scotland

DESIGNER: Charles Rennie Mackintosh (1868–1928)

Charles Rennie Mackintosh viewed this house as an opportunity to create "interior architecture". He designed all of the fixtures, fittings and furniture, giving the house an overall sense of harmony. In this way, the interior of the home reflected his artistic personality and the modernity and taste of its inhabitants.

In 1906, Mackintosh and his wife Margaret Macdonald remodelled a standard Glaswegian terraced house to create a modern home of simplicity and space – a dramatic contrast to the industrialized city of Glasgow. Mackintosh denoted space by changes in colour – he moves from the darker browns and greys of the hall and staircase to the pristine whiteness of the private living areas. The room is L-shaped, divided not by walls but a low arch – a continuous cornice focuses attention on the living area, helping to define a sense of vertical space. This design was a radical departure from traditional nineteenth-century room usage. And like the use of the cornice, Mackintosh's designs for the furniture and fittings are not merely decorative, they are functional. Furniture is not used to denote status and prestige but arranged to distinguish different areas of use within the room. Furniture is often built-in – shelves, cupboards and the fireplace all contain display space. Like so many Mackintosh interiors from this period, the room is predominantly white. Colour is mainly used to enhance and mark out space.

This interior represents progressive taste for 1906 – its simplicity is extreme for the period, but it is also worth noting that as an Arts and Crafts architect, Mackintosh always placed some fine art and decorative pieces within his design, such as a stencilled decoration he designed with his wife, or Japanese prints. With its use of space and simplification of form, Southpark Avenue articulated ideas that would define the Modernism of the interwar years.

Greene and Greene were key exponents of the American Arts and Crafts movement, which came to maturity in the early years of the twentieth century. They were heavily influenced by the writings of William Morris and the work of British architects such as Voysey, whose buildings they could have seen in the pages of the British magazine *The Studio*. Like many other Western architects, they were inspired by Japanese culture and artifacts. More specific American influences and attitudes also shaped their work, most notably the designer Gustav Stickley. The Gamble House remains an important example of a new native Arts and Crafts style. Built for David Gamble – of Procter and Gamble as a retirement home, it reflects a desire to produce an American architecture for American people. In designing the interior of the Gamble House, Greene and Greene took into account four principles: climate, environment, use of local materials, and the culture of the inhabitants.

The plan focuses around a central hall, allowing free circulation of air – crucial in Pasadena's hot climate. The living zone was built on one side of the hall, with the kitchen and dining area on the other. These interlinked spaces give an underlying unity to the overall design. The house is particularly notable for its use of art glass, seen here in the doors, and the desire to include up-to-date technology, such as electric lighting covered by the famous Tiffany glass shades.

Gamble House

DATE: 1907–08

Pasadena, California, USA

DESIGNERS: Charles Sumner Greene (1868–1957) and Henry Mather Greene (1870–1954)

Grand Salon d'un Collectionneur

DATE: 1925

Exposition des Art Décoratifs, Paris, France

DESIGNER: Jacques-Emile Ruhlmann (1879–1933)

During the early part of the twentieth century, French decorative art and interior design was acknowledged to be the most advanced in the world. With its rich tradition of craftsmanship, France dominated a market for luxury and sumptuous interiors throughout the 1920s and 1930s. Jacques-Emile Ruhlmann was among the most famous French designers in this field. A Parisian, Ruhlmann designed carpets, furniture and textiles from his workshop – Etablissements Ruhlmann et Laurent – using a stripped-down version of classicism, which we now describe as Art Deco. Ruhlmann was one of a group of designers whose work was acclaimed at the Exposition des Arts Décoratifs in Paris in 1925.

Ruhlmann produced the highly decorated, luxurious one-off items that Modernists such as Le Corbusier found inappropriate to the modern age. However, because he attempted to moderate the decorative excesses of Art Nouveau and to replace it with a more restrained classically based design aesthetic, his work can be seen as a progression, part of a move towards a *"rappel à l'ordre"* that took place after 1918.

Ruhlmann continued to work within a palette of rich and expensive materials, achieving his effects by the traditional use of craft techniques. His design for Hotel d'un Collectionneur is typical. A severely stripped classical pavilion, in plan it appears as a central octagon within a square. Inside, a sumptuous interior is focused around a salon with a bedroom, boudoir and dining room. The classically inspired furniture made from burr, walnut, ebony, and ivory, all expensive woods, typifies the Art Deco approach.

Led by the Russian émigré Berthold Lubetkin, Tecton was the most important Modernist practice in prewar Britain. This architectural group was responsible for some of the most distinguished and rigorously designed Modernist buildings for a range of progressive clients during the 1930s. As soon as it was completed, Highpoint One was immediately recognized as a major triumph for modern architecture in England. It was visited and admired by Le Corbusier and many other important Modernists.

Backed by the industrialist Zigsmund Gestetner, Highpoint One was designed as a commercial venture to provide a block of fifty-nine apartments that combined accommodation with communal facilities, such as tea room, winter garden, roof terrace and tennis courts. The idea was that the communal entrance and gardens would develop into places where residents could socialize. Light and open space would enable easy interaction within the community of flat dwellers.

In this way, Highpoint One reflected the influence of Russian housing models where the provision of communal facilities was meant to encourage an eventual transition to a socialist way of life.

Although it was intended to attract people from varied backgrounds and classes, Highpoint One quickly became a community of artists, designers and intellectuals. It nonetheless provided an important model for social housing in postwar Britain.

Highpoint One

DATE: 1933–35

London, England

DESIGNER: Berthold Lubetkin (1901–90), Tecton Partnership

Director's Office

DATE: 1923

The Bauhaus, Weimar, Germany

DESIGNER: Walter Gropius (1883–1969)

Walter Gropius founded the Bauhaus in 1919, holding the position of director until 1928. He aimed to introduce a radical new form of design education that would equip students with the skills and insight necessary for the new industrial society of the twentieth century. Every aspect of the Bauhaus reflected these aims, including the design of the interior.

Gropius' office is an interesting example of an early Bauhaus project. Although it includes light fittings inspired by industrial models, and simple geometric furniture, also displayed prominently are wall hangings and rugs from craft students Else Mogelin and Gertrud Arndt, whose work reflects the influence of Paul Klee.

This photograph was used for publicity when Gropius organized a Bauhaus exhibition in 1923. Gropius had a talent for public relations and wanted the Bauhaus to be viewed sympathetically. The Bauhaus always struggled with funding – during the 1920s Germany was already facing the problem of monetary inflation. Gropius organized an open week for the school in which visitors could visit the workshop, see his office, buy student work and attend lectures. It was a tremendous success, attracting 15,000 visitors to Weimar, including leading figures such as J. J. P. Oud, the Dutch De Stijl architect. Gropius was sensitive to public opinion and industry. The success of the exhibition confirmed his view that the Bauhaus should concentrate on the design of objects for mass production, rather than crafts.

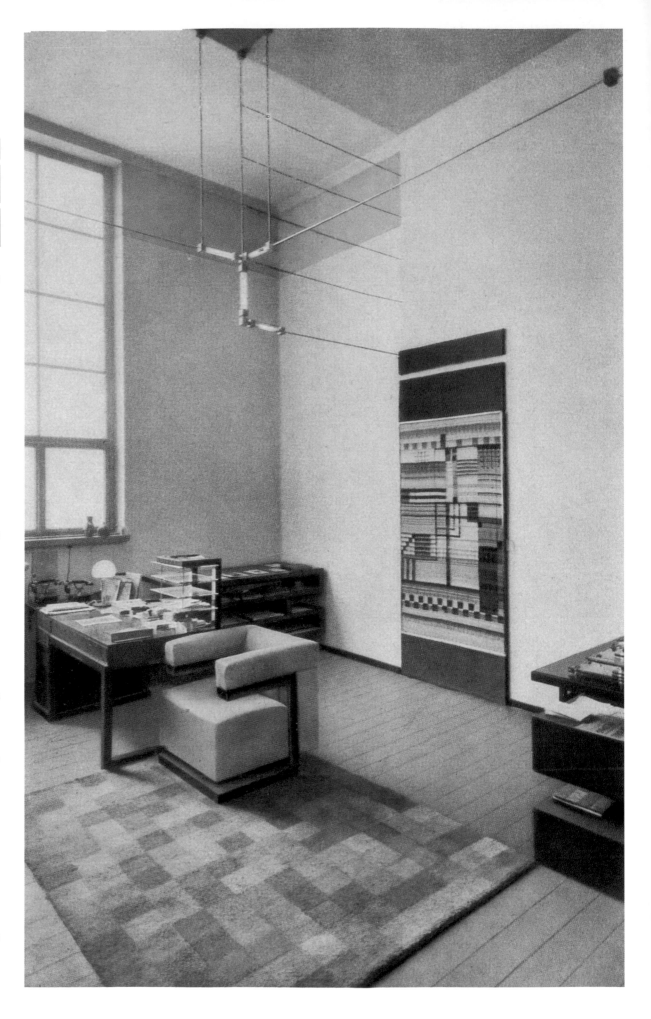

Eileen Gray did not subscribe to the Modern Movement ideology of the machine and mass production. Her work remained exclusive, concentrating on a select group of interiors for a small but influential group of clients, and on the design and production of custom-made furniture, lamps, mirrors and hand-woven carpets. The Villa E.1027 was an exception to this in that Gray did not only design the interiors, she also designed the house, perched on an inaccessible part of the Mediterranean coastline, as a summer retreat for herself and her lover Jean Badovici.

Gray named the house E.1027 after the letters of the alphabet which made up their initials: E for herself, 10 for J (the tenth letter of the alphabet), 2 for B and 7 for G. She designed every aspect of the furnishings and interior. The floor coverings, murals, furniture and light fittings were all made in her Paris workshops. Gray did not only exploit new materials, such as perforated metal sheeting and aluminium, but also invented new forms – sliding screens, false ceilings for storage space and extending wardrobes.

In 1938, after a short visit, Le Corbusier wrote to Gray praising the house in glowing terms for "the organization, inside and outside, which gives to the modern furniture – the equipment – such dignified form".

Villa E.1027

DATE: 1925

Roquebrune, Cap Martin, France

DESIGNER: Eileen Gray (1878–1976)

Pavilion de l'Esprit Nouveau

DATE: 1925

Paris, France

DESIGNER: Le Corbusier (1887–1965)

The 1925 Exposition des Arts Décoratifs was planned as a major international exhibition to signal a new spirit of progress after the devastation of the First World War. Most of the exhibits tended toward the well known and conservative, with two significant exceptions – Le Corbusier's building and the Melnikovs' Russian Pavilion. These two examples offered the public a glimpse of the future, a model of the new architecture of the twentieth century.

The pavilion took its name from *L'Esprit Nouveau*, a magazine Le Corbusier founded in 1920 to publicize his own work and that of like-minded contemporaries. In the grounds of the 1925 Exposition site stood a prototype in which Le Corbusier wanted to show that an interior could be standardized yet still satisfy human needs. The interior space is notable for its free plan – in Le Corbusier's words: "*une surface pour circuler*" – rather than a series of individual box rooms. Two storeys high, the upper storey is a mezzanine offering a vista of open white space below. Le Corbusier does not use solid walls to divide the space; instead furniture and sliding screens create distinct areas.

The contents of the Pavilion were just as radical. Le Corbusier designed some of the furniture himself, including the steel cupboards and tubular steel-framed tables. His approach to furnishing the space reflected a belief that industry had refined certain objects to their optimum form, for example, laboratory porcelain and glassware, the English club armchair and the Thonet bentwood chair. They all represent Le Corbusier's perfect standardized solution to the problems of comfortable sitting, living and entertaining. The interior also reflects Le Corbusier's interest in painting, featuring works by Léger, Ozenfant and Le Corbusier himself, as well as sculptures by Laurens and Lipchitz.

Finally, the interior does not just show new forms of enclosed space. Le Corbusier wanted to integrate the occupier with nature – the Pavilion also incorporates the garden.

Erno Goldfinger was born in Budapest, studied in Paris and came to England in 1934 as a refugee. He built this house in Hampstead for his wife, the painter Ursula Blackwell, and their three children. It was the centre house in a terrace of three, overlooking Hampstead's famous heath. For its design Goldfinger moved away from white concrete to a more sophisticated amalgamation of Modernist approaches to material, space and furniture. He also referred to traditional English forms of housing: Willow Road was a Modernist version of a Georgian terrace.

From the tiny entrance hall the visitor climbs a tightly coiled spiral staircase to the main floor, which contains the most significant rooms. Here the dining room, studio, living room and kitchen are designed as zones within a single volume of space which wraps around the staircase in a "C" shape forming distinct areas which can be closed off by folding screens. There is a sense of progression from the entrance into these spaces. The house constitutes a fascinating record of the taste of British progressive architects in the 1930s. Goldfinger designed most of the furniture, some of which is reminiscent of the work of Charlotte Perriand and Le Corbusier. Other more quirky and Surrealist-inspired details include the fireplace set into a convex screen and mounted within a projecting frame which appears to float in front of the main wall surface.

2 Willow Road

DATE: 1937–39

Hampstead, London, England

DESIGNER: Erno Goldfinger (born 1902)

Johnson Wax Building

DATE: 1936–39

Racine, Wisconsin, USA

DESIGNER: Frank Lloyd Wright
(1867–1959)

The Johnson Wax Building was designed as the headquarters of one of the USA's largest companies and for it Frank Lloyd Wright created a very special interior. The building represented in many ways a continuation of his standard repertoire of themes: an intimate interior enclosed by a skin-like wall, but it was also a radical departure from his previous use of the square and cube in his architecture since here he makes great use of the curve. The streamlined brick exterior encloses a large open-plan office space notable for the use of distinctive mushroom-shaped columns which support the ceiling. Another special feature is the lighting with the centre section of the ceiling constructed from glass while the walls are periodically broken up with narrow seams of Pyrex glass ribbon windows. In common with other projects Frank Lloyd Wright was responsible for all the interior fixtures and fittings in the space.

Fiat Factory

DATE: 1915–21

Turin, Italy

DESIGNER: Giacomo
Matte Trucco (1869–1934)

In 1923, Le Corbusier published a photograph of the Fiat factory in his seminal book, *Vers une Architecture*. As the first major reinforced concrete building of the twentieth century, the Fiat factory was for Corbusier and subsequent generations emblematic of Modernity and the way forward for architecture. This great structure made from reinforced concrete was commissioned by Fiat's owner Agnelli after his visit to the USA to study modern methods of industry and the mass production techniques developed by rival companies such as Ford. Agnelli was deeply impressed with the scale and power of New York as a modern city. He returned to Italy determined to introduce these innovations to Fiat. Agnelli, who had great ambitions for his company, wanted a new factory to be simultaneously an industrial building and a corporate flagship advertising Fiat. Agnelli's brief therefore specified the latest technology, lighting and machinery and the inclusion of a racing track on top of the building to test the latest Fiat cars.

Casa Devalle

DATE: 1939–40

Turin, Italy

DESIGNER: Carlo Mollino
(1905–73)

In the 1930s, Carlo Mollino set out to extend the Modernist agenda. Mollino made trips to see the work of Antoni Gaudí in Spain and knew the work of Alvar Aalto, both of whom he deeply admired. He was a man of diverse talents – a poet, writer, sportsman, iconoclast and non-conformist. A deeply private individual, the complex strands of Mollino's personality express themselves through a range of buildings, interiors and furniture, all of which continue to exercise an important influence on design.

One of Mollino's obsessions was drawing and photographing nude women. His interiors extend the theme of the body, exploring open curving space and the idea of organic movement.

Mollino had studied the Modernist idea of opening up the interior space of the home but, unlike Mies van der Rohe or Le Corbusier, he did not focus on the placement of objects as sculpture. He filled his interiors with texture: drapes, cushions and screens creating sensual surfaces. This is one of Mollino's personal photographs of the bedroom of Casa Devalle, showing it as the ultimate erotic experience. Here, veiled curtains wrap a bed against velvet walls, a theme extended to Mollino's buttoned-lips sofa – his homage to Dali's original design. Mollino has deliberately blurred the erotic distinctions between masculine and feminine, combining hard industrial doors and walls with sensual surfaces and flowing fabrics and everywhere the extensive use of mirrors reflects and breaks up the space and contributes to the overall feeling of erotic tension.

The Italian architect Adalberto Libera designed this house for the poet and aesthete Curzio Malaparte who, disillusioned after his imprisonment by the Italian Fascist government, needed a spiritual retreat. The house, completed in 1942, was a highly personal reflection of Malaparte's poetic life in which metaphysical and Surrealist elements pushed Italian rationalism to a new intensity. Libero was part of the Gruppo Seven, founded in 1927 by Italian architects whose combination of Modernism and the classical tradition was adopted as the official Fascist architectural style.

The design of Casa Malaparte – sited on a spectacular cliff top overlooking the sea on the island of Capri – plays with the conventions of what a house should be. There is, for example, no obvious entrance. The approach – a winding rocky path cut out of the cliff – leads to a widening staircase that shifts to a vast rectangular roof terrace projecting out to the sea. Beneath the roof, two floors of rooms present a sequence of spaces that progress from land to sea, and from the public – the sitting room is enormous, resembling an Italian piazza – to a series of private symmetrical rooms. These spaces are pure white and rectilinear with parallel bedrooms on either side of the main axis of the house. However, the last room overlooking the sea remains private, accessible only from Malaparte's bedroom. This dramatic study spans the width of the house with a window looking onto the Mediterranean.

Casa Malaparte

DATE: 1938–42

Capri, Italy

DESIGNER: Adalberto Libera (1903–63)

Danish National Bank

DATE: 1971

Copenhagen, Denmark

DESIGNER: Arne Jacobsen
(1902–71)

This interior is one of Jacobsen's last works. Completed in 1978, seven years after the designer's death, the design for the Danish National Bank shows all the maturity and confidence of a master designer. Born in 1902, Jacobsen grew up with the ideas of the Modern Movement. Although his native Denmark was relatively isolated, with its own traditions of neoclassicism, as a young man Jacobsen had first-hand experience of the new. In 1925 he visited the Paris Exposition and saw for himself the work of Mies van der Rohe and Le Corbusier.

Jacobsen became well known in the 1930s for a style of architecture that merged the Danish vernacular with Continental Modernism. Together with architect Gunnar Asplund, he explored a "Scandinavian" design aesthetic, revealed in Jacobsen's work for Arhus Town Hall in 1937.

In the postwar period, Jacobsen continued this assimilation in his design for the main building of Denmark's National Bank. The building is enclosed by two glass façades stretched between two enclosed gables. The customer enters the lobby of the bank via a low entrance space. The lobby itself extends twenty metres (65 feet) high through all six storeys of the building where the walls and floor are covered in Norwegian Porsgrunn marble. Jacobsen's practice was largely confined to his homeland, but he completed two interesting buildings in Britain during the 1960s: St Catherine's College, Oxford, and the Danish Embassy in London.

The designer and entrepreneur Sir Terence Conran was responsible for a revolution in retail design during the 1960s. In 1964, when he opened his first Habitat shop in London's Fulham Road, he brought the concept of the total lifestyle to a mass market. His aim was simple: recognizing that the young affluent consumer in the 1960s was being offered little to appeal to new lifestyles and aspirations, Habitat presented a solution to the interior design and decoration of the home. Habitat not only sold furniture but wallpapers, curtain fabrics, crockery, lighting and kitchen equipment. With its white painted walls and red quarry tiles, the shop's design suggested the effect its customers were encouraged to achieve in their own interiors.

Goods were informally stacked on the floor or grouped on industrial shelving, creating a relaxed environment that people found sympathetic. Habitat produced its own designs as well as stocking a range of what Conran identified as design classics – for example, the reissue of Marcel Breuer's Cesca chair from the 1920s. Also innovative was the production of a mail order catalogue which expanded Habitat's market to include the whole country. The catalogue was designed to look fresh, modern and appealing and it proved an immediate commercial success.

Habitat

DATE: 1964

London, England

DESIGNER: Sir Terence Conran (born 1931)

Mr Freedom

DATE: 1968–69

London, England

DESIGNER: Jon Wealleans
(born 1949)

Jon Wealleans designed this clothes boutique for Tommy Roberts on London's Kensington High Street, then a centre for the new Pop culture of swinging London. Wealleans had recently visited Disneyland and the west coast of America. His design was a fusion of theme park, neon, rock'n'roll and the inspiration of new wave Italian design. Filled with oversize soft sculptures and pictures of Mickey Mouse, it was London's first retail Pop

interior. The shop reflected the instant and immediate qualities of Pop, including murals borrowed from Roy Lichtenstein, like a continually changing stage set with Wealleans supplying drawings for objects such as a giant coat hanger which were designed and installed within a week.

Mr Freedom became more than just a shop. People used it as a meeting place and it included a café. It was chaotic but made people smile. A

typical example of sixties naiveté, the business was totally disorganized and the shop ultimately closed. For a while, however, Mr Freedom and the clothes of Pamela Motown and Jim O'Connor dressed the likes of Peter Sellers and Elton John, and contributed to the mythology of Swinging London. The shop's cult status also attracted buyers from a new enterprise in Milan – Fiorucci – who bought up the stock to take home in suitcases.

The Factory was Andy Warhol's famous New York studio. The converted Manhattan warehouse functioned as a studio, a film set and the setting for Warhol's infamous parties. The Factory was about lifestyle in the 1960s, pioneering the reclamation of industrial space and the idea of interior design as art installation. Warhol attracted many of New York's fringe community, among them Billy Name, who was to become an integral figure in the life of The Factory, documenting, organizing and contributing ideas, notably for the famous Cow wallpaper. Warhol gave him a camera and made him the group's photographer. The resulting grainy black and white photographs have become the essential documentation of Factory life. Name had set himself up in his own apartment as a hairdresser and many of The Factory crowd used it as a meeting place. Warhol liked the way Name had decorated the space with silver foil and when shortly afterward Billy Name moved into The Factory, he set about covering the walls in the same way. It was exactly the kind of unplanned event that Warhol enjoyed. The idea of anti-design, of do-it-yourself, ran against the manicured and lavish interiors for which New York was then famous and the silver interior has come to express the spirit of Pop design.

The Factory

DATE: 1964

East 47th Street, New York City, USA

DESIGNER: Billy Linich (aka Billy Name) (born 1940)

Joseph Shop

DATE: 1988

Sloane Street, London,
England

DESIGNER: Eva Jiricna
(born 1939)

Eva Jiricna was born and educated in the Czech Republic. She left her home country in 1968, shortly before the Russians invaded Prague, to take up a post at the architectural office of the now-defunct Greater London Council. She is best known for her sophisticated and understated work for the Joseph fashion shops. Her interest in architecture has always had an engineering bias, with a concern for materials and structure. It was this aesthetic which attracted the attention of Joseph. Regarded by many as a fashion retailer of international significance, Joseph's ability to spot and nurture talent is well known. For his chain of shops he chose Jiricna to create a cool, industrial modern space as the backdrop for the more extravagant world of fashion. The focal point for the shop is the staircase. Walls and fixtures are painted grey which allow the skeletal steel and glass staircase to stand out as the most important element. Jiricna's staircases are intended to appear as though they are floating, thus all the structural elements are reduced to a minimum – the glass and perspex strips sit on circular panels which rest on a horizontal truss connected to the glass-panelled balustrade. The quality of this beautiful detailing makes this staircase more than a piece of engineering – its sculptural effect has been widely imitated in shops throughout the world.

Imagination Offices

DATE: 1989

London, England

DESIGNER: Herron Associates

Imagination, run by Gary Withers, is one of Britain's most prestigious design companies. In the late 1980s, the company wanted to expand into larger premises and bought two buildings connected by an alleyway behind London's busy Tottenham Court Road. It was an awkward site with two red-brick blocks running parallel, but Ron Herron's solution was masterful, opening up the dead central space by roofing it over with a skin of translucent plastic fabric. The result is a soaring white atrium, criss-crossed by a network of lightweight, semi-transparent bridges of steel and aluminium. Walls which were once external are now inside and opened up to public view. They are painted white to lighten the space and to stress their new role as interior walls.

For the Imagination offices, Herron has used interior design to revive an old building by opening up these previously hidden facades. At the same time he has acknowledged the past life and memory of the building while adding something completely new.

Royalton Hotel

DATE: 1988

West 44th Street,
New York City, USA

DESIGNER: Philippe Starck
(born 1949)

The Royalton was more than a new hotel design: it marked the revival of the hotel as a social focus for "happening" people – a place for the designer generation of the 1980s to stay and be seen. Before Starck, the hotel was a necessity, but it was not hip. Now, people not only stayed in the Royalton, they socialized in the bar and restaurant. It became a meeting place, more like a bar or club than the traditional exclusive and business foyer of the hotel. Starck transformed this space with his typical concern for customized detailing. He introduced new designs for the lights, furniture, toilets and the restaurant. He dispensed with the reception desk as the traditional focus of the hotel foyer and introduced informal seating arrangements and steps, which layered the space and provided an intimate atmosphere in which guests could meet and be seen.

Barney's

DATE: 1994

Beverly Hills, Los Angeles, California, USA

DESIGNER: Peter Marino (born 1949)

Barney's has a long-standing reputation for being the most stylish of Manhattan's big stores, a view that was enhanced by the redecoration of its Fifth Avenue branch in 1994. With its policy of promoting leading edge fashion Barney's has redefined the idea, not just of the clothes shop, but the department store itself. With such an approach, Barney's challenges the established New York giants, Macy's, Saks and Bloomingdales, targeting a more youthful and style-conscious clientele. Part of Barney's expansion programme included opening a store in America's richest and most prestigious shopping area, Beverly Hills in California. The store was lavishly fitted, with no expense spared, from the lift interiors to the floor finishes, to create a "new look" department store for the 1990s.

The inspiration for the store was the Alphonso XIV hotel in Seville, Spain. The Spanish influence permeates the design. The exterior combines brick, stucco and limestone, while the roof is covered with Spanish tiles. The main feature of the store is a central open staircase, which affords the customer glimpses of every level and of other shoppers. The staircase and ground floor are fashioned from a Spanish stone called "Blanco Macael". Other flooring is made from wood from France.

Kidosaki House

DATE: 1982–86

Tokyo, Japan

DESIGNER: Tadao Ando
(born 1941)

Tadao Ando is one of Japan's most celebrated architects. Although much of his work, including this house, can be found in Tokyo, his practice is based in Osaka away from the pressures of city life. The Kidosaki house is a typical example of his philosophy. Located in a quiet suburb of Tokyo, Ando's design provides a home for three families, each with separate living spaces within the main volume of the house. The house itself is a perfect twelve-metre cube surrounded by a wall that runs along the perimeter of the site. The living room looks out through floor-to-ceiling windows onto a courtyard, which introduces an element of nature within the cityscape.

The interior is beautifully simple. Ando's concern is to reduce form to its essentials. He uses light to articulate and highlight form, reflecting both modern design and also traditional Japanese ways of living. Ando is part of what the architectural critic Kenneth Frampton described as "Critical Regionalism", the combination of Modernism with the vernacular and rural traditions of design. One of the key themes in Ando's interiors is a rejection of the chaos of modern metropolitan life. His solution is to create haven-like interiors, often hidden away surrounded by walls and gardens, that offer the occupant a peaceful refuge.

Throughout his life Carlo Scarpa failed to receive much recognition as an architect, but he has since been acclaimed by architects and designers all over the world for his use of formal experimentation and sensitive detail. He offered a model for interior designers because his architecture deals with intervention, the conversion of existing buildings. Many of these projects included museums, the best-known being the Museo Correr and La Foscari Palace, both completed in the mid-1950s in Venice. Scarpa's work showed how it was possible to achieve a creative interweaving of tradition and innovation respecting the original building without allowing the past to overwhelm the new. This approach has become increasingly significant. In 1955 Scarpa began work on the extensions to the Museum Canova to redisplay the work of this master of late eighteenth-century white marble sculptures. Scarpa's achievement was the design of an exhibition space which used unusual light sources by cutting into the space windows and openings which ingeniously spotlit Canova's masterpieces. Scarpa also worked on the Castelvecchio Museum in Verona and as design consultant for the prestigious Venice Biennale international modern art showcase.

Canova Museum

DATE: 1955–57

Possagno, Italy

DESIGNER: Carlo Scarpa (1906–78)

Silver Jewellery Shop

DATE: 1987

DESIGNERS: Branson Coates Practice, London, England

Doug Branson and Nigel Coates run one of London's best-known architectural practices. They established their reputation in the 1980s with a series of innovative interiors in London and in Tokyo, which were widely admired and influential.

The jewellery shops of London's exclusive Bond Street have traditionally been fitted with plush carpets and expensive wood fittings. The Branson Coates design for the Silver Jewellery Shop introduced a rather different approach: instead of pilasters, torch lights are fastened to a rail with laboratory clamps; instead of volutes, curlicue metal; instead of panelling, a row of safes; and instead of Gothic gloom, sombre industrialism. The display cabinets are placed in a free-standing wall that cuts across the length of the shop. Their design uses standard fittings based on laboratory clamps which were then patinated. The jewellery is displayed on cushions which can be arranged at will.

Sober colours were used to dramatize the jewels. The walls were painted plaster grey by Nick Welch and the granite-toned colours blend with the grey-tinted walnut floor. Branson Coates is also well known for commissioning British designers for their interiors. The Silver Jewellery shop features chandeliers by Andre Dubreuil, a mirror by Andrew Logan and a mask made from a fish skull by Simon Costin. Nigel Coates has also used his own furniture for the shop, including his Chariot and Horse chairs.

The Hacienda

DATE: 1982

DESIGNER: Ben Kelly
(born 1949)

Manchester, England

Before the Hacienda, nightclub design either resembled the glitz and glam of *Saturday Night Fever* or the "paint it black" Punk style. Ben Kelly and his former partner Sandra Douglas created a new aesthetic for the nightclub, establishing the Hacienda as one of the most important interiors of the 1980s. It was commissioned by Factory, an independent record label which had achieved cult status with a series of seminal bands, such as Joy Division and New Order, and which also had ambitions to transform design.

Kelly had previously produced design work for Vivienne Westwood. He used an industrial aesthetic, including road bollards and road markings, with a new palette of colours, such as oranges, greens and reds – now widely accepted but then radically different.

Kelly was inspired by the ideas of Punk. The name of the club was not a kitsch reference to Spanish holidays but appropriated from the writings of the Situationists. The names of the bars, Kim Philby and The Guy Traitor – a reference to Anthony Blunt – were also not quite the names one would expect for a nightclub venue. The project pulled together a unique set of talents and helped to establish the originality of British interior design in the early 1980s.

Casa Neuendorf

DATE: 1989

Majorca, Spain

DESIGNERS: John Pawson
(born 1949) and Claudio
Silvestrin (born 1951)

John Pawson and his former partner Claudio Silvestrin developed a style of interior architecture that reduced the elements to a minimum. In such interiors, unnecessary elements have been stripped away, following the long tradition that links their work to Japanese living spaces, Shaker homes and the twentieth-century architecture of Mies van der Rohe in the Barcelona Pavilion, of Shiro Kuramata and Luis Barragân. The Neuendorf house is about architectural reduction: it concentrates on the organization of space and attention to the smallest detail, from the specification of the interior finishes to the positioning of a light switch. For this house, they sought to achieve a spiritual and calm effect, a holiday retreat in which the starkness of the approach is offset by the sensuous use of materials, including white marble and polished wood. The house was designed as a holiday home for a German art dealer and his family. It enjoys a spectacular site, set in an olive grove overlooking the sea. A 100-metre-long wall climbs the slope, beside a path of elongated steps, leading to a narrow vertical gap, piercing the façade of the house. Visitors are then led into a large atrium, an empty cube within a cube of massed walls, where local limestone is used throughout for the floor, and to form massive tables, benches and basins. The external walls are covered with a render reddened by local clay. Sunlight is manipulated by the thick walls and the few deep windows are positioned to frame views of the landscape. The long and narrow pool projects from the terrace towards the horizon, ending in a waterfall.

John Young is a partner in one of Britain's most distinguished architectural practices, the Richard Rogers Partnership. Designed as an apartment for himself and his wife, this project is a monument to Young's fascination with technology. Practically every element in the apartment is manufactured from industrial materials: the structural elements are the architecture. The main living space consists of an open-plan "L" shape forming a single living, cooking and work space. The area is single height except for the short arm in the L, which is double height and contains a mezzanine level that functions as a sleeping area. The space is articulated by the furniture and by the use of staircases all of which, in Young's hands, become works of art as well as an exercise in engineering. The living room is dominated by a suspended staircase, the truss of which is painted Day-Glo yellow. The banister steel is made from wire suspended between narrow steel balustrades in contrast to the teak treads. Connected to the mezzanine is a bathroom, a pod of glass bricks with a glass roof and a sunken cedarwood Japanese bath tub. The spiral staircase, which wraps around the exterior, also gives access to another pod-like form, the glass observatory on the roof of the building. In this interior functionalism becomes a form of high art – every possible feature is pared back to the structure and made into a memorable interior through its spaciousness and simplicity of materials.

Apartment London

DATE: 1989

Hammersmith, London, England

DESIGNER: John Young (born 1944)

Galvez House

DATE: 1968–69

Mexico

DESIGNER: Luis Barragán
(born 1902)

Inspired by traditional Mexican architecture, Luis Barragán's work is notable for its use of intense colours. By fusing elements of Modernism with references to the vernacular architecture of his childhood, Barragán has succeeded in creating a series of memorable buildings of atmosphere and spirituality.

Because of the climate, Mexican architecture focuses upon the interior. Barragán often uses series of platforms leading to heavily walled interiors. Spaces are defined by walls and accentuated by use of light. By the careful placing of top lights and windows, Barragán frequently manipulates the projection of light onto walls. Colour is used to add a spiritual dimension to the interior and further define the space. Barragán's individual palette often includes deep rich reds, acid tones of yellow, green and pink. It is his use of colour which has so deeply influenced the work of many contemporary interior designers. Traditional vernacular devices are balanced with Barragán's love of the abstracted forms of Modernism. The effect of Barragán's work has been compared to the balance and stillness of a De Chirico painting – it is always emotionally charged, offering a sense of refuge and memory.

Mash and Air

DATE: 1997

Manchester, England

DESIGNER: Marc Newson
(born 1963)

Oliver Peyton is the proprietor of two of the most influential restaurants in London in the 1990s, The Atlantic Bar and Grill and Coast, both of which are designed by Marc Newson. In 1997 Peyton opened Mash and Air in Manchester. It occupies a vast, four-storey mill, which was transformed by Newson. Newson's work for Coast was widely admired for its stylish coolness and finesse, but for Mash and Air he produced something very different. Here, he exploited the industrial feel of the building which included huge circular brewing equipment in the central space, a transparent piece of machinery revealing stainless steel and bright orange colour. Floor to ceiling windows enable the space to be light and airy and offer sweeping views. Newson has designed the interior to create the feeling of entering another world, a theatrical and surrealist effect in which the designer reveals an obsessive attention to detail. In the Mash and Air interior, from the lighting to the lime-green men's toilet, not one millimetre has escaped his attention. The tables appear like mushrooms growing out of the floor, and some of the eating banquettes are dropped into recesses with the tables at ground level, cut out of the stone work and cantilevering over the eating area so that the diners climb down to their table.

The Graan-silo Squat

DATE: 1991

Westerdoksdijk 51,
Amsterdam, The
Netherlands

Not all interiors in this section are designed by professionals. In 1989 a group of people occupied a derelict silo, an 1896 grain-drying tower in Amsterdam, with the intention of converting this huge industrial space into living areas for the homeless. This project was documented by the historian and writer David Carr-Smith and he provides a rare insight into this unique project. Converting this hostile industrial environment into habitable living space resulted in an astonishing transformation. To make this kitchen between their two-level apartment, Mark Horner and Brian Zaetlinck had to dismantle sixteen vertical metres of steel installations, install drains and power, lay wooden floors and salvage the fittings for the kitchen from the skips of urban refuse. Their work reveals an inventiveness and resourcefulness that blends domestic needs with the sheer grandeur and danger of the space, where steel pillars and girdered walls can be seen alongside the carpets and domestic objects of the home. It delivers a simple message that some people have the creativity and resourcefulness to design their own living spaces.

Chiat Day is a large international advertising agency with offices in Europe and America. It has become well known for its pioneering work in developing the concept of the new paperless office, turning the traditional working environment into a series of spaces that can accommodate a variety of activities instead of being, to quote Jay Chiat, "waste dumps of dead paperwork". What Chiat Day wanted was a total rethink of the way offices were organized and designed, exploring a new and experimental "non-territorial" office etiquette. Staff were no longer given designated spaces; rooms were flexible with walls and floors saturated with data-power ports so that people could hook up to the system anywhere within the office. But electronic technology is only part of the answer. The success of such a bold move relies on the role of the designer in the manipulation of this new spatial diversity. For its New York offices Chiat Day commissioned Gaetano Pesce, one of Italy's leading architects, widely admired for his visionary and forward-thinking attitudes. Pesce's solution was to take the rather mundane building shell and reconfigure the plan to create imaginative treatments of the internal partitions. He introduced a number of idiosyncratic details including the vivid floors, made of pigmented resin, poured to a thickness of seven millimetres over a concrete slab. In the thirty minutes it took to set, written messages and whimsical drawings were imprinted by hand. Pesce also used diverse wall finishes such as padding and thick felt and "brickwork" made from casts of television remote controls, and, in keeping with his interest in iconography, silhouetted doorways that recall advertising campaigns for important clients. A large staff locker room replaced the individual office desk and here Pesce introduced muted lighting to create a sense of privacy along with wooden cabinets to dispel the old image of uniformity usually associated with the locker room.

Chiat Day Offices

DATE: 1993–96

New York City, USA

DESIGNER: Gaetano Pesce (born 1939)

PART 4

furniture

ANT CHAIR

STACKING STOOL

SUPERLEGGERA CHAIR

FURNITURE DESIGN OFFERS AN OPPORTUNITY in small scale to explore new design and style directions, and for the twentieth century, with its agenda of dramatic visual and cultural change, this assumed a particular importance. Furniture maps out the territory of twentieth-century design and key pieces signal to us important changes in production, technology, taste and cultural aspirations. In this context the chair came to represent an opportunity to produce radical and daring experiments exploiting the new vocabulary of form and materials. Furniture was the prototype for a new way of living and offered possibilities for experimentation that architecture did not.

At the beginning of the century a large scale furniture industry was in place, but production methods were still essentially reliant on traditional, labour-intensive techniques. There were some technical innovations, notably the simple and minimalist bentwood chair by Thonet. This chair pioneered the standardization of simple parts and could be exported in knock-down form, which saved on space and generated huge export sales. In general, however, nineteenth-century furniture for the domestic consumer concentrated on large scale, elaborately decorated pieces using a language of ornament taken from a variety of largely historical sources. The Arts and Crafts Movement introduced a new direction. Pioneer designers and retailers like William Morris revived interest in the simple forms of late nineteenth-century furniture and the tradition of vernacular furniture. This tradition included furniture types whose production had continued in an unbroken line for hundreds of years. Practical and comfortable wooden chairs like the ladderback and the Windsor had been used to furnish the country cottage and the kitchen; now they found a place in the new artistic home and represented the values of truth to materials and honest form. This simple and undecorated furniture influenced many leading designers who designed their own variations on this vernacular theme, including the famous London store Heals. Elaborate and richly decorated furniture did not however disappear from the market and was given new impetus with the emergence of Art Nouveau, the century's last "decorated style". Leading continental exponents of Art Nouveau produced expensive and exclusive furniture whose influence filtered down to the furniture trade and was a trend which continued in the 1920s with the geometric formalism of Art Deco.

The taste for furniture as decoration and display remains with us in the 1990s, but a more radical direction for furniture in the twentieth century came with the Modern Movement. One of the earliest and most important experiments in this regard was the famous Blue and Red Chair, 1918, by the Dutch De Stijl designer Gerrit Rietveld. With this chair Rietveld developed the

paintings of his famous contemporary Piet Mondrian in three dimensional form, using abstracted pure form, geometric shapes and primary colours. At the same time leading avant-garde architects were reshaping the architectural landscape but they quickly realized that there was no commercially available furniture that could be successfully integrated into the new open plan, white living spaces. Le Corbusier's solution was to design appropriate furniture himself and, together with his cousin Jeanneret and the young Charlotte Perriand, he produced furniture as "machines for sitting in" to complement the house as a "machine for living in".

POWERPLAY ARMCHAIR

This pioneer work in furniture can be seen as both an attempt to create a mass product, but also to extend this experiment on a broader scale to the house and the built environment as a whole via standardization, prefabrication and factory production. This furniture evoked the machine: it suggested industry and engineering and the European admiration for *Amerikanismus* – the world of Henry Ford, of skyscrapers and new beginnings. Important in this context is the furniture designed at the Bauhaus, notably the tubular-steel cantilever chair by Marcel Breuer. The streamlined, sculptural and continuous lines of such chairs became the perfect expression of the new modernity and set in place a new direction for furniture design.

Meanwhile other exponents of Modernism continued to use natural materials and organic forms, most famously expressed in the 1930s by Alvar Aalto and in the 1950s by the work of Arne Jacobsen. These traditions provided a heritage inherited by the postwar world. Now the agenda for furniture included the demands of a new consumer culture expressed by the 1960s aesthetic of Pop and the availability of new technology. Synthetic glues allowed dramatic plywood shapes and plastic polypropylene introduced cheap, light, mass-produced chairs by Italian companies such as Kartell. While designers continued to develop the themes of the Modern Movement other priorities emerged with the appearance of Postmodernism. Consumers and designers looked again at colour, decoration and pattern. Furniture, epitomized by the 1980s Italian group Memphis, shifted from the classic to become playful, witty and childlike. At the same time the aesthetic of mass production was challenged by a number of important craftsmen–designers, including Ron Arad and Tom Dixon. Their starting point was the one-off piece, using recycled materials and sculptural effects using metal; their influence soon affected the mainstream. Today the industrial forms and materials of the Modern Movement are simply another style option for the consumer, alongside the quirky and the expressive, and the traditional upholstered furniture that has changed little since the nineteenth century.

WW STOOL

Chair
No. 14

DATE: 1859

DESIGNER: Michael Thonet
(1796–1871)

MATERIAL: bent beechwood

MANUFACTURER: Gebrüder
Thonet, Vienna, Austria

The Thonet bentwood chair remains one of the most successful chairs of the twentieth century and is still produced in modified form. Michael Thonet was born in the small German town of Boppard, a centre for furniture-making. Using the techniques he had seen developed by barrel makers and boat builders, Thonet experimented with steaming and bending strips of beech wood into curves. By holding them in wooden clamps and using strips of tin plate, he bent solid beech strips beyond their natural flexibility.

In 1836 he introduced the first chair made of laminated wood, and in 1856 he was granted a patent for industrial bentwood processing. Thonet had grand ambitions for his product, exhibiting the chair at the 1851 Great Exhibition in London.

Thonet was also responsible for another key innovation. With an eye on the export market, he came up with kit furniture, rationalizing the chair design into four simple parts so that thirty-five unassembled chairs took up only thirty-five square metres of a ship's cargo space. When the chairs reached their destination, caning was done by hand, largely by women in factories or working at home.

The chair was cheap to buy and its success meant large quantities could be produced. In the twentieth century its qualities were recognized by modern designers. It was one of the few pieces of commercial furniture that Le Corbusier bought for his interiors and is a rare example of design continuity and survival.

Horta Museum

DATE: 1898–1901

Brussels, Belgium

DESIGNER: Victor Horta
(1861–1947)

Although Art Nouveau conveys solidly Gallic connotations, Paris was not the only centre for the new style. Other European cities played a key role in the development of Art Nouveau, most importantly the Belgian capital, Brussels. During the 1890s, Victor Horta designed a series of houses for private clients, for which he not only designed the building but every aspect of the interior, including carpets, lighting, stained glass and furniture. In these houses, which include his own, since converted into the Horta Museum, he developed a mature version of the Art Nouveau style, using whiplash tendrils and elaborate naturalist forms, which were applied to furniture, fittings and interior details in order to achieve a unified interior. Also shown here is Horta's use of white enamel bricks, initially bought for the outside but here used as an original wall finish. Horta became one of Europe's most sophisticated exponents of Art Nouveau and indeed the famous whiplash curve that epitomizes his style also became the "Horta Line" in his honour – a tribute to the rich eclectic style for which he was renowned.

In 1902 Horta was commissioned to design the Belgian Pavilion at the Turin exhibition, a showcase for Art Nouveau. Increasingly, however, Horta found himself isolated and after World War One, when Art Nouveau was no longer fashionable, he undertook little design work. In 1920 he become a professor at the Académie des Beaux-Arts in Brussels, where he remained until 1931.

Letchworth Bedroom

DATE: 1905

DESIGNER: Ambrose Heal
(1872–1959)

MANUFACTURER: Heal and
Son, London, England

Heal's was and is one of the best known furniture shops in London. Under the directorship of Ambrose Heal, the company allied itself to progressive design. Heal learnt his trade as an apprentice to a furniture workshop in Warwick. When he joined his father's business in 1893 he was allowed a small area in the shop to show his own designs. His work was heavily influenced by the Arts and Crafts Movement, but far from being an amateur designer,

Heal quickly attracted international interest in his designs, exhibiting them in Paris and London.

In 1905, Ambrose Heal was asked to design a range of furniture for the Letchworth Exhibition. The furniture would be displayed in a cottage designed by FW Troup. Letchworth was one of the new "Garden Cities" that were springing up over Britain, and the furniture was intended to appeal to the middle-classes who inhabited such leafy suburbs.

Heal's designs were beautifully made and linked to a vernacular tradition of furniture making which had so inspired the Victorian design reformers. His furniture emphasized simple and rational forms with no surface decoration and plain finishes. These qualities, in spite of the name, place the Heals range alongside radical continental design. The Cottage Furniture range, which was shown to the public in 1919 through an illustrated catalogue, summed up his approach.

Shaker

DATE: nineteenth century

USA

Original Shaker furniture and reproductions now command high prices and have attracted a dedicated following. The Shakers were originally an English nonconformist sect founded by Ann Lee in Manchester. In the late eighteenth century, in search of religious freedom, Mother Lee and a group of followers emigrated to the East Coast of America where they established a series of communities. The Shakers rejected all modern inventions, living a life of refined austerity which they translated into their furniture and household objects. Shaker craftsmen encapsulated their moral beliefs in spare and simple interiors and furniture – ladder back chairs, tables and boxes – which owed something of their aesthetic to late eighteenth-century English furniture. What they added was an idiosyncratic element of invention, introducing ideas such as fitted furniture and the distinctive rails on which they hung clothes and chairs.

Shaker communities have dwindled during the course of the twentieth century and very few remain. However, Shaker style has remained influential to twentieth-century designers. Their furniture rejected decoration and used the language of form to express moral purity. It is not difficult to see why they attracted the admiration of so many modern designers.

Red and Blue Armchair

DATE: 1918

DESIGNER: Gerrit Rietveld (1888–1964)

MATERIAL: painted wood

The visual impact of the Red and Blue Chair has ensured that it remains a standard image in any history of twentieth-century design, and with the Schröder house it has become a metaphor for the Modern Movement.

Rietveld was a member of De Stijl (the Style), one of the most coherent groups within the Modern Movement. Although Gerrit Rietveld was a key player in De Stijl, his work remains rooted in the craft tradition in which he trained. Until 1911, when he opened his own cabinet-making business in

Utrecht, his early years were spent as an apprentice cabinet-maker to his father.

His approach changed dramatically in 1918 when he came into contact with the early members of De Stijl. Their search for a universal form of expression led them to experiment with primary colours, basic geometric shapes and abstracted pure forms. The most recognizable expression of these aims can be found in the paintings of Piet Mondrian. This work was an inspiration to Rietveld, who took literally the De Stijl message that "the new consciousness is ready to be

realized in everything, including the everyday things of life".

Rietveld developed the ideas of De Stijl in a three-dimensional form, the most famous expressions of which were the celebrated Red and Blue chair of 1918, and the Schröder House built six years later in Utrecht.

It is simplistic but nonetheless true to describe these designs as three-dimensional Mondrian paintings. However, it is worth pointing out that his work remains more interesting on a visual level than as a design solution for the needs of the twentieth century.

Marcel Breuer started his career at the most famous design school of the twentieth century – the Bauhaus in Germany. Enrolled in 1920, Breuer spent most of his time in the cabinet-making workshop. Almost immediately his work was recognized as highly original.

The story of how he discovered bent tubular steel has become part of the mythology of the Modern Movement. Legend has it that Breuer simply purchased an Adler bicycle and was so inspired by its strength and lightness, that he determined to apply the same techniques to furniture. Although many other designers experimented with the idea of a single, curved chair shape that did not use traditional legs, it was Breuer's B 64 – nicknamed in the 1960s after Breuer's adopted daughter, Francesca – which became the decade's most-famous cantilevered design.

Breuer did not train as an architect and only started to design buildings after he left the Bauhaus in 1928, when he moved to Berlin. While his architectural projects during this period were restricted to interiors and competition entries, they were as radical as any in the avant-garde. Breuer was unusual in that, unlike Gropius and Mies van der Rohe, his furniture preceded his architecture. In this way it can be seen as a rehearsal for his buildings. Streamlined, continuous metal furniture that flowed seamlessly became the perfect expression of the Modern Movement and informed Breuer's interiors and structures. In 1937, at the invitation of Walter Gropius, he taught architecture at Harvard. It was there that Breuer became an important bridge between Europe and America. Partly due to his early workshop training, Breuer proved a popular and practical teacher. In this sense Breuer became more important for his influence on a key generation of American architects – among them Philip Johnson – than for his own buildings.

Cesca Chair (B32)

DATE: c.1926

DESIGNER: Marcel Breuer (1902–81)

MATERIAL: chrome-plated steel, wood and cane

MANUFACTURER: Gebrüder Thonet, Frankenberg, Germany

Chaise Longue

DATE: 1928

DESIGNERS: Le Corbusier (1887–1965), Pierre Jeanneret (1896–1967), Charlotte Perriand (born 1903)

MATERIAL: chrome and painted steel with leather and fabric upholstery

MANUFACTURER: Thonet Frères, Paris, France

During the mid to late 1920s, some of the most talented European architects, including Marcel Breuer and Ludwig Mies van der Rohe, produced chair designs in tubular steel and leather that remain some of the classic pieces of twentieth-century furniture.

Perhaps the greatest and most enduring piece of Modernist furniture produced at this time is the chaise longue designed in 1928 by a previously little-known French designer called Charlotte Perriand, seen lying on her creation in a photograph by Pierre Jeanneret. When Perriand approached the prominent architect Le Corbusier with her portfolio, she was told that "we don't sew cushions here!". Her desire to make her mark within the masculine world of architecture was rewarded when she was eventually employed by Le Corbusier to design items of furniture for the villas he was building.

Le Corbusier had a holistic approach to architecture, in which furnishings were physically integrated into the fabric of the building. Le Corbusier termed the fixtures of a house "*équipment d'habitation*" or literally, equipment for living.

The designs that were produced by Perriand, and jointly signed by her, Le Corbusier and his cousin Pierre Jeanneret, are some of the purest expressions of the modernist aesthetic, in which simplicity and function are the governing considerations. The feet of the chair mimic the profile of an aeroplane wing and establish the piece as an icon of the "machine age".

Perriand's designs were first manufactured by Thonet and later by the Swiss company Embru. The chaise longue remains in production today in a modified form by Cassina.

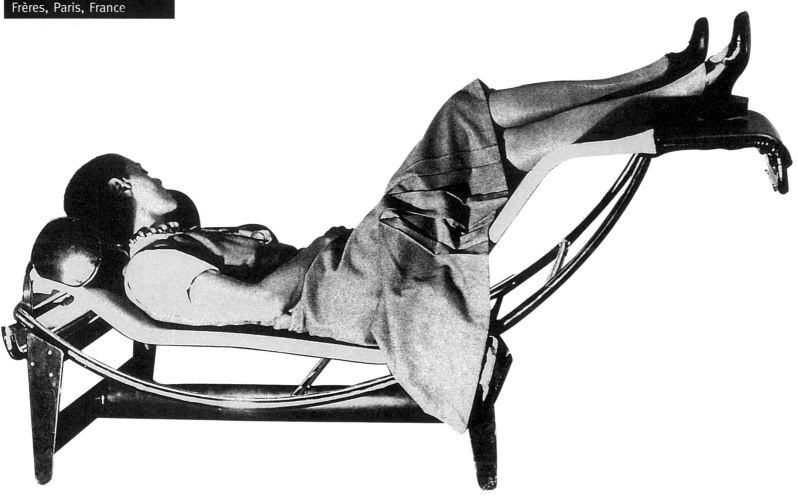

Tom Wolfe, in his critique of Modernism – *From Bauhaus to Our House* – described the way in which Mies van der Rohe's Barcelona chair became an icon of new values and aspirations for postwar America: "When you saw that holy object on the sisal rug you knew you were in a household where a fledgling architect and his young wife had sacrificed everything to bring the symbol of the godly mission into their home."

Originally the Barcelona chair was designed for the German Pavilion at the 1929 International Exhibition in Barcelona. The German Pavilion was the only Modernist building in the exhibition and it created a sensation. Inside the austere structure, Mies displayed his famous chair as thrones for the Spanish king and queen and, although it was designed within the Modernist aesthetic, the X-frame recalls medieval seats of power.

The chair was produced in America from 1948 and came to express modernity, taste and high quality, and signified the values of the mighty corporations to all who bought it. Mies had attempted to rethink furniture and seek out a dramatically different approach to the prevailing craft tradition. Both his architecture and his furniture evoked the machine. It suggested industry and engineering and the European admiration for *Amerikanismus*, the world of Henry Ford, of skyscrapers and new beginnings. Ironically, the Barcelona chair was the result of painstaking hand-craft techniques using traditional materials.

Barcelona Chair

DATE: 1929

DESIGNER: Ludwig Mies van der Rohe (1886–1969)

MATERIAL: chrome-plated steel with leather upholstery

MANUFACTURER: Bamberg Metallwerkstatten, Berlin, Germany, later Knoll Associates, New York City, USA

Fauteuil, Modèle Petit Confort

DATE: 1928

DESIGNERS: Le Corbusier (1887–1965), Pierre Jeanneret (1896–1967), Charlotte Perriand (born 1903)

MATERIAL: chrome-plated steel and leather upholstery

Le Corbusier's furniture – or "equipment" – must be understood as an extension of his architectural aims of this period. When Le Corbusier realized that his clients could not buy furniture that would complement the flowing space of his houses, he developed a range of a furniture – machines for sitting in – to co-exist with machines for living in. Placed in the interiors of houses such as the Maison Cook (1927),

the Villa Church (1927–28) and the Villa Savoye (1929) this furniture became discrete sculpture, articulating the free-flowing space of the interior, and rendering the house a totally designed entity.

The furniture was not the work of Le Corbusier alone. He worked in collaboration with a young furniture designer, Charlotte Perriand, who had been experimenting with tubular steel

as a material, as well as with his cousin and partner Pierre Jeanneret. It is to these three that the furniture should be attributed, and some to Perriand alone – a fact recognized only recently.

The "confort" armchair was made in both small and large versions. The prototypes had sprung rear legs with feather-filled cushions. It is now reproduced in modified form by the Milanese company, Cassina.

In 1925, Eileen Gray and Jean Badovici designed a house – the Villa E.1027 near Saint Tropez – which featured furnishings made in her Paris workshops. Gray exploited new materials, such as the tubular steel used for the table shown here. It was originally designed as a bed table with the ring foot pushed under the bed for ease of use with adjustable tabletop height. It was later used as an occasional table for the living room.

The E.1027 Table relates to the cantilever chair experiments of the 1920s in that it also explored the idea of a table without conventional legs exploiting the streamlined possibilities of tubular steel. Gray, however, did not share the machine age preoccupations of many of her contemporaries in the European Modern Movement. Her driving force was less concerned with industrial techniques than with a search for visual perfection. The table was put into production again from the late 1970s.

E.1027, Side Table

DATE: 1927

DESIGNER: Eileen Gray (1879–1976)

MATERIAL: tubular steel and acrylic glass

MANUFACTURER: Atelier Eileen Gray–Galerie Jean Desert, Paris, France

Stacking Stool "L" Leg

DATE: 1932–33

DESIGNER: Alvar Aalto
(1898–1976)

MATERIAL: plywood

MANUFACTURER: Artek,
Helsinki, Finland

Aalto's great achievement was the production of designs that were simultaneously ahead of their time and timeless. Designed as fixtures for his buildings, the furniture reflects exactly the same aesthetic as the architecture – they remain part of the same vision.

The beauty of his plywood furniture meant that it became more than just furniture – it was appreciated and collected as sculpture for the modern interior. In this context, for example, his plywood kitchen stools were specified as seating for Manchester's Hacienda nightclub in the 1980s, by designer Ben Kelly, and for kitchens, restaurants and homes all over the world. Aalto's designs have found a place in the modern domestic interior and inspired countless imitations in stores such as Ikea.

Aalto's choice of natural materials – such as wood – and his simple use of curves reflects both an interest in organic forms and the need for a human and humane aesthetic.

In 1925 he married the architect Aino Marsio, his most important collaborator. It was Marsio who ran the Artek Wooden Furniture company, which marketed Aalto's designs that found almost immediate commercial success around the world.

Arne Jacobsen's achievement as an architect was to fuse the traditions of his native Denmark with those of mainstream Modernism. In common with many Scandinavian architects of his generation, Jacobsen also concerned himself with the design of the interior and its fixtures. Most of his designs for silverware, textiles and furniture were site specific but their appeal to a wider audience was immediate.

In 1952 he designed The Ant, a light, stackable chair, the seat and back of which were moulded from a single piece of plywood supported by a tubular steel frame. The chair was designed for the Fritz Hansen furniture factory, which had experimented with steam-bent plywood for a number of years. The Ant was Jacobsen's contribution to the language of modern, industrially manufactured furniture and it inspired a series of successors from 1952 to 1968 whose common elements were the continuous seat and back. These chairs marked an important turning-point in Jacobsen's career and they mark his shift from a distinguished Danish designer to a figure of international importance.

The 3107 Ant Chair, pictured here, produced as the Series 7, was designed for the Rodovre Town Hall as a stacking chair. it is now manufactured in many different versions and numerous colours, and remains the most sold chair in Denmark. With their new materials and organic forms these chairs were original and fresh, sensual and even sexy objects. It is no coincidence that the photograph of the naked Christine Keeler posing on a fake Ant chair has become a legendary icon of the Swinging Sixties.

Ant Chair

DATE: 1955

DESIGNER: Arne Jacobsen (1902–71)

MATERIAL: moulded plywood and chrome steel

MANUFACTURER: Fritz Hansen, Denmark

Landi Chair

DATE: 1938

DESIGNER: Hans Coray
(born 1906)

MATERIAL: aluminium alloy
and rubber

MANUFACTURER: Blattmann
Metallwarenfabrik,
Switzerland

The Landi, created for the Swiss National Exhibition of 1939 – the Schweizerische Landesausstellung – became the most successful outdoor chair of the twentieth century. Although aluminium was extremely costly to use for furniture, it was a major Swiss export and so was felt appropriate for an exhibition aimed at raising national prestige. At the time the Landi, made from aluminium alloys stretch stamped and baked in the factory, represented a technological tour de force. The arm and leg units were manufactured separately and finished with clear lacquer. The extraordinary aesthetics look forward to postwar plywood experiments of the Eames era. Strong, comfortable and genuinely rust- and waterproof, the Landi was an immediate success and, although designed for outdoor use, quickly found its way into homes, restaurants and cafés. It has been in continuous production since 1938.

Utility was a fascinating design experiment brought about by the horrific circumstances of wartime Britain. In 1940, when the worst of the Blitz bombing had taken its toll on civilian lives and property in densely populated urban areas, the Prime Minister, Winston Churchill, was determined that civilian morale should be maintained by a limited availability of consumer goods. The Government established the Utility scheme. The brief was simple: all

furniture, clothing and other products, such as ceramics, would be specially designed and produced, and available on a ration basis, subject to need.

The scheme enlisted a small group of designers, many of whom had been involved in Britain's design experiments with the new European Modernism. These designers included Gordon Russell, whose factory had pioneered modern furniture in the 1930s, but the results merged the rationale of the

British Arts and Crafts tradition with the utilitarian demands of the war. It was no accident that one of the ranges was called Cotswold – a nineteenth-century centre for Arts and Crafts experiments. Typical of these designs was the introduction of this dining chair, based on earlier work of the British Arts and Crafts designers, but here using simplified construction methods and a synthetic leather seat cover.

Dining Chair, Model 3a

DATE: 1943

DESIGNERS: Utility Design Team

MATERIAL: oak and leather cloth seat

MANUFACTURER: Utility Scheme, London, England

Superleggera Chair

DATE: 1955

DESIGNER: Gio Ponti
(1891–1979)

MATERIAL: tinted ash
and cane

MANUFACTURER: Cassina,
Meda, Italy

Gio Ponti was a true Renaissance man. Not only was he active as a teacher and writer, he was also a gifted painter and designed products, lighting and furniture. Even in the context of so many talented Italian designers, Ponti remains a unique individual, remarkable for his integration of ceramics, furniture, theatre design, town planning and graphics with architecture.

During the 1930s he had worked with Cassina, one of Italy's most respected furniture manufacturers, and this relationship continued in the postwar period. Cassina wanted a light, versatile chair that would suit the smaller apartments of the 1950s where space was at a premium, so Ponti produced a seminal design, the Superleggera chair of 1955. For this he was inspired by the tradition of light wooden chairs, used by local fishermen he had seen as a child. He had worked on versions of this vernacular design as early as 1947. His final work for the Superleggera produced a classic but modern chair that proved extremely popular with Italian consumers. In 1957 it won the prestigious Compasso d'Oro prize. Ponti's trademark combination of tradition with modernity can be seen in Milan's Pirelli Tower (1956), where modern concrete is capped with a cantilevered roof in the shape of a cardinal's hat.

It is not surprising that this simple and spare table was designed by a garden designer and a sculptor who had worked in the 1920s as an assistant for Alexander Calder. This table became Isamu Noguchi's best-known design and received international publicity for its minimalist aesthetic that fitted so well into the culture of the 1950s. It was designed using two identical elements for the base, one of which was inverted and glued to the other. Interestingly, it was this same quality of minimalism that caused Noguchi many problems and inspired the imitations that dogged his career as a designer. In fact it was a copycat design of an earlier piece that prompted Noguchi to produce this table. As soon as it was designed it sold in huge quantities, helped by the fact that Herman Miller were able to promote this table as knock-down furniture.

Coffee Table IN-50

DATE: **1945**

DESIGNER: Isamu Noguchi (1904–88)

MATERIAL: ebonized birchwood and glass

MANUFACTURER: Herman Miller Furniture Company, Michigan, USA

P40
Reclining
Armchair

DATE: 1954

DESIGNER: Orsaldo Borsani
(1911–85)

MATERIAL: metal and
upholstery

MANUFACTURER: Tecno,
Milan, Italy

One of the most striking designs of the decade, this chair relies on an engineering aesthetic – with its adjustable seat and back, and flexible armrests, it resembles an aircraft seat. The chair was influenced by the techniques used in the automobile industry: foam rubber, then a new

material from Pirelli, was used to pad the seat, the footrest was retractable and the chair could be adjusted into 486 different positions. Tecno, the manufacturer, started life as the Atelier Varedo, run by Gaetano Borsani, a progressive 1920s designer, who won a silver medal at the Monza Triennale of

1927. Borsani opened his first shop in Milan's prestigious Via Montenapoleone after the war. He later established Tecno, which was run by his two sons, designer Orsaldo and financial director Fulgenzio. Tecno concentrated on the design and production of furniture for offices and factories, including Olivetti.

Eames Storage Unit 421-C

DATE: 1949–50

DESIGNER: Charles Eames (1907–78) and Ray Eames (1916–88)

MATERIAL: plywood, varnished steel, fibreglass, masonite, and rubber

MANUFACTURER: Herman Miller Furniture Company, Michigan, USA

In 1941 Charles married Ray Kaiser and together they became America's most important furniture designers. Their work dominated postwar design not only in their own country but internationally, and their experiments with new materials, particularly plywood and plastic, established an aesthetic that came to express the spirit of the 1950s. The Eames Storage Unit (ESU) illustrated here is closely linked to the house the Eames built for themselves in California (see p. 60) using steel-frame prefabricated units with infill units painted in bright colours. These units can be placed in the Modernist tradition of using standardized, industrial techniques for domestic furniture. The idea was that by using prefabricated parts, the user could assemble virtually limitless combinations according to practical needs and personal taste. In its catalogue the manufacturer Herman Miller illustrated the various options which the range made possible, but this early experiment was difficult to market. The self-assembly element proved difficult and required skilled installation, a DIY concept which 1950s people found unappealing. Although the Eames design inspired many later copycat versions, the ESU was not a commercial success in its own right and was discontinued.

Generally, however, Charles and Ray Eames were extremely fortunate in that they acted virtually as in-house designers for Herman Miller, America's most prestigious furniture company. The company's respected design profile meant that Eames furniture was painstakingly produced and marketed, featuring then, as it still does now, in books, magazines and high-profile interiors.

No. 22 Diamond Chair

DATE: 1952

DESIGNER: Harry Bertoia
(1915–78)

MATERIALS: steel with
upholstery and rubber

MANUFACTURER: Knoll
Associates, New York City,
USA

Many would argue that this is less of a chair than a piece of sculpture. It was designed to be viewed from all sides and extended Bertoia's earlier experiments with visual transparency, sculpting with metal wire. Certainly that was how he viewed his work. He had trained as a sculptor and shortly after designing this chair returned to that activity for the rest of his life. For many people, however, this wire chair has come to express the aesthetic of postwar design – new materials, a new lightness of form and a promise of the future.

From the late 1930s, when he moved to the Cranbrook Academy, Bertoia found himself at the centre of new American developments in design. At Cranbrook he met his friend Charles Eames, with whom he collaborated briefly, and Florence Knoll. It was she who later offered him the commission to work on the chair of his choice and design. It took two years of production work to launch the Diamond range, using fabricated wire mesh to create a network of diamond patterns formed into these distinctive seating shells which float in space. The range was always expensive, relying on handmade welding. Although they were Bertoia's last furniture designs they remain classic chairs of the postwar period.

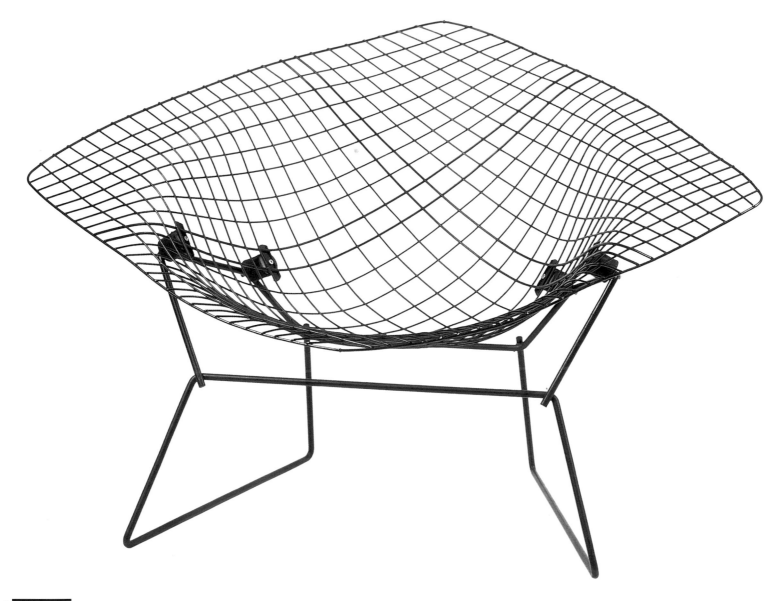

Arabesque Table

DATE: 1949

DESIGNER: Carlo Mollino (1905–73)

MATERIAL: maple plywood and glass

MANUFACTURER: Apelli, Varesio and Company, Turin, Italy

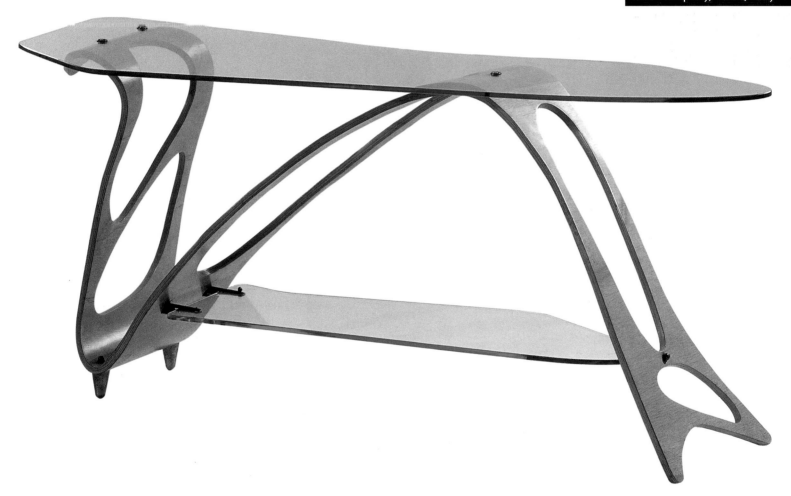

Born in Turin, the city at the centre of Italy's new industrialization with such landmarks as the Fiat factory, Carlo Mollino enjoys a cult status among architects and designers. His father, Eugenio, was an architect and engineer who instilled in his son an admiration of all things modern. He introduced Carlo to stunt flying – the designs of much of his streamlined furniture clearly echo the wing structures of these early planes.

Mollino was a designer who saw his work as part of a personal lifestyle dedicated to speed. He competed in international car racing competitions, mountain skiing and flying. Of greater significance was an obsession with the erotic and the female body, from which he drew much formal inspiration. Eroticism is a recurring theme throughout his work in architecture, furniture and interior design. His archive contained thousands of photographs he took of the female nude placed in what he called "bachelor rooms" – specially designed environments for which he designed furniture and fixtures.

Mollino designed the first Arabesque table in 1949 for the living room of Casa Orenga in Turin. The shape of the glass top was taken from a naked woman's back in a drawing by the Surrealist artist Léonor Fini, while the perforated table frame has a similar organic quality to the reliefs of the sculptor Jean Arp.

Much of Mollino's architecture and interiors have been destroyed, leaving only the photographs and furniture remaining. However, his influence on postwar designers has been an enduring one.

Action Office

DATE: 1964

DESIGNER: George Nelson
(1907 86)

MATERIAL: aluminium, steel,
wood, plastic and leather

MANUFACTURED: Herman
Miller Furniture Company,
Michigan, USA

Herman Miller was America's most prestigious postwar furniture company. Their ambitious agenda for furniture design included a research department established in 1960 to introduce a new approach to the design of office furniture. George Nelson, the company's director of design from 1946–66, was given the brief to design a new system of modular units that could be adapted to the different requirements of people and work. The Action Office consisted of a chair on wheels, different tables, and stackable shelf sections accompanied by a variety of accessories. The common component was the aluminium base, which acted as a support for the different units, including the option to use two as the support for a larger conference table. In the 1960s Nelson was a pioneer is developing office systems that suited the new flexible work environments of the large company or small office. Although it was later promoted in a more simplified form, the Action Office established a new standard for the design of office furniture and the system proved extremely popular.

There had been earlier experiments with inflatable designs, for example emergency rafts for aeroplanes. Blow, however, was the first time that inflatable furniture was made popular and available, thanks to new plastic technology which used electronic welding by radio frequency to seal the chair seams. It was a collaboration between four architects designing their first piece of furniture. The publicity it received did much to establish Zanotta in the 1960s as a company with fresh, exciting ideas .

The aesthetic of Pop design led to a quest for furniture that was cheap, witty, fun and disposable. Inflatable furniture was an obvious extension of these ideas. The chair was bought as a flat pack kit which was inflated at home – when moving, it was simply deflated and folded flat.

Visually, the styling is reminiscent of the Modernist chairs of the 1930s, notably those of Eileen Gray. It also connects with the inflatable Pop art experiments of Claes Oldenburg. The Blow chair became one of the instantly recognizable icons of the decade, appearing in films of the period to express the new spirit of the times, and in endless design magazines.

The Blow was an impractical piece of furniture. It was easily damaged, and so came equipped with its own repair kit. However, it is important to remember that it was relatively cheap to buy and intended to have a short lifespan – when it was beyond repair it was simply replaced.

Although revived as a design classic in the 1980s by Zanotta, the real impact of plastic, inflatable furniture was for fun – play items for the beach and swimming pool.

Blow Chair

DATE: 1967

DESIGNERS: Jonathan De Pas (1932–91), Donato D'Urbino (born 1935), Paolo Lomazzi (born 1936), and Carlo Scolari (born c.1930)

MATERIAL: transparent PVC plastic

MANUFACTURER: Zanotta, Nova Milanese, Italy

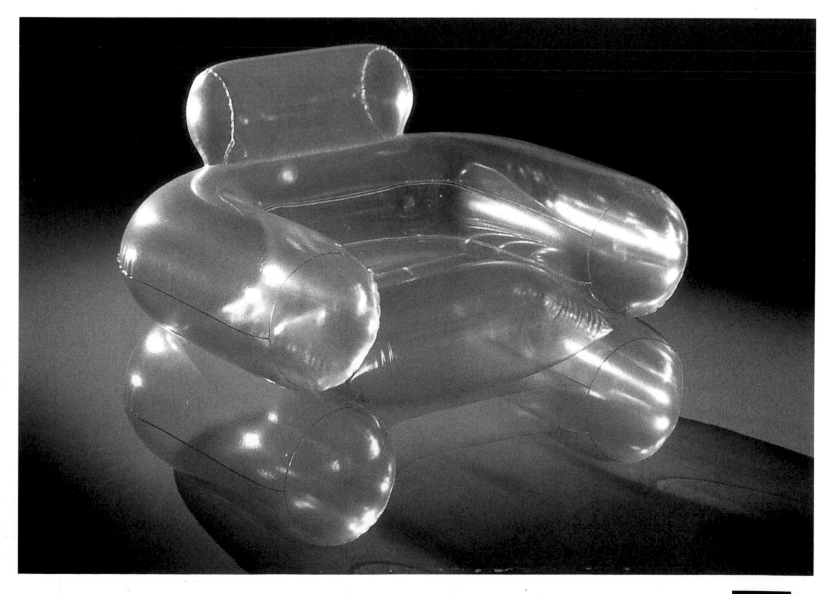

4867 Chair

DATE: 1965

DESIGNER: Cesare "Joe" Columbo (1930–71)

MATERIAL: plastic

MANUFACTURER: Kartell, Milan, Italy

Joe Columbo has become a legendary Italian designer, arguably the most original and inventive of his generation and his early death has contributed to this reputation. His creativity was incredibly versatile, perhaps the result of training both as a painter and an architect in Milan. The 4867 was Columbo's first experiment with new technology: it was the first chair made of ABS plastic to be injection-moulded in one piece, although a hole in the back was needed to remove the chair from the mould.

Kartell was founded in 1949 by Giulio Castelli to produce household objects using the newly patented plastics. Castelli's father had been involved in the early Italian plastics industry and Kartell used this experience to design functional objects, such as plate racks and kitchen pails, but commissioning leading designers to work on the aesthetics. The 4867 chair was Joe Columbo's response to a new material which could be curved in three dimensions and allowed the designer the freedom to create fresh, different shapes.

Facciamo progetti per il presente

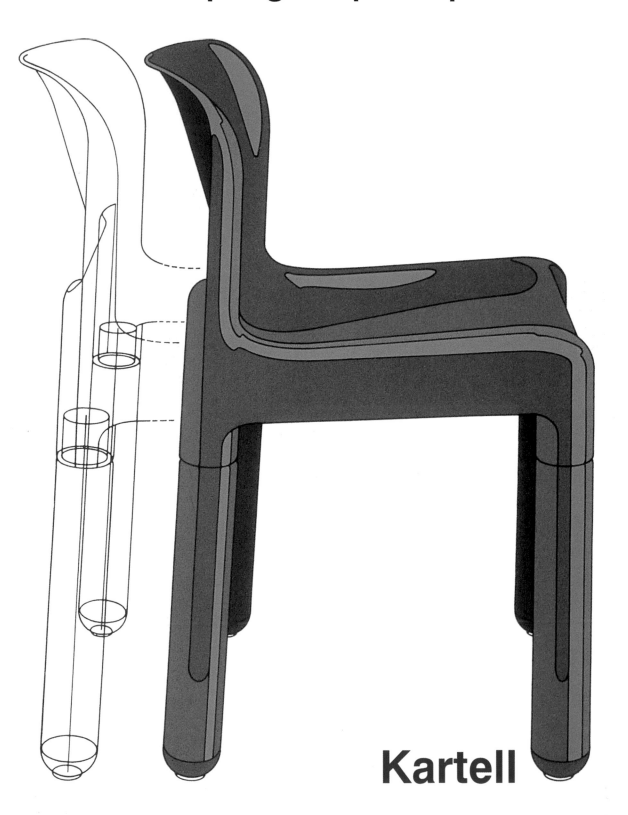

Kartell

AEO
Armchair

DATE: 1973

DESIGNER: Paolo Deganello
(born 1940)

MATERIAL: painted metal,
fabric covered upholstery
and steel

MANUFACTURER: Cassina,
Meda, Italy

In 1972 the Museum of Modern Art in New York held an exhibition called "Italy: The New Domestic Landscape". If indeed there was any doubt, this exhibition established Italian design as the most innovative and creative in the world. During the 1960s Italian design established a reputation for radical, leading edge work and many young designers had formed design groups of which Archizoom Associati was one of the best known. They acted less as conventional design practices than as think-tanks, producing prototypes, art installations and events. With typical Italian pragmatism, the more mainstream companies did not ignore these activities and often worked in collaboration with young designers.

This experimental chair, designed for Archizoom Associati, is such a collaboration, investigating structure and form. Piero Daganello divided the chair into separate elements: an organic plastic base, in which was placed the iron frame covered with stretch cloth supporting a soft cushion. The back is a loose canvas cover which slips over the frame. AEO stands for Alpha and Omega – the first and last letters of the Greek alphabet. The chair was designed to sell as a flat-pack.

Cab Chair

DATE: 1976

DESIGNER: Mario Bellini
(born 1935)

MATERIAL: enamelled steel,
leather upholstery

MANUFACTURER: Cassina,
Meda, Italy

Mario Bellini ranks alongside Sottsass, Branzi and Magistretti as one of Italy's most important postwar designers. Bellini not only enjoys a prestigious reputation for the quality of his furniture and products, but also his writing. From 1986–91, Bellini was editor of *Domus* magazine, arguably the world's best-known design publication. In 1987, his international status was confirmed when the Museum of Modern Art in New York City awarded him the rare distinction of a one-man show.

The experience of working for Olivetti influenced the design of one of Cassina's best-selling chairs, the Cab. Here a flexible leather skin sheaths a simple metal frame in a way that recalls the casing of a typewriter.

Bellini's career spans architecture and product design – exemplifying the Italian tradition for designers to train originally as architects. This seamless relationship between the two professions is expressed in the Bellini quote: "To be a good furniture designer, you have to be an architect. Everything meaningful that's been designed has been by meaningful architects."

In 1981, Ettore Sottsass, one of Italy's best-known designers, launched a new design group in Milan. Rather tellingly, it was called Memphis – the home town of Elvis Presley, the king of American music, and the sacred capital of the Egyptian Pharaohs. Memphis was an immediate success. Set against the prevailing late-1970s mood for the "classic" and "good taste", Sottsass and his collaborators produced something exciting, fresh and new. Their furniture used a new palette of colours and materials, mixing plastic laminates with expensive wood veneers in bright reds, blues and yellows. These objects evoked the wit and fun of children's toys, and used references to the past, reworking the coffee bar era of the 1950s. Memphis challenged basic assumptions: for example, why should the shelves of a bookcase be straight, or the legs of a chair identical?

Sottsass drew on his own experience of the 1960s. He commented that much of his inspiration came from watching girls on London's Kings Road and his fascination with the monuments and structures of ancient cultures. The Carlton Bookcase is one of the most famous of the Memphis objects. Like so much of Sottsass' work, the piece combines his interest in Indian and Aztec art, 1950s popular culture, and his roots in 1960s Pop.

Carlton Sideboard

DATE: 1981

DESIGNER: Ettore Sottsass (born 1917)

MATERIAL: wood and plastic laminate

MANUFACTURER: Memphis, Milan, Italy

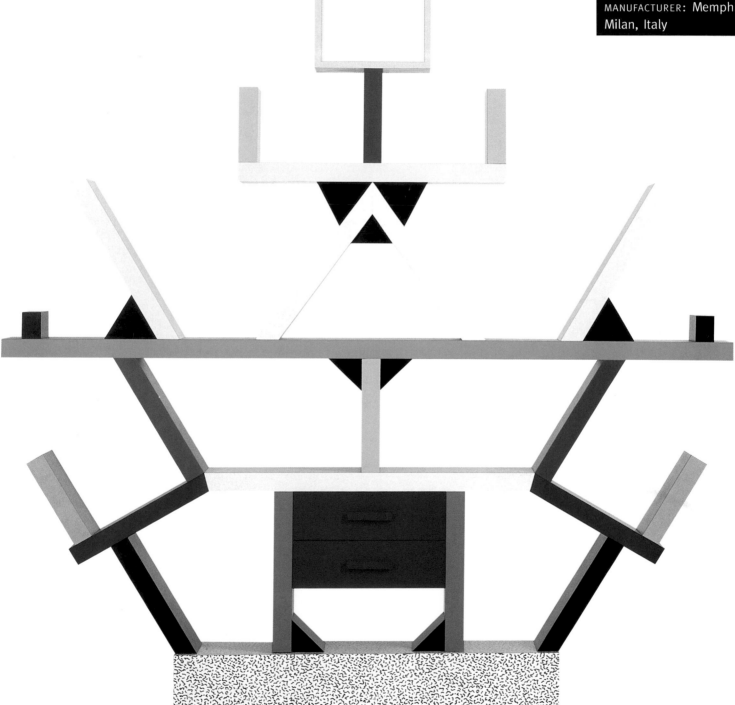

Nomos Table

DATE: 1986

DESIGNER: Foster and Partners, London, England

MATERIAL: glass and chromed steel

MANUFACTURED: Tecno, Milan, Italy

Nomos uses the high-tech components of engineering construction for this furniture system designed by Foster and Partners for the Italian furniture company Tecno. Sir Norman Foster's office is well known for its daring technical structures and Nomos started life as a table design for Foster's own office and for the Renault factory in Swindon, England. The basic idea was simple: a top resting on a metal frame with a central spine, two lateral brackets and four inclined shaft legs. The effect is not unlike the backbone and ribs of the human body. It is an inventory of precision components that can be combined to create total environments for groups of varying sizes, self-sufficient even to the extent of providing built-in and background lighting. Using different leg configurations, the table height can be adjusted and the system can expand horizontally as well as vertically, it can also accommodate a variety of surface finishes from glass to wood, marble, metal and plastic.

Nomos was designed to cope with the rapid changes in information technology and includes a built-in vertebrae-like conduit to carry cabling from desk terminals, allowing the floor space underneath to remain free. Although the range was designed as a high perform-ance office system, many people liked its aesthetic so much that it was used as a domestic table in the context of the home.

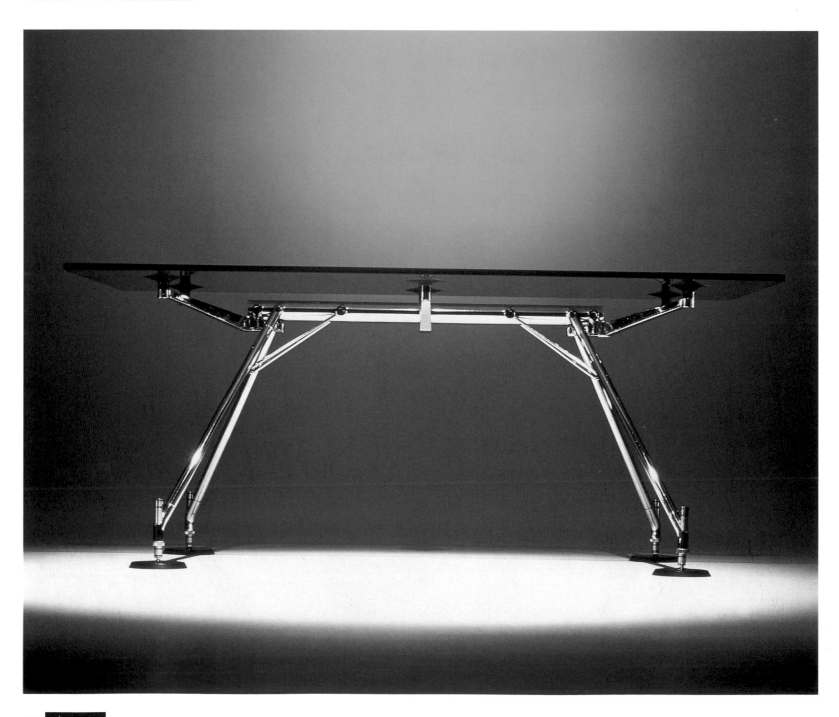

Gae Aulenti remains a rare phenomenon: a female designer. Trained as an architect in Milan, she made her greatest impact as an exhibition designer but worked on other projects including a collaboration with Richard Sapper in 1972 on a proposal for new urban transportation systems, presented at the 1979 Milan XVI Triennale. Working from the 1950s she enjoyed a quiet profile, admired for her furniture designs and commissions for interiors and showrooms for Knoll, Fiat, Olivetti, and Pirelli. Then she was chosen to design the new Paris museum Musée d'Ursay, which was sited in an old railway station.The brilliant success of this project placed her in the international design spotlight. Gae Aulenti's work reveals a complex sensibility, wishing to make contemporary objects rational, yet also accessible and human. The coffee table is one of her most famous designs using industrial components. The wheels form the base for a more traditional glass table top.

Table With Wheels

DATE: 1980

DESIGNER: Gae Aulenti (born 1927)

MATERIAL: glass, metal and rubber

MANUFACTURER: Fontane Arte, Milan, Italy

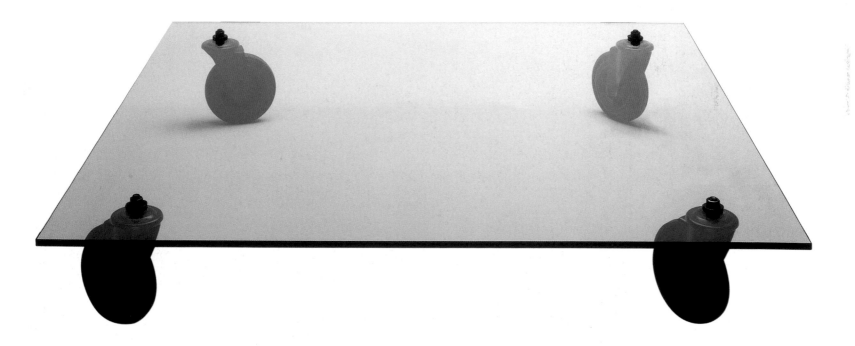

S Chair

DATE: 1987

DESIGNER: Tom Dixon
(born 1959)

MATERIAL: metal and wicker

Tom Dixon was part of a group of young British designers in the 1980s who, inspired by the do-it-yourself aesthetic of Punk, started working with recycled materials and welded metal. These designs crossed the boundaries of sculpture, design and craft and became known as "creative salvage", a name Dixon chose for his first design company.

Largely self-taught as a designer, Dixon might have remained part of an interesting, if marginal, design trend. However in the late 1980s he crossed over from one-off furniture into more commercial design. The S Chair is an example of this change, combining Dixon's idiosyncratic vision with a more accessible version of his earlier work.

Dixon based the distinctive organic curve of the chair on a sketch he made of a chicken and for the S chair he worked on over fifty different prototypes. These were made using many different materials, including rush, wicker, old tyre rubber, paper and copper, which Dixon produced in his studio called SPACE. In 1987, the well-known Italian furniture company Capellini bought the design and put it into mass production; since then it has been acquired by many leading international museums including the Victoria and Albert Museum in London and the Vitra Museum in Germany. In 1994 Dixon opened the SPACE shop as an outlet for his designs and as an exhibition venue for new talent. In 1996, he launched a new product range called Eurolounge.

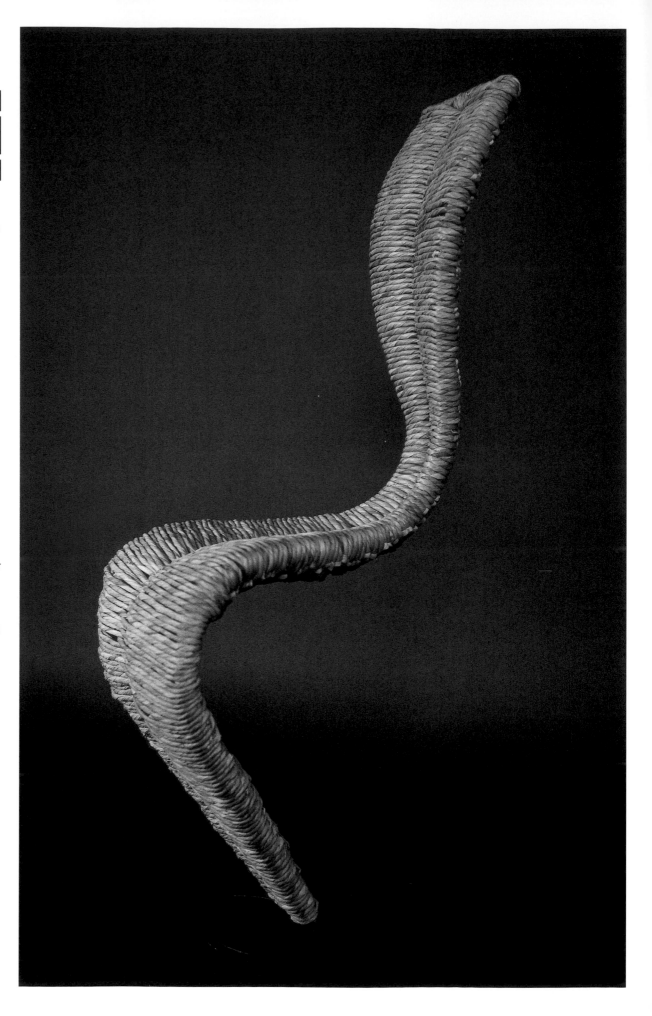

Born in Israel, Ron Arad moved to London in 1973, studied at the Architectural Association and in 1981 opened a furniture shop in Covent Garden. Called "One Off", the showroom became a significant part of the new British design wave of the 1980s and established Arad as Britain's most creative designer–maker. His early work used industrial materials and recycled parts, notably the famous Rover chair, which placed the car seat into a tubular steel frame. His showroom attracted many other designers with whom he collaborated or whose work he sold, including glass furniture by Danny Lane and metal furniture by Tom Dixon. Arad was therefore at the centre of new and exciting developments in London.

Always an inventive maker, Arad worked extensively in his metal workshop, welding large pieces together to make installations and furniture. Here Arad has reduced the traditional armchair to simple folded forms which challenge the conventional idea of comfort and use. Unlike many of his contemporaries in the 1980s, Arad made the significant jump into the international arena. His work was profiled in many leading museums, including the Pompidou Centre in Paris, and his annual exhibitions at the Milan Furniture Fair attracted a great deal of favourable attention. Leading Italian manufacturers, including Driade, Vitra and Poltronova, have commissioned him to design furniture for limited production.

Well Tempered Chair

DATE: 1986–93

DESIGNER: Ron Arad (born 1951)

MATERIAL: high grade sheet steel and thumb screws

MANUFACTURER: Vitra AG, Basel, Switzerland

Sofa

DATE: 1988

DESIGNER: Jasper Morrison
(born 1959)

MATERIAL: wool upholstery
and wood frame

MANUFACTURER: Sheridan
Coakley Products, London,
England

Jasper Morrison is now widely regarded as one of the world's leading young furniture designers. His work in the 1980s marked a new direction away from the complexities of Postmodern design towards simple, classical sculptural shapes that established a cooler and highly individual style.

In 1982 Morrison graduated from Kingston University before moving on to the Royal College of Art in London. He opened his own design studio in 1987. Morrison designed a series of pieces for British company Sheridan Coakley before quickly attracting the attention of manufacturers abroad, including Vitra and Capellini. He also worked for the popular Swedish retail store Ikea.

Morrison's series of sofas, using brightly coloured stretched upholstery, typically in oranges and purples, fitted perfectly with the taste for spare, simple interiors in the late 1980s and early 1990s. Additionally, Morrison has applied the same aesthetic to other objects, including sculptural door handles for the German company Franz Schedier GmbH and a simple wine rack made from brightly coloured plastic.

Frank Gehry can be placed in the great tradition of American individualist architects that includes Frank Lloyd Wright. His other trademark is the use of everyday materials in distinctly non-everyday ways – an approach which inspires his furniture design. Once again, the influence of the Pop aesthetic is important here. For Gehry, furniture should include the elements of surprise and challenge. The Powerplay chair reflects these ideas, and can be read as a cheeky reworking of his earlier design, the Wiggle – a cardboard version of the Rietveld Zig-Zag chair, which demystified a Modernist icon by using such a cheap everyday material. With the Powerplay Chair, Gehry uses bent wood.

Powerplay Armchair

DATE: 1992

DESIGNER: Frank Gehry (born 1929)

MATERIAL: high-bonding urea, laminated and bent maple wood strips

MANUFACTURER: Knoll Associates, New York City, USA

W W Stool

DATE: 1990

DESIGNER: Philippe Starck
(born 1949)

MATERIAL: lacquered
aluminium

MANUFACTURER: Vitra AG,
Basel, Switzerland

Philippe Starck is now one of the best-known contemporary designers in the world. His office has produced a number of high-profile commissions, including work on the private apartment for former French President François Mitterrand in the Elysée Palace and the fashionable Royalton Hotel in New York City, which has become a standard for the new metropolitan meeting place.

In the early 1980s, however, the project that brought him to public attention was a small Paris café near the Pompidou Centre called Café Costes. What was so interesting about the project was the fact that Starck designed all the fittings, including a three-legged chair, which became an international best-seller and has come to signify modern design in restaurants and venues all over the world.

Since then he has gone on to design many well-known objects, including his Juicy Salif Lemon Press for Alessi and the WW Stool, part of a series of designs that use anthropomorphic forms. The WW is a reference to the German film director Wim Wenders for whom he designed this office chair, defining the idea of a stool as a sculptural and growing form which resembles the roots of a living plant.

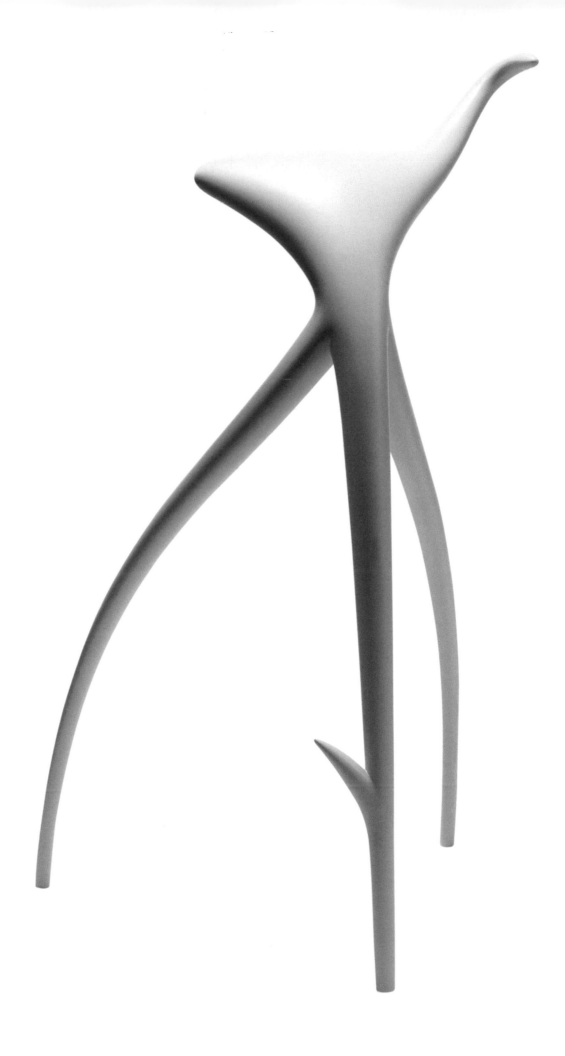

Sardine Collector's Cabinet

DATE: 1995

DESIGNER: Michael Marriott (born 1963)

MATERIAL: MDF, sardine tins, wing nuts

MANUFACTURER: Space UK, London, England

In 1996 the Crafts Council in London put on an exhibition called "Recycling: Forms for The Next Century". As the title suggests the show explored the new interest in alternative design, in the reuse of materials and the search for a design future that took on board concerns for the environment and a less aggressive use of raw materials. This exhibition highlighted the work of Michael Marriott, a graduate from the furniture department of the Royal College of Art, whose quirky and fun objects caught the imagination of many people. His cabinet used a medium-density fibreboard structure to house used sardine cans as the drawers. This witty, simple and elegant solution suggested another agenda for design that looked back to the 1960s alternative tradition of Victor Papanek and the Whole Earth Catalogue.

In his work Marriott exploited the tradition of found objects. For him, found materials produced not only beautiful accidental effects but also established familiarity with the object. He recognized a culture with a wealth of wasted resources, and that he could capitalize on such materials with interesting qualities. So far the results have included a table using an old oil drum, castors and chipboard top, and a wall light using a traditional glass lemon squeezer, plywood and shelf brackets.

lighting

HANGING LAMP

TIZIO TABLE LAMP

UNTIL THE INVENTION OF ELECTRICITY, the industrialized world relied on oil lamps or gas for lighting. Electricity – instant and clean – changed all that and introduced lighting as an integral and important design area for the twentieth century.

Lighting design in the twentieth century has always been closely related to the development of bulb technology. The tungsten bulbs most of us still use in the home are virtually the same as those Edison and Swan invented in 1879, using a coiled tungsten filament as light source, surrounded by a mixture of gases that slow the process of oxidization that will eventually end the bulb's life. Tungsten lights range from clear, candle bulbs to crown-silvered versions for use in reflector lamps. They are cheap and flexible, the average life span is about a thousand hours; however, they are not energy efficient, with only six per cent of their energy emitted as light and the remainder emitted as heat.

By the 1880s one of the first electric lighting systems for the home was introduced by Lord Armstrong at Cragside in Northumbria, in the North of England. By 1900 electric lighting had spread to such an extent that a growing industry producing light fittings had begun to develop, but the overall design aim was the same: to reduce the light emitted and conceal the bulb.

One of the best-known lamp-producing companies was Tiffany, which by 1905 employed over 200 craftsmen to produce light fittings that were designed in stained glass. These shades and table lamps have come to represent one of the most important contributions to Art Nouveau style. Other important pioneers included William Arthur Smith Benson, arguably the first modern lighting designer, whose London shop and catalogue sold light fittings made not by hand but with industrial techniques.

More radical solutions were also being explored and in the early 1920s and 1930s the Modern Movement introduced new attitudes to lighting design. Early signs of change came, most notably, from Peter Behrens for the German company AEG. Behrens' early lights rejected the naturalism of Art Nouveau, and instead concentrated on industrial concerns, simple mass-produced forms using industrial materials. Designers at the Bauhaus also started to look at light bulbs not simply as objects to produce light but as objects with their own aesthetic appeal.

These designers did not want to hide the bulb but wanted it to lead the design. Designers produced tube lighting arranged as formal sculptures and introduced some of the most innovatory advances in the design of industrial lighting into the house. These included the use of opaque and frosted glass in simple globe forms, integrated switches and the use of aluminium for reflectors. At this date they relied heavily on lighting developed for the factory and the office which could be adapted for the new home.

Technical developments after the War included the widespread use of fluorescent tubes, which although introduced in 1938 were based on the nineteenth-century research of a German scientist called Heinrich Gessler. They quickly become the main form of lighting in shops and offices. Fluorescence works on a completely different principle from tungsten, using an electrical discharge. At the end of each tube, electrodes send out electrons, which react with mercury vapour to create ultraviolet light. This is turned into visible light by a coating of phosphor on the inside of the glass tube. The advantage of such lights is that they are cheap to buy and run, installations are easy to maintain, there is a large choice of sizes and shapes, and the tubes are energy effective. However, such lights have their drawbacks – they are difficult to control and toxic materials are present, so all tubes require special disposal. Tungsten halogen bulbs were originally used in car headlights and then shop lighting display. They came in two types, mains voltage and low voltage, which was introduced in the 1980s. Halogen bulbs work in the same way as a conventional bulb except for the addition of gas and this gas helps to regenerate the tungsten. The advantage is that the light is stronger and it

BAY TABLE LAMP

LIGHTCOLUMN

allows the designer to use smaller bulbs and therefore a greater flexibility of light fittings. The disadvantage is that they are delicate and more sensitive, and the short lifespan of the bulbs, which produce a large amount of heat, gives low energy efficiency.

During the 1960s and 1970s lighting manufacturers took advantage of the new reflector bulbs to develop single spot systems or track lighting. They were an immediate commercial success and dominated certain aspects of the market until well into the 1980s. The 1980s and 1990s saw important new lighting developments with the introduction of halogen and mini-fluorescents. Both these technologies have inspired designers such as the German Ingo Maurer and caught the public imagination, showing new possibilities in lighting design. Low-voltage versions of the halogen are small and popular for interiors because they offer strong directional lighting, and low-voltage lighting is safe to touch. They are easy to control and energy efficient but they need a transformer, which must be incorporated into the design or into the plug. Current new directions on the market include the appearance of a range of low-energy bulbs, brought about by a new public concern about energy conservation.

TREFORCHETTE

Tiffany
Lamp

DATE: C.1910

DESIGNER: Louis Comfort Tiffany (1848–1933)

MATERIAL: stained glass, lead and bronze

MANUFACTURER: Tiffany Glass Company, New York, USA

Tiffany and Company was founded in 1837 and became a fashionable New York department store specializing in decorative silverware. It quickly achieved an international reputation for the quality of its products, opening branches in London and Paris. In 1885 Louis Comfort Tiffany, the founder's son, established his own enterprise, the Tiffany Glass Company in New York. A hugely successful studio, it marketed his trademark architectural stained glass and other decorative objects for the home.

By 1900 Tiffany had developed what was to become one of the most famous Art Nouveau products: a series of oil, then electrical, lamps. Originally the lamps had been developed as an economical use for the offcuts of coloured glass from the stained-glass workshop. The coloured-glass lamps produced a warm, glowing light and turned Tiffany lamps into an art form in their own right. Though expensive, they quickly became popular. Using rich, iridescent colours, the decoration drew on the Art Nouveau concern for naturalistic form, insects, flowers and the swelling shapes and abstracted forms of the body. Tiffany glass fitted perfectly into the architecture and interior design of the new century.

Ceiling Light

DATE: 1890s

DESIGNER: William Arthur Smith Benson (1854–1924)

MATERIAL: brass and glass

MANUFACTURER: Benson and Company, London, England

William Arthur Smith Benson was arguably the first person to design modern electric light fittings for the home: it was an achievement appreciated by his contemporaries both in his home country and abroad. When, in the early 1900s, the famous German critic Hermann Muthesius published *Das Englische Haus*, his study of avant-garde British design, he dedicated the last pages of the book to images of Benson's electric lights. From the 1870s Benson had been at the centre of the British Arts and Crafts movement when, as a student at Oxford, he had met members of the William Morris circle, including the painter Burne-Jones. Benson designed wallpapers, furniture and lighting for William Morris, and, after Morris's death in 1896, became a director of William Morris and Company. Morris inspired him to set up a metal workshop in Hammersmith, West London, and later a larger factory in Chiswick, where Benson not only designed lighting but also furniture.

Alone among the Arts and Crafts designers, Benson was prepared to use machine production, and introduced the innovation of marketing his lights using his own catalogue and opening a shop, Benson and Co in Bond Street, in which to sell them. He was a natural inventor, patenting his ideas and working on many products including Thermos jugs. In 1914 he became a founder member of the Design and Industries Association, which was set up to pioneer new standards of design in British industry.

Bauhaus Table Lamp

DATE: 1923–24

DESIGNER: Karl J. Jucker and Wilhelm Wagenfeld (1900–90)

MATERIAL: clear and opalescent glass, brass and steel

MANUFACTURER: Bauhaus metal workshop, Dessau, Germany

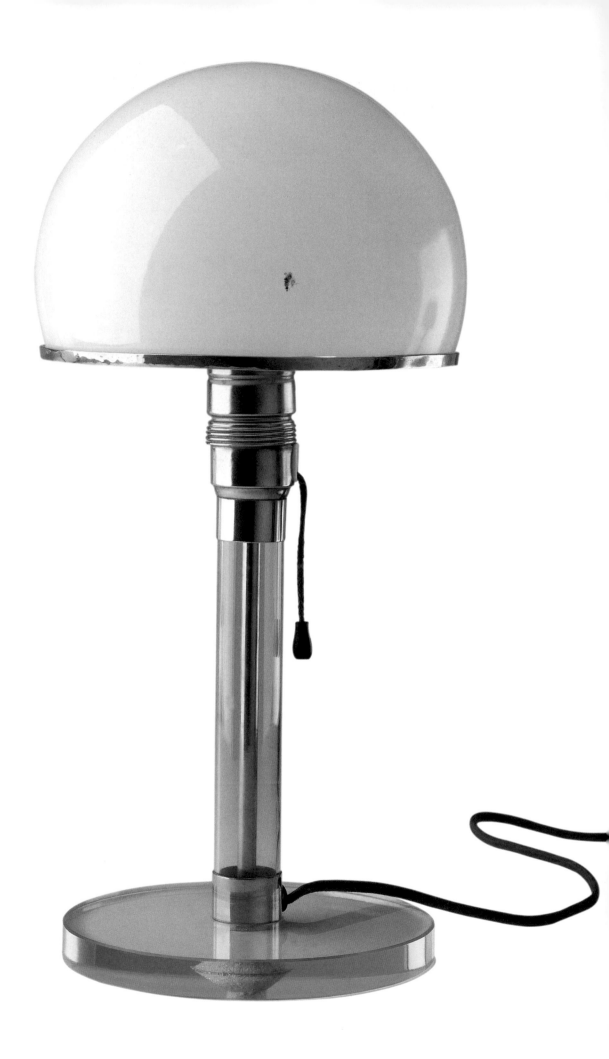

This design was one of the most simple and successful lamps to come from the Bauhaus metal workshop, then under the direction of László Moholy-Nagy. It was designed by two students, Willhelm Wagenfeld and Karl Jucker. Wagenfeld became one of Germany's best-known industrial designers, applying the Bauhaus principles of Modernist forms and materials to lighting design and glassware for the home. Nothing is known about Jucker's career after 1925. The only surviving information about his work documents a number of his innovative student designs for light fittings from 1922 to 1925. The two students' collaboration on the lamp, however, attracted a great deal of interest almost immediately. It was shown at the Leipzig Trade Fair in 1924 and published the following year in a book of new work from the school. The lamp looked startlingly modern and industrial: the shade was borrowed from existing factory lighting and steel tubing concealed the wiring. However, it represented a paring down of quite conventional Art Nouveau shapes. The industrial effects were achieved by laborious hand production, which meant that it was never available as a mass-produced, cheap, modern product for the home.

Hanging Lamp

DATE: 1920–24

DESIGNER: Gerrit Rietveld
(1888–1964)

MATERIAL: glass and wood

In 1920, Rietveld experimented with a version of this hanging lamp for a doctor's clinic in Maarssen, one of the earliest interiors inspired by the Dutch De Stijl Movement. Constructed using standard light bulbs and electric wiring, various versions of this minimalist design appeared. Different versions using three or four lights were used in the Schröder House (see p. 48) and the office of Walter Gropius at the Bauhaus (see p. 51).

The light fittings that appeared at Bauhaus in around 1920 do not hide technology, but incorporate it into the design. Using tungsten bulbs, and with its radical shape, the lamp was available in different combinations incorporating the same basic elements – the bulb and two square wooden fixings.

Other designers also found the aesthetic of tubular tungsten bulbs appealing – Max Krajewski's 1927 installation at the Bauhaus and Eileen Gray's tube light of the same year employ the same design vocabulary.

Kandem Table Lamp

DATE: **1927**

DESIGNER: **Marianne Brandt (1893–1983)**

MATERIAL: **metal nickel-plated and lacquered**

MANUFACTURER: **Korting and Matthieson, Leipzig, Germany**

Marianne Brandt's simple and radical design for the Kandem lamp became the world's first commercially successful bedside downlight and between 1928 and 1932 over fifty thousand were sold.

Walter Gropius, the director of the Bauhaus, wanted to establish his school as the principal centre of Modernist ideas. The Metal Workshop (*Metallwerkstatt*) was particularly important in this context. Dedicated to the research and production of prototypes for industry, it was described as "a laboratory for mass production". Part of that strategy was the organization of live projects in partnership with industry, the most successful of which was a series of light fittings put into commercial production.

Marianne Brandt is particularly important: not only was she one of the few women in the Metal Workshop between 1923 and its closure in 1932 (in 1928 she was temporarily in charge of the department) but she also designed most of the lighting. She remains a rare example of a woman industrial designer.

The success of the Kandem was based on its functional adjustable shade and the ingenious invention of a push button switch to make switching it on and off easier when one is half awake. Its form has influenced the language of lamp design ever since.

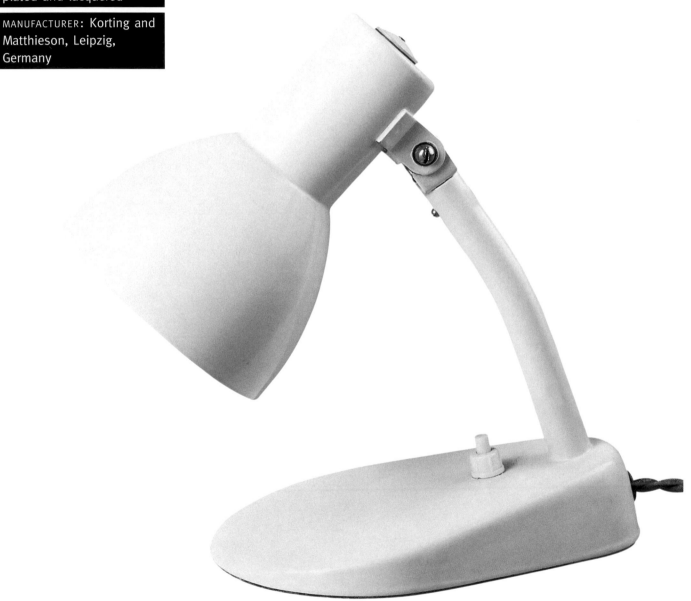

In the 1930s Britain produced a rational, modern lamp for mass production, intended as a functional light for both office and home. The Anglepoise was designed for the Herbert Terry company by George Carwardine, an automotive engineer, and a director of Carwardine Associates of Bath. His background is revealed in the Anglepoise, which became one of the most popular desk lights in the world. It was modelled on the ergonomics of the human arm, with springs instead of counterweights to hold the arm in position. The lamp has sold in England for over sixty years in enormous quantities and represents an independent British tradition of rational design.

Anglepoise Lamp

DATE: 1932

DESIGNER: George Carwardine (1887–1948)

MATERIAL: lacquered metal and Bakelite

MANUFACTURER: Herbert Terry & Sons, Redditch, England

Hanging Lamp

DATE: 1926

DESIGNER: Poul Henningsen
(1894–1967)

MATERIAL: opal glass
and brass

MANUFACTURER: Louis Poulsen
& Company, Copenhagen,
Denmark

The end of the 1920s saw the emergence in Scandinavia of a new type of lighting. Experiments in the design of lamp fittings concentrated greater emphasis on the quality of light, rather than simply designing around the bulb. Poul Henningsen trained as an architect but quickly attracted international attention with the design of a new range of light fittings. Reflectors of different sizes were combined so that the lamps would give off direct and indirect light simultaneously without any glare. These ergonomic qualities made them popular as dining table lights. They appeared in the Danish Pavilion for the 1925 *Paris Exposition des Arts Décoratifs*, where they were awarded several prizes. They were soon specified and used by Modernist architects and designers all over the world, as well as attracting a popular market in Scandinavia. They remain in production: a modern classic of design.

The Arco lamp, designed in the early 1960s, is another collaboration between the Castiglioni brothers, Achille and Pier Giacomo. Although designed to light the dining table and therefore adjustable to three different heights, it was more generally used as a floor light and proved to be extremely popular. It has since become a classic of its time and has come to define the radical, bold and witty style of the Castiglioni brothers.

Both men were inspired as students by the work of Marcel Duchamp and the tradition of the "found object" – a theme which Achille was to explore for the rest of his career. Light bulbs, transformers and – for his famous chair – tractor seats provided him with sources of inspiration. This approach to design, Achille explained, gave his work "resonances of previous artefacts so that there is an almost ready-built relationship with the user".

The Castiglioni brothers were extremely fortunate that their original approach to design was supported by a series of committed Italian manufacturers prepared to spend the time and money on product development.

Arco Floor Lamp

DATE: 1962

DESIGNER: Achille (born 1918) and Pier Giacomo Castiglioni (1913–68)

MATERIAL: white marble base, stainless steel stem, polished aluminium reflector

MANUFACTURER: Flos, Brescia, Italy

Boalum Lamp

DATE: 1969

DESIGNER: Livio Castiglioni (1911–79) and Gianfranco Frattini (born 1926)

MATERIAL: PVC plastic and metal

MANUFACTURER: Artemide, Milan, Italy

Made from industrial translucent plastic tubing held in place by a series of metal rings into which light bulbs were fitted, the Boalum is the typical Pop design. It expressed radical new form and relied on the consumer to define the object's shape. The consumer could hang it vertically or arrange it as a piece of sculpture on the table or floor.

Theoretically the user could purchase more units and decide the length of the light based on units, each of which was 2 metres (6½ feet) in length.

Boalum showed that designs using industrial components need not be hard and aggressive: here was an object that was glowing and animal-like. It gave off a soft and gentle light more reminiscent of a Japanese lantern than the glare of a laboratory or factory. The design combined the talents of two of Italy's famous designers. Although Livio Castiglioni worked independently, he was part of the trio of famous brothers who included Achille, also well known for his lighting designs. This was Livio's only collaboration with Gianfranco Frattini.

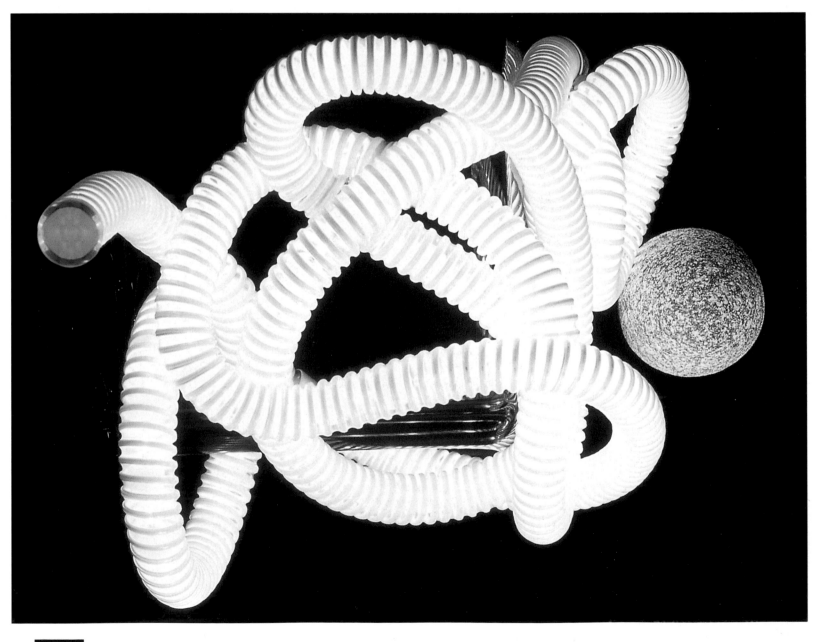

Parentesi Lamp

DATE: 1970

DESIGNER: Achille Castiglioni
(born 1918) and Pio Manzù
(1939–69)

MATERIAL: stainless steel
with spotlight

MANUFACTURER: Flos,
Brescia, Italy

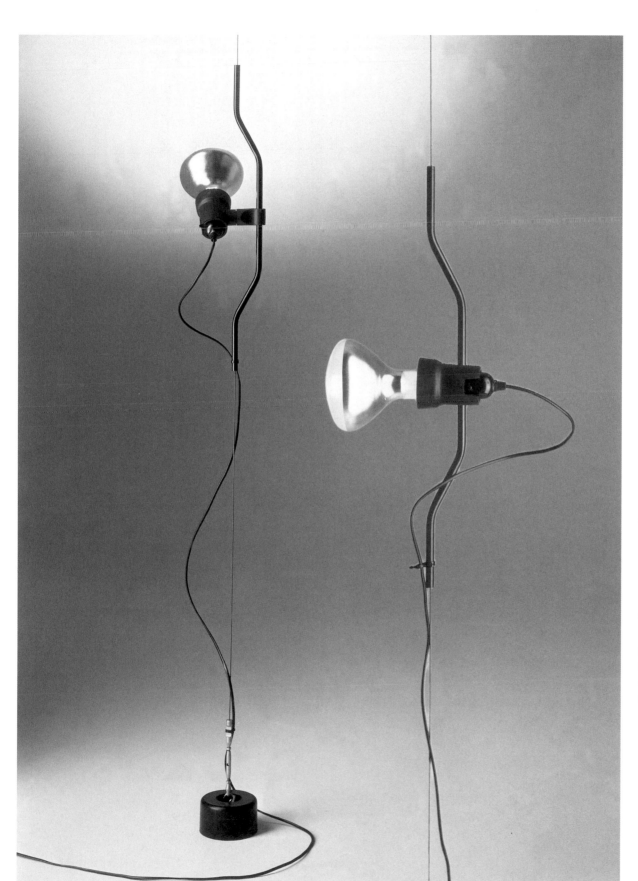

Achille Castiglioni's unique and fresh
vision found expression in a series
of seminal light designs that he
continued to produce in the 1990s.
Parentesi, designed in 1970, is one
of his best-known lights and for this
design he collaborated with Pio
Manzù. Manzù had trained at the
well-known Ulm School of Design
and then worked for the Fiat Design
Centre, producing the original
concept drawings for the Fiat 127
car. Tragically, he died in a car
accident in 1969 and the lamp was
completed by Castiglioni. Manzù,
however, was probably responsible
for the Parentesi's reflector bulbs,
which had previously only been
used as automobile lighting.
Hitherto, light fitting manufacturers
had taken advantage of the new
reflector bulbs and used them
largely for single spot fittings or for
the newly developed track systems.

Characteristically simple and
stylish, Parentesi used tensioned wire
suspended from the ceiling. It was a
direct-light lamp with flexible movements and a light intensity adjuster.

Luminator

DATE: 1955

DESIGNERS: Achille Castiglioni (born 1918) and Pier Giacomo Castiglioni (1913–68)

MATERIAL: steel

MANUFACTURER: Gilardi e Barzaghi, Milan, Italy

The Castiglioni brothers designed several of the lights in this section. They came from an artistic family: their father was a classical sculptor and the three sons, Pier Giacomo, Achille and Livio, all studied architecture at Milan Polytechnic. They made a unique contribution to Italian design in general but to lighting design in particular. The collaboration from 1945 between Achille and Pier Giacomo was to prove especially fruitful.

In the postwar years of 1950s "*ricostruzione*", or reconstruction, the light fitting assumed a special significance in the Italian quest to rebuild the economy. Italian industry needed to produce low-tech objects for export for which the added value of design and style could command high prices. The Luminator was an immediate success. Manufacturing costs were low: apart from a simple three-legged stand, the only other feature was a wire that flowed from the base of the tube with a simple control switch. The result was an elegant uplighter that was widely exported.

The Luminator was also the first domestic light to exploit the latest tungsten bulb with a built-in reflector on top. The lamp's visual appearance, with its simple vertical steel tube supported on a slim tripod, reflects this technical inspiration. But the Castiglionis produced an object which was much more than a clever technological innovation: the Luminator helped to define the qualities of postwar Italian design with its use of stylish and expressive sculptural form combining good looks with function and structure.

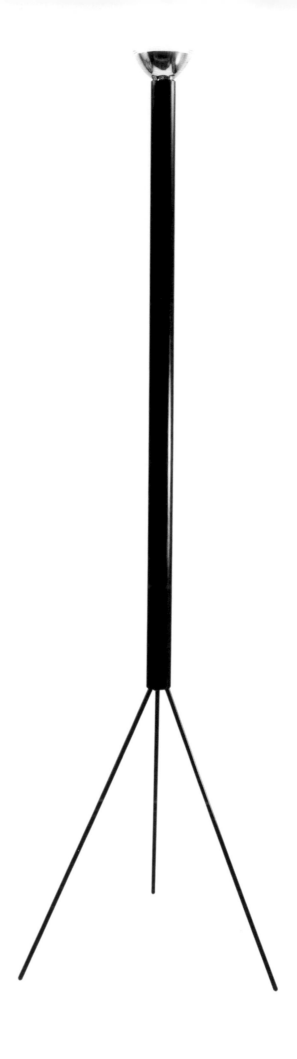

Model H

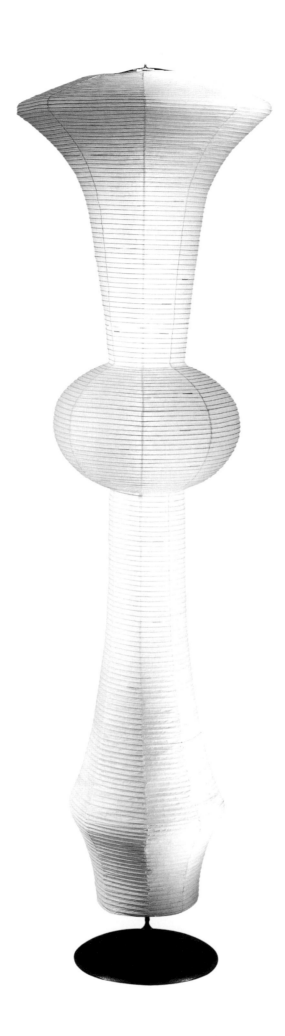

DATE: shade 1954, base 1962

DESIGNER: Isamu Noguchi (1904–88)

MATERIAL: mulberry bark paper, bamboo and steel

MANUFACTURER: Ozweki and Company, Gifu, Japan

Isamu Noguchi's original training as a sculptor informed the design of both his furniture and his lighting. With this floor lamp he explores the lamp shade as both a sculptural form and as a modern reinterpretation of the traditional Japanese paper lantern. In 1951, Noguchi travelled to Japan, and studied such lanterns constructed from a framework of bamboo covered with paper. Called *chochins*, these lanterns were traditionally unornamented and used to diffuse candlelight. Inspired by their simplicity, Noguchi explored ways in which he could use them in a contemporary context and adapt them for electric light. Like the original Japanese chochin, Noguchi's lights were designed to be collapsible, reflecting a widespread trend towards the purchase of consumer goods in flat packs. Using a mulberry bark paper, his lights could be folded into an envelope. Over twenty-five years he produced a whole series of designs based on the paper shades, which he called Akaris. In the 1960s he produced versions using fluorescent lights and devised a standing lamp using a flat metal base to support the shade.

Noguchi's ideal was to produce floating sculptural forms that reflected the inspiration of modern designs but were inspired by the vernacular craft traditions of Japan. Although his designs were notable for their simple and beautiful effects, they were always produced as expensive limited edition lights. In the 1960s his work was quickly imitated in countless less expensive forms.

Gibigiana Lamp

DATE: 1981

DESIGNER: Achille Castiglioni (born 1918)

MATERIAL: metal reflector with mirrored surface, aluminium support with enameled metal

MANUFACTURER: Flos, Brescia, Italy

Wit and humour form a key part of Castiglioni's approach to design, expressed here by a shape that evokes an animal or bird. The Gibigiana is an adjustable table lamp. It produces reflected light and incorporates a dimmer. The lamp also demonstrates successful use of the relatively new technology of the halogen bulb that reflects light against a mirror and concentrates it on a particular spot – a function conveyed in the lamp's unusual name, which is the Italian expression for light reflected from a surface.

The angle of reflection is controlled by a circular dial on the "head" of the lamp, while the intensity of the light is controlled by a lever which runs up and down the base. The Gibigiana sought to combine a quirky appearance with a high specification, quality finish not normally associated with this kind of domestic product.

Richard Sapper trained as an engineer in Munich and began his career working for Daimler. He went on to apply these technical skills to consumer products and later worked with many blue-chip companies including Artemide and, since 1980, IBM. Sapper is responsible for many twentieth-century design classics. In the 1960s he worked on ground-breaking products for the television and radio manufacturer Brionvega, which made the company world-famous. His approach promoted the idea that the technological function of a product should determine its appearance, and the Artemide Tizio lamp follows this principle. It is classic Sapper: finished in matt-black aluminium, the lamp has a formal beauty that incorporates balanced, lightweight engineering forms to produce an elegant shape with arms that move smoothly and offer a number of different, stable positions. It is also a technical success in that it uses a low-voltage halogen bulb, which gives a concentrated light source.

The Tizio became one of Artemide's best-selling designs and won the *Compasso d'Oro* prize in 1979.

Tizio Table Lamp

DATE: 1972

DESIGNER: Richard Sapper (born 1932)

MATERIAL: ABS plastic and aluminium

MANUFACTURER: Artemide, Milan, Italy

Bay
Table
Lamp

DATE: 1983

DESIGNER: Ettore Sottsass
(born 1917)

MANUFACTURER: Memphis,
Milan, Italy

Ettore Sottsass' expressive genius
made an important contribution to
virtually every decade since the War.
His versatility is breathtaking and
his ability to explore with a fresh
eye almost every category of
product design is now legendary. In
the early 1980s Sottsass led Milan's
Memphis group, an international
collective of designers who
reshaped the approach to colour,
decoration and materials. Memphis
is better known for its furniture and
decorative patterns, but Sottsass
also exploited traditional Italian
expertise in coloured glass. Murano,
the Venetian island, is famous for
glass-making, for the quality of its
craftsmen and for their use of
distinctive bright blue and red glass.
In the 1950s and 1960s this
tradition had inspired many
designers but by the 1980s such
coloured glass was no longer
fashionable. Sottsass focused
attention again on coloured glass as
a contemporary design material. He
worked first on a series of objects
using glass modelled in a manner
not unlike children's plasticine, and
later on light fittings, including the
Bay Table Lamp shown here,
exploring the potential of glass for
decorative domestic lighting. This
lamp's formal sculptural qualities,
based on simple geometric shapes,
recalled Sottsass' 1960s work, but
the playful, almost childlike,
assembly of parts, combined with
striking red and blue glass, made
the lamp a new and influential
object for the 1980s.

Miss Sissi Table Lamp

DATE: 1991

DESIGNER: Philippe Starck
(born 1949)

MATERIAL: coloured
technopolymer plastic

MANUFACTURER: Flos,
Brescia, Italy

This table lamp – replete with
mysterious name – is a signature
Starck product: a clever reworking
of an otherwise conventional
design. Starck has an unfailing
talent for taking an everyday object
and investing it with wit and irony.

Giving both direct and diffused
light, this tiny lamp – only eleven
inches in height – is available in
white and a range of bright colours.
It proved an immediate commercial
success, becoming one of the best-
known interior design accessories of
the 1990s.

Ya Ya Ho Lighting System

DATE: 1984

DESIGNER: Ingo Maurer (born 1932)

MATERIAL: glass, ceramic, metal and plastic

MANUFACTURER: Design M Ingo Maurer, Munich, Germany

Such was the originality of Ya Ya Ho that it turned the German designer Ingo Maurer into an overnight success. The light became his signature piece and it was hailed as one of the freshest and most original lighting designs of the decade. Ya Ya Ho stretched out fine wires of low-tension cabling onto which were attached halogen lamps, counterbalanced to create the effect of a sculptural mobile. The clip-on miniature light sources can be arranged by the consumer at will, a flexibility reminiscent of the famous lighting icons of the 1960s, including the Boalum light (see p. 152).

Maurer exploited the 1980s development of the halogen family of bulbs and the new mini fluorescent lamps. Initially, halogen technology was rather primitive, and indeed rather dangerous, until the introduction of transformers. Maurer wanted to promote a situation where lighting could be reduced to a series of simple components offering a wide variety of designed forms and lighting effects, using low-voltage lighting sources that enable the consumer to touch and move the lights freely.

Birds, Birds, Birds

DATE: 1992

DESIGNER: Ingo Maurer
(born 1932)

MANUFACTURER: Design M
Ingo Maurer, Munich,
Germany

During the 1980s, Ingo Maurer created a sensation with a series of lights that combined state-of-the-art technology with an approach that brought lighting closer to installation art than design. German-born Maurer had worked in America for several years and began his career as a lighting designer in the 1960s. His work during this decade explored themes of Pop Art, experimenting with scale, decoration and the recycling of found objects. The ideas and theories of this seminal decade were to emerge in a different form twenty years later when his projects in the 1980s established him as an international designer. When it was shown at the annual Arteluce exhibition in Milan, international critics began to compare Maurer's work to other original lighting designers such as the Castiglioni brothers. They admired the way that Maurer introduced a playful, almost throwaway approach to design, which used new technology but did not allow it to dominate the final result.

Maurer works with a team of designers who include electronics engineers and has worked on a range of domestic lights.

Treforchette Table Lamp

DATE: 1997

DESIGNER: Michele de Lucchi
(born 1951)

MATERIAL: PVC shade and
table forks

MANUFACTURER: Produzione
Privata, Italy

Produzione Privata is an experimental range that produces objects from the combination and assembly of simple, pre-existing components. This is a new and limited edition range of objects, which comes from the studio of one of Italy's best-known designers, Michele de Lucchi.

In the 1980s, de Lucchi established himself as a designer of international importance with his work for Studio Alchimia and, more famously, for the Memphis group under Ettore Sottsass. During this period his work on experimental, but essentially one-off, pieces was balanced by his career as an industrial designer for a series of high-profile Italian companies, including Kartell, Artemide and Olivetti. Produzione Privata is a return to more intimate and small-scale experiments, which reflect de Lucchi's interest in the twentieth-century idea of the found object. This concept was developed in the 1920s by Marcel Duchamp, who exhibited wine racks and urinals as art pieces. In his design for Treforchette, Michele de Lucchi is searching for a new direction that assembles ordinary objects in an unexpected way. He has used a simple circle of PVC for the shade, which is supported by two "ready made" metal cutlery forks. His intention is to rediscover in this way the potential of the ordinary and the everyday.

Lightcolumn

DATE: 1995

DESIGNERS: Philips Corporate Design

MANUFACTURER: Philips, Eindhoven, The Netherlands

In 1891 Philips and Company was established in Eindhoven, The Netherlands, as a light-bulb factory. Although the company quickly diversified into products such as radios, they remain leading exponents in the field of lighting technology. Lightcolumn exploits improved technology to disperse and adjust the intensity of the light source and create a light that evokes natural light. Developed by Philips as a series of decorative components it uses organic, sculptural structures to blend with their surroundings. Each choice of components creates a different lighting effect. The intention was to enable urban planners to provide an environment with a more modern feel with "natural" lighting.

PART 6

homeware

SOUP LADLE

THROUGHOUT HISTORY, products for the home have reflected both the culture of a society and the technology of an age. Social and technological developments brought about by the Industrial Revolution, for example, had a significant effect on the way tableware was manufactured and used. The rise of the middle class increased the demand for good quality tableware, while the introduction of mass-production techniques allowed factories to manufacture to a standardized quality and design.

GLASS TEAPOT

In the nineteenth century Victorian values of display and the availability of cheap servants enabled formal rituals of eating and organized leisure to develop in the home. Each activity and area in the home was clearly separated: for example, the kitchen and the parlour, so objects were designed for their particular place and purpose. The new requirements of twentieth-century society broke these traditions.

In the twentieth century, developments in material technology, together with changes in social patterns, have further influenced the look of products. The relaxation of dining rituals, the growing desire for convenience and practicality, and the introduction of new materials such as stainless steel, heat resistant glass

PASTA SET 9092

and synthetic plastics have all led to designs that are multi-functional, more durable, easier to clean and, in some cases, disposable.

There was another important shift in attitudes to homeware which derived from the reform of kitchen design. Now the kitchen was as precisely calculated and equipped as a scientist's laboratory; the principles of factory organization could be applied to the family home. This involved the careful integration of areas for preparation, cleaning and cooking, with work surfaces and appliances positioned at the same height. The most influential of these models was the so-called "Frankfurt Kitchen", used for standardized houses built to replace the slum areas of the city after World War One. It was intended to improve hygiene and facilitate the work of the housewife, but also to upgrade her status: the housewife was no longer a domestic maid but a manager.

Modern Movement designers looked to mass production to improve the design and quality of products for the home. Leading designers no longer saw their remit within the context of traditional craft products but within the factory, using cheap industrial materials to best effect. The glassware designed by the husband and wife team Alvar Aalto and Aino Marsio-Aalto is one such example. Aino Aalto directed her talents to pressed glass: a cheap material whose production flaws she sought to conceal with the use of simple, curved bands and basic shapes. Tableware was designed using easy to clean, simple shapes that could be bought in single pieces to build up the set requirement, breaking the long tradition of buying ceramic services in large sets. In this context the pioneer Bauhaus School is particularly important. Here students were encouraged to design objects with a new modern agenda and to consider always the question of its potential for mass production.

Almost every category of object for the home was redesigned in this way. In Italy, for example, items such as the Moka coffee maker were designed to make the transition from kitchen cooker hob to table, the Caccia cutlery set was produced to offer an alternative to traditional, high-maintenance use of silver for knives and forks. New materials also began to make an impact: the 1920s heat-resistant glass was used for cooking and storage, designed again to be flexible as oven-to-table ware and fridge-to-table. Plastic was another key material. In the postwar period it began to replace glass in the design of storage containers, most famously by the Tupperware company; other key materials were ceramics for bowls and metal for kitchen implements such as salad servers and spoons.

While many leading designers worked to produce rational and functional mass-produced objects other designers continued to work in the more traditional areas of craft and decoration. The famous Marion Dorn geometric rugs of the 1930s are a good example of this

GRAVES KETTLE

as are the decorated patterns of Eric Ravilious and Susie Cooper, which made Wedgwood ceramics so distinctive. The Scandinavian countries in particular led the way in creating well-designed objects for the home. The quality of Scandinavian glass and tableware attracted international admiration in the postwar period and this work is typified by the architect Arne Jacobsen's designs for objects, ranging from coffee pots to simple taps.

The rise of the designer decade in the 1980s brought homeware into even sharper focus. Nowhere is this better illustrated than in the products from the Italian company Alessi. They quickly recognized that people now wanted objects for the home that represented many functions. They wanted the products of named designers like Michael Graves and Philippe Starck and items that were not only functional but pieces of sculpture – true objects of desire. A new and affluent section of society sought a market that would provide them with Jasper Morrison wine racks in bright plastic and Ettore Sottsass wineglasses alongside an ever increasing choice of cheap tableware and cutlery designs sold by modern retail shops such as Ikea. Consumers have learnt to negotiate the old and the new within the home.

ODEON CUTLERY

GINEVRA CARAFE

Soup Ladle

DATE: 1879

DESIGNER: Dr Christopher Dresser (1834 1904)

MATERIAL: silver-plated steel and ebonized wood

MANUFACTURER: Hukin and Heath, Birmingham, England

Christopher Dresser was unique among nineteenth-century designers. He has come to be seen as an important pioneer of modern industrial design, producing simple, functional items for mass production at a time when contemporaries such as William Morris and John Ruskin were advocating a return to craft production, based on the model of the medieval guild.

Trained as a botanist, Dresser studied at the South Kensington School of Design where he established himself as a star pupil and later taught. His design rationale was derived from his study of nature, producing a language of geometric pattern and form that could be applied to industrial design. His interest in Moorish patterns and Japanese art led him to develop a geometric, simplified visual grammar that he applied to startlingly modern and functional silverware such as teapots, toast racks and soup tureens. Dresser published his ideas in a series of books on design that were influential both in the United Kingdom and abroad.

Although the majority of Dresser's output was conventional by nineteenth-century standards, some of his metalware featured astonishingly original shapes that predated the work of the Bauhaus by almost thirty years. His designs represent important archetypes in the development of twentieth-century Modernism. His work combined the latest in materials technology, such as the electroplating of metals, with the most up-to-date manufacturing techniques. His minimalist designs had no contemporary counterparts in Victorian England – many of his uncompromising forms would not be matched until the 1920s.

Archibald Knox is probably best known for his turn-of-the-century metalware designs for Liberty's, the famous London department store. His talent as an architect and designer was, however, much more widespread and he is recognized as one of the great exponents of the British Arts and Crafts movement.

In common with his contemporaries, Knox explored the Celtic traditions of his native Isle of Man. This can be seen in his use of complex flowing patterns. However, his style was much more than simple revivalism and although still inspired by the glowing colours and the flowing, sinuous forms of Celtic decoration, Knox went on to create a language of ornament that saw an increasing simplification and refinement of forms.

Designed in 1900, Knox's watercolour sketch for the rug shown here still appears fresh and timeless. Such work positioned Knox not only as a leading Arts and Crafts designer but as a practitioner who helped to establish a new direction in design for the next century.

Design For a Rug

DATE: 1900

DESIGNER: Archibald Knox (1864–1933)

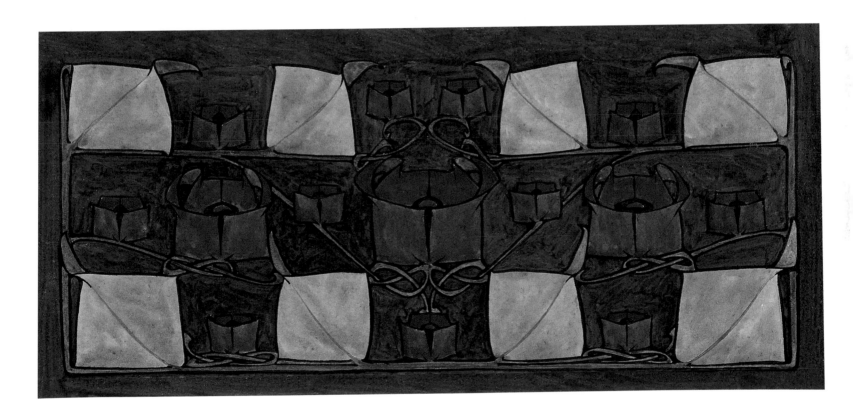

Cutlery for Lilly and Fritz Waerndorfer

DATE: 1904

DESIGNER: Josef Hoffman (1870–1956)

MATERIAL: silver

MANUFACTURER: Wiener Werkstätte, Vienna, Austria

The architect and designer Josef Hoffman was a leading member of the Vienna Secession, a group of avant-garde designers who were opposed to established and academic forms in architecture and design. In 1903, together with Koloman Moser and Fritz Waerndorfer, Hoffman founded the *Wiener Werkstätte* (Vienna Workshop)

and remained its artistic director until 1931. The *Werkstätte* was inspired by the British designer C. R. Ashbee's Guild of Handicrafts and Hoffman was strongly influenced by the English Arts and Crafts Movement, particularly Charles Rennie Mackintosh and the Glasgow School.

Hoffman's furniture and metalwork designs are strictly based on geometric

and rectilinear shapes, giving them an austere and elegant simplicity – a radical contrast to the florid forms prevalent in Art Nouveau that dominated progressive design at the turn of the century.

Hoffman is viewed as one of the founding fathers' of twentieth-century design and his work remains a source of inspiration to contemporary designers.

Electric Light Bulbs Fabric

In the immediate aftermath of the Bolshevik Revolution of 1917 many Russian artists rejected the bourgeois practice of art and pledged their skills to serving the Soviet state. Their designs were intended to symbolize the new Soviet society and to help foster the transition to a new way of life.

In the first few years after the Revolution, much emphasis was made by the State on the need for new imagery and products to convey the ideology of the Revolution to the ordinary people. The desperate economic situation meant there was little industry and no money to build grand architecture. Inevitably Russian Constructivist designers turned their attention to graphics, textiles and ceramics to express their vision of the future. The most famous members of the group included El Lissitsky, Vavara Stepanova and Liubov Popova. However, virtually no biographical information has survived on Strusevich.

The work of the Constructivists was characterized by bold abstract motifs that found their way into the design of theatre sets, tapestries, rugs, wallpapers and fabric designs. The visual language of Constructivism was largely based on the use of multiple flat planes derived from the Cubism of Picasso and Braque. However, the Constructivists almost always insisted on an abstract and logical application of line and colour, and – the key element – the underlying suggestion of the Revolution's ideology. The design carried a message to the people, represented here in the use of light bulbs as the repeat pattern illustrating the electrification programme of the Soviet Five Year Plan of 1928–32. The use of industry and technology as imagery symbolized a break with the decadent, bourgeois ornamental traditions of the nineteenth century.

DATE: 1928–30

DESIGNER: S Strusevich (active 1920s)

MATERIAL: printed cotton

MANUFACTURER: Sosnevsk Amalgamated Mills, Ivanava, Russia

Glass Teapot

DATE: 1932

DESIGNER: Wilhelm Wagenfeld (1900–90)

MATERIAL: glass

MANUFACTURER: Jenaer Glaswerk Schott and Genossen, Jena, Germany

Although Wagenfeld went on to design electrical products for Braun in the 1950s, he is best known as a designer of glassware and ceramics. He studied at the Bauhaus – where he later taught – and remained a lifelong advocate of the principles of uncluttered simplicity and functionalism in design which the school fostered. Wagenfeld was teaching at the Berlin Kunsthochschule (art college) when he developed the tea service. It remains one of the purest expressions of Wagenfeld's industrial aesthetic, in which every aspect of the relationship between form and function is figuratively and literally transparent. Working with the same heat-resistant glass used to make test tubes, his brief was to design glassware, such as the teapot (shown here with a later cup and saucer) that could be used both in the kitchen and on the table. His pioneering use of new materials brought Bauhaus ideals to the mass-market. Despite his unflinching devotion to Modernism, Wagenfeld nonetheless enjoyed a successful career in German industry during the Third Reich. After the war he opened his own design workshop where he continued to produce work for leading clients until 1978.

The Kubus range of stacking glass containers demonstrates the Bauhaus principle that design could be reduced to pure geometric form that would lend itself to mass production and, therefore, a mass market. When in 1935 Wagenfeld was appointed the artistic director of Vereinigte Lausitze Glaswerke, he became responsible for the introduction of Modernist ideals into inexpensive pressed glass products. Based on a rectangular module, his Kubus containers remain the best-known of hundreds of design he produced for the company. They were designed for use straight from the fridge to the table and when not in use could be stacked together to form neat geometric shapes for ease of storage. Because it is non-porous and easy to clean, glass is ideally suited for kitchen use. The Kubus range included ten separate refrigerator storage containers, seven boxes and three jars, all with air vents and interchangeable lids.

Kubus Stacking Containers

DATE: 1938

DESIGNER: Wilhelm Wagenfeld (1900–90)

MATERIAL: pressed glass

MANUFACTURER: Kamenz Glassworks, Vereinigte Lausitze Glaswerke, Weiswasser, Germany

Burg Giebichenstein Dinner Service

DATE: 1930

DESIGNER: Marguerite Friedlaender-Wildenhain (1896–1985)

MATERIAL: porcelain

MANUFACTURER: Staatliche Porzellanmanufaktur, Berlin, Germany

The Burg Giebichenstein Service takes it name from the school of Applied Arts in Halle–Saale – known as the "little Bauhaus" – where Friedlaender headed the ceramics department from 1926 to 1933. Born in Lyon to English and German parents, Friedlaender studied in Berlin and then at the Bauhaus, where she was taught by the master potter Gerhard Marcks. Friedlaender was commissioned by the Staatliche Porzellanmanufaktur in Berlin to design a modern, functional dining service that took into account the trend toward less formal dining. She dispensed with the elaborate serving dishes usually available in such services, rationalizing her range to plates and bowls in basic shapes and in a variety of sizes. The simplified geometric forms of the pieces are emphasized by concentric grooves in the porcelain that acted as a restrained form of decoration.

Friedlaender married the potter and ex-Bauhaus student Franz Rudolf Wildenhain in 1930. Three years later, when she was dismissed from her teaching post by the Nazis, they were forced to flee to the Netherlands where they established the Het Kruikje (Little Crock) pottery. Friedlaender also carried out commissions for the Spinz factory in Maastricht. In 1940, Freidlaender emigrated to California where she taught at Oakland's College of Arts and Crafts and established the Pond Farm Workshops. Her industrial ceramics are regarded as some of the most important and influential of the Modern Movement.

The early years of the twentieth century saw the establishment in many European countries of organizations intended to promote good design in industry. The Swedish Society of Industrial Design encouraged manufacturers to employ leading artists and designers to create new products. In 1930, Gustavsberg, the country's leading ceramic manufacturer, commissioned Wilhelm Kåge to design a new modern tableware with a radical new brief. Rather than purchasing a complete service, as was usual, Praktika was sold using the retail concept of open stock, enabling customers to buy the tableware piece by piece. It was also designed to stack easily for more efficient storage and offered versatile pieces – for example, bowls which could also serve as covers for the storage jars. Praktika used clean basic forms, light colour and simple ornamentation. It was not, however, a commercial success when it was introduced, and only gained popularity with the public when it was reissued after the Second World War.

Praktika Tableware

DATE: 1933

DESIGNER: Wilhelm Kåge (1889–1960)

MATERIAL: earthenware

MANUFACTURER: Gustavsberg, Sweden

Savoy Vase

DATE: 1936

DESIGNER: Alvar Aalto
(1898–1976)

MATERIAL: blown glass

MANUFACTURER: Karhula
Iltala, Karhula, Finland

The famous Karhula glass manufacturer in Finland launched a competition to find new glassware designs to show at the Finnish section of the 1937 Paris International Exhibition. Alvar Aalto's design won first prize. Aalto submitted a series of drawings called Eskimoerindens Skinnbuxa (Eskimo leather pants) and his curving forms broke the glass design tradition of symmetrical form.

Sometimes known as the Savoy, because they were used in the well-known Stockholm restaurant of the same name, the interior of which Aalto had designed, the vases were an immediate success and have remained in production ever since. Aalto developed a unique architectural style based on irregular and asymmetric forms and the imaginative use of natural materials.

The organic and non-rational form of the Savoy vase can be seen as a rejection of the geometric formalism adhered to by the majority of Aalto's contemporaries. Its fluid form is similar to that of Aalto's bent laminate birch chair designs from the same period, and calls to mind the free-form shapes of Surrealist painting.

Aino Marsio was the wife of the famous Finnish architect Alvar Aalto. Like the wives of many other designers, her distinguished work has often been overshadowed by that of her more famous husband. Marsio was, nonetheless, a distinguished designer in her own right who also played a key role in Alvar's career, working in his office from 1924 until her death in 1949. Together they set up Artek, a company to market their designs. Marsio enjoyed a long and successful collaboration with the glass manufacturer Karhula, beginning in 1932 when she won a design competition sponsored by the company to create a range of cheap, mass-produced pressed glass. Originally called Bölgeblick, the name of a café in the 1930 Stockholm Exhibition, the range included a pitcher, glasses, bowls, dishes and a creamer. It used thick glass made in three-piece moulds that left clear seams down the side. The distinctive "stepping rings" were not an original idea: in 1930 the Swedish designer Edvard Hald had used a similar technique for his Orrefors Glass Works bowls.

Aino Aalto's glass went into production in 1934 and two years later won a gold medal at the Milan Triennale. The range, still admired for its simple practical forms, has enjoyed enduring success.

Pressed Glass 4644

DATE: 1932

DESIGNER: Aino Marsio-Aalto (1894–1949)

MATERIAL: pressed glass

MANUFACTURER: Karhula Iltala, Karhula, Finland

Rug

DATE: 1932

DESIGNER: Marion Dorn
(1896–1964)

MATERIAL: wool

MANUFACTURER: Wilton Royal
Carpet Factory Limited,
United Kingdom

During the 1930s, Marion Dorn's rugs
and textiles were the preferred choice
of leading British Modernist architects
who wanted interior furnishings
sympathetic to their work. It was
Dorn's rugs that appeared in Syrie
Maughan's famous White Room at
The Savoy Hotel, and in the foyer of
Oswald P. Milne's redecorated
Claridges Hotel, both in London.

Trained as a painter, Dorn's
output was prolific. She designed
fabric for the London Underground
seats as well as fabrics, wallpapers
and furniture. She was also
commissioned to work on the great
ocean liners of the period, including
Cunard's *Queen Mary*. During the
1930s, she completed over one
hundred rug designs for Wilton
Royal, which led to her being
described in the *Architectural
Review* magazine as "the architect
of floors". Her long and fruitful
collaboration with Wilton
concentrated on handmade rugs,
usually produced in limited editions.
Dorn's rugs were used in the new
Modernist interiors to define
particular spaces, often placed at
key points with furniture arranged
around the rug or left in isolation as
a decorative feature. The patterns
were generally bold geometric
shapes but her use of colour was
restrained, employing tones of
white, cream, black and brown.

Travel Tableware

DATE: 1938

DESIGNER: Eric William Ravilious (1903–42)

MATERIAL: earthenware

MANUFACTURER: Josiah Wedgwood and Sons Limited, Etruria, Stoke on Trent, England

Although Eric Ravilious died tragically young while on a flying mission as a war artist during World War Two, the impact of his graphic style was an enduring influence in the immediate postwar years.

Ravilious was an illustrator and wood engraver who had been taught at London's Royal College of Art by the leading British artist Paul Nash. Like his fellow student, Edward Bawden, with whom he painted the murals in the canteen at Morley College in London, Ravilious provided illustrations for a number of publishing houses during the 1930s, most notably Jonathan Cape. His simple but pleasingly decorative style was well suited to industries that were attempting to raise the standards of modern design in 1930s Britain.

In 1936, Ravilious was commissioned to design a Regency Revival dining table and chairs for Dunbar Hay and Company, a shop established by Athole Hay and Cecilia Dunbar Kilburn (Lady Semphill) that marketed works of applied art. It was through Lady Semphill that Ravilious was introduced to Tom Wedgwood in 1935. For the next few years Ravilious designed Wedgwood's most successful printed ceramics, some of which would retain their popularity well into the 1950s.

American Modern Table Service

DATE: 1937

DESIGNER: Russel Wright
(1904–76)

MATERIAL: glazed earthenware

MANUFACTURER: Steubenville
Pottery, East Liverpool,
Ohio, USA

More than any other American designer, the work of Russel Wright has come to represent an image of informal living in the 1940s. He started his career as an apprentice to Norman Bel Geddes but unlike his contemporaries, who applied their talents to transport and products, Russel Wright concentrated on the design of homeware – particularly tableware. His American Modern service, designed in 1937 and in production from 1939 to 1959, was a huge commercial success. It sold over eighty million pieces making it one of the most popular tableware sets ever designed. The American Modern also signalled a more widespread change in American design. Wright rejected the popular machine aesthetic in favour of sculptural, organic forms for his ceramics. In the 1930s the work of Surrealist painters, such as Salvador Dali, and the sculpture of Jean Arp was widely exhibited in New York. Their use of biomorphic shapes had a gradual impact on design. At the same time the leading American architect Frank Lloyd Wright was shifting direction towards a more natural architectural form, exploring traditions and roots of American visual culture. American Modern brought these new ideas to the public – the shape of the water jug, for example, was compared to a traditional eighteenth-century coal scuttle, while other pieces defined the new colour and organic style of the period.

Susie Cooper was a unique designer in many respects: a rare example of a successful female designer, she was not exclusively an "art" potter but designed primarily for mass production.

She was born in Burslem in the heart of the Staffordshire potteries. Her first job was as an assistant designer for A. E. Gray but she soon began producing and decorating her own pieces. In 1929, she opened the Susie Cooper Pottery, which produced a number of hugely popular decorative pieces in her own distinctive stylized version of Modernism.

Although she worked initially as an art potter, Cooper's career took a different turn into the mass market after the war. Turning her attention to bone-china tableware during the 1950s, her modern colours, clear lines and graphic patterns inspired by nature captured the spirit of the times.

In 1966 she became a partner with the Wedgwood group, remaining their principal designer until 1972.

Beechwood Tableware

DATE: 1939

DESIGNER: Susie Cooper (born 1902)

MATERIAL: china

MANUFACTURER: Crown Works, Stoke On Trent England

Prestige 65 Pressure Cooker

DATE: 1948

DESIGNER: unknown

MATERIAL: plastic handles and metal body

MANUFACTURER: Platers and Stampers Limited, London, England

Prestige 65's simple and stylish design proved very popular when it was launched in 1949. Made from polished steel with black plastic handles and incorporating a cooking trivet to release the steam on the lid, it looked modern, practical and extremely durable. In the 1950s pressure cookers enabled the housewife to cook a variety of foods quickly and cheaply, fulfilling something of the function of today's microwave oven. In practical terms the pressure cooker meant that you did not have to heat the oven to cook only a single item or to prepare food in different pans on the hob, since it was fitted with three separate areas for cooking individual foods. In theory, using the Prestige 65 allowed the cook to prepare a complete family meal using a single cooking utensil; and the 1950s saw the publication of a number of specialist cookbooks suggesting appropriate menus. Using high pressure steam also had another advantage: cooking vegetables in this way was quick and healthy since it preserved nutrients and vitamins. A pressure cooker was therefore not only a functional and practical household object but was contributing to the health and wellbeing of the consumer – a factor which proved an extremely strong selling point.

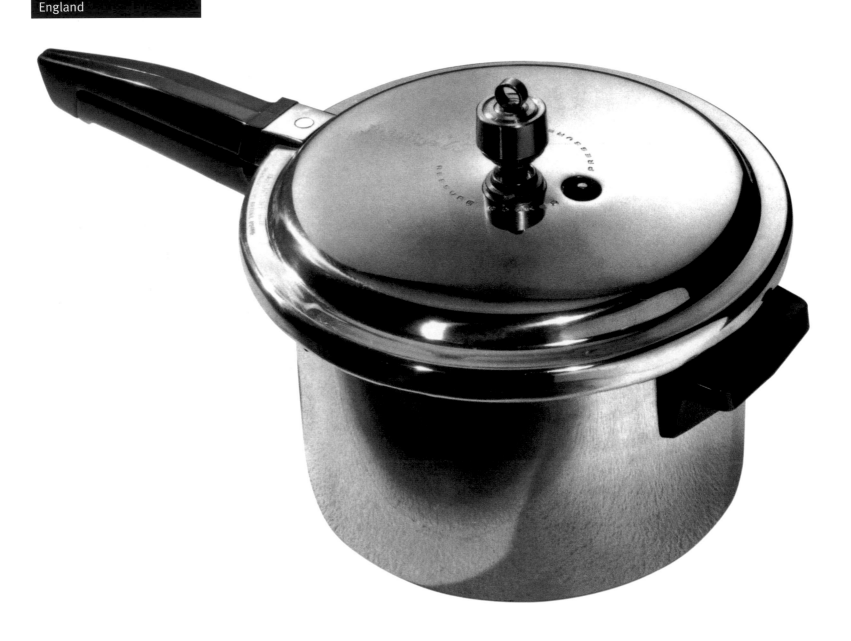

Cornish Kitchenware, adapted in the 1920s from traditional blue-dipped ware, made its first appearance in the 1927 T.G. Green catalogue. Made from white earthenware dipped into blue glaze, the range was introduced to provide work for the factory's turners, whose jobs were then under threat because of the widespread economic slump. T.G. Green, anxious not to lose its skilled workforce, used Cornishware as a way of exploiting their expertise. Originally consisting only of utilitarian jars and jugs, it was extended to include tableware such as mugs, plates and teapots. Aimed at the middle-income mass market, the range offered functional, cheap tableware for breakfast and informal meals. The title "Cornish" was a marketing strategy used to evoke farmhouse and country associations, while the use of blue reinforced the fresh feel of the dairy.

Cornishware's distinctive blue and white bands owe something to the Continental development of well-designed, mass-produced Modernist tableware at this time. It became a British design classic, and early examples are avidly sought by collectors and featured in museums. In 1967 Royal College of Art graduate Judith Onions redesigned many of the Cornishware shapes and its commercial success continues.

Cornish Kitchenware

DATE: 1927

DESIGNER: unknown

MATERIAL: earthenware

MANUFACTURER: T.G. Green and Company, Church Gresley, Derbyshire, England

Victory V

DATE: 1941

DESIGNER: unknown

MATERIAL: printed cotton

MANUFACTURER: Calico
Printers Association,
England

This novelty fabric was part of a
series of patriotic prints produced
during the Second World War under
the auspices of the Utility scheme, a
programme of design controlled by
the Government to produce consumer
goods for the civilian population.

During this period everyone from
the Queen to the ordinary citizen
was issued with ration coupons,
which they were required to produce
when purchasing goods. It was a
simple but fair system, aimed at
tackling the severe shortages in the
shops. Any imported material was
strictly rationed, including dyestuffs,
which may account for the dark
brown of this fabric. With a
distinctly patriotic theme it used
Winston Churchill's famous Victory
salute as a pattern repeat designed
in various forms, including falling
bombs, RAF fighter planes and an
"X-ray image" of women's hands –
a technique which probably owed
something to the Surrealist
photographic experimentation of
Man Ray in the 1930s.

Crystal Design

DATE: 1951

DESIGNER: S.M. Slade

MATERIAL: Celanese

MANUFACTURER: British Celanese, United Kingdom

This pattern comes from a *Souvenir Book Of Crystal Patterns* from the 1951 Festival of Britain. It represents an interesting design experiment. This famous festival, held on London's South Bank, was intended to promote British achievements and trade in a national and international context. Part of the brief was to feature the radical scientific work undertaken at that time in Cambridge on the structure of crystals. This research lent itself to a commission inviting designers to produce patterns for the home for carpets, curtain fabric and laminates using the distinctive forms and shapes of crystals revealed under the microscope. The fabric shown here exploits the contour type of diagram and fits perfectly with the prevailing current taste for bright colours and the freeform outlines of organic shapes.

These designs proved extremely popular with the consumer and were widely imitated in a whole range of carpets and fabrics for the 1950s home.

3089 A.B.C. Graduating Table Bowls

DATE: 1969

DESIGNER: Enzo Mari
(born 1932)

MATERIAL: plastic melamine

MANUFACTURER: Danese,
Milan, Italy

Until the 1960s, plastic had a negative image, as a material of little value. However, young designers of the decade did not see plastic as a cheap alternative for more expensive materials but an opportunity for strong colour and form, which helped to create the new aesthetic of Pop. Manufacturers were keen to exploit the market for new plastic goods and one example was the Italian company Danese. Founded by Bruno Danese in Milan in 1957, the company specialized in small household goods such as glasses, bowls and vases. Enzo Mari worked for Danese from its beginning and, in 1964, he produced a series of objects, including desk accessories and vases, which helped to define the company's reputation for stylish innovations in plastic.

Interested in semiology, Mari is among the more intellectual of his generation of designers. His book analysing design as a linguistic system, *Funzione della ricerca estetica,* was published in 1970. Mari's approach to plastic design was technologically inventive and original, demonstrated here in a series of cylindrical table bowls with a concave central well, incorporating pierced holes on each side. In 1972 the bowls were included in a seminal exhibition on Italian design at the Museum of Modern Art, New York called "Italy: The New Domestic Landscape". The exhibition brought Mari wide recognition as one of Italy's most important designers.

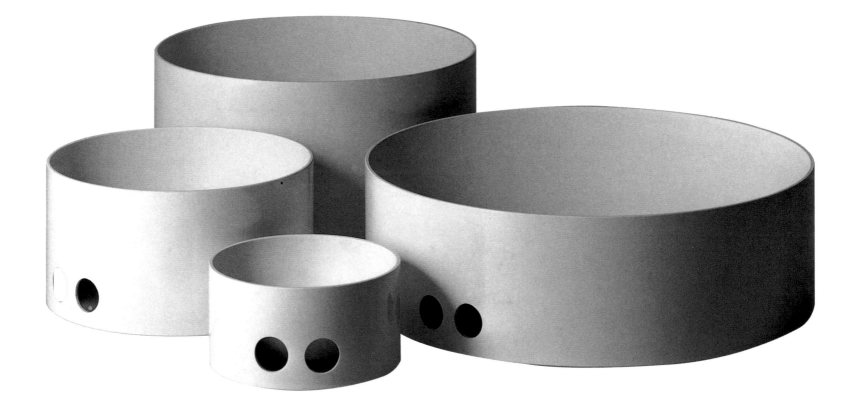

The American Earl Tupper first developed a range of containers made from polyethylene in 1945. Designed with air-tight seals to keep food fresher for longer periods of time, they revolutionized the storage of food in the home. The commercial success of Tupperware was based on the idea of home party-selling, which began in 1946 and was introduced to Britain in 1960.

The Tupperware range has been extended from basic kitchen storage and utensils to include cooking, table, and picnic ware, and children's products – including toys. The designs are constantly updated to incorporate new fashions in shapes and colours.

Picnic Set

DATE: 1950s

DESIGNER: Tupperware

MATERIAL: plastic

MANUFACTURER: Tupperware, Orlando, Florida, USA

Terrazzo Fabric

DATE: 1943

DESIGNER: Josef Frank (1885–1967)

MATERIAL: printed linen

MANUFACTURER: Svenskt Tenn, Stockholm, Sweden

In the years after World War One, Josef Frank emerged as one of Austria's leading avant-garde architects, building apartment blocks, houses and offices using modern styling and techniques. In 1927 he came to the attention of Mies van der Rohe who invited him to take part in a Deutsche Werkbund exhibition; but his career was to be cut short in the 1930s, when Nazi domination made his position as a Jew untenable.

In 1933 he and his Swedish wife emigrated to Stockholm where he worked for Svenskt Tenn, Sweden's leading interior design company. Along with his Scandinavian contemporaries, Frank helped establish a distinctly Swedish approach to Modernism – an approach to design that was less hard line, that used nature and the vernacular as sources, and developed sculptural, organic shapes.

Although Frank spent the war years in America, he maintained contacts with Sweden. In 1944 he sent Estrid Ericson, Svenskt Tenn's founder, a series of fifty new designs for her fiftieth birthday. Among them was Terrazzo. This is an unusual design in that Frank's sources were mainly derived from nature, using flowers, birds or animals. The pattern here is made up of polished stones with a background of terrazzo – an Italian floor finish using pieces of marble. Although the patterned stones appear to be random they make up a repeating geometric pattern which acts as a surface net to hold the design together.

Arne Jacobsen was foremost among Denmark's modern architects. This range of utility objects in stainless steel conformed entirely to Modernist principles of beauty through honesty to materials and method of manufacture, while at the same time being inexpensive and available to the mass of the populace.

The Cylinda Line series – all based on the form of a cylinder – was developed with Stelton over a three-year period. The range included saucepans, ice tongs, ashtrays and coffeepots.

Cylinda Line Tea Service

DATE: 1967

DESIGNER: Arne Jacobsen (1902–71)

MATERIAL: stainless steel

MANUFACTURER: A. S. Stelton, Denmark

Caccia Cutlery

DATE: 1938

DESIGNER: Luigi Caccia Dominioni (born 1913), Livio (1911–79) and Pier Giacomo Castiglioni (1913–68)

MATERIAL: stainless steel

MANUFACTURER: Alessi, Crusinallo, Italy

Luigi Caccia Dominioni, who gave his name to this set of tableware, was trained as an architect and worked on many projects with the better-known Castiglioni brothers. When their collaboration on the Caccia cutlery was shown at the Milan Trienniale in 1940 it was described by Gio Ponti in *Domus* magazine as "the most beautiful cutlery in existence". In this exhibition Italian architects addressed the problems of producing objects for industrial production – tableware and new cutlery designs on show explored the possibilities of die casting and new materials such as steel. When it was originally launched it was available only in silver. However, Alessi saw its mass-market potential when, fifty years later, they commissioned Dominioni to complete the set using original drawings from the period.

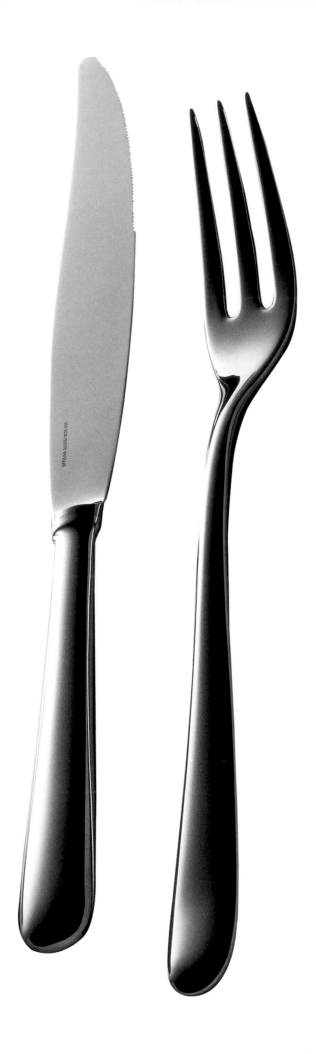

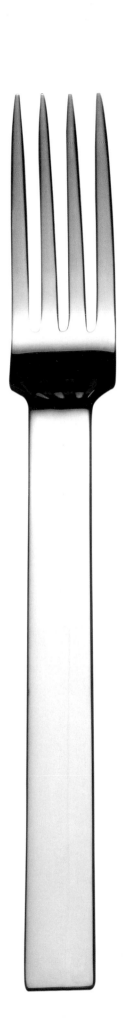

Odeon Cutlery

DATE: 1992

DESIGNER: David Mellor (born 1930)

MATERIAL: stainless steel and plastic

MANUFACTURER: David Mellor, Sheffield, England

Cutler, industrial designer and more recently retailer, David Mellor has had a profound influence on postwar British design. He trained as a silversmith in his native Sheffield and then at the Royal College of Art in London. During the 1950s and 1960s Mellor designed street lighting, bus shelters, road traffic signs for the Department of the Environment and a pillar box for the Post Office. However, his contributions to environmental design have been overshadowed by his importance as a designer, manufacturer and retailer of high-quality silver and stainless steel.

In 1970, Mellor established his own factory at Broom Hall in Sheffield, a city long associated with the steel and cutlery industries. From here he has directed every aspect of the design and production of his innovative cutlery. He has revolutionized the manufacturing process, introducing purpose-built machinery and a flexible work force in which each cutler is trained to carry out every stage of the production. Through his shops in London and Manchester, Mellor has successfully marketed his own cutlery and kitchenware as well as those by other designers and craftsmen, selected for their functional and aesthetic excellence.

Mellor has produced an exceptionally diverse range of cutlery designs, from the Embassy silver service, commissioned in 1965 for use in British embassies throughout the world, to a special service designed to meet the needs of the disabled.

Pasta Set 9092

DATE: 1985

DESIGNER: Massimo Morozzi
(born 1941)

MATERIAL: stainless steel

MANUFACTURER: Alessi,
Crusinallo, Italy

Established in the 1930s, the Italian company Alessi enjoyed a reputation for good quality metalware that continued into the postwar period. In 1983 they launched a new and hugely successful series of products for the home called Officina Alessi. They saw an opportunity to expand their range and to exploit the growing interest in design in the 1980s. Alessi commissioned leading International architects and designers to produce specially designed, distinctive products exploiting

Alessi's traditional expertise in the use of stainless steel, brass, copper and silver. In some ways the choice of Massimo Morozzi was typical of the Alessi approach in that previously Morozzi was a leading Italian avant-garde designer, producing radical and experimental work that did not make him the obvious candidate for a pasta set. Alessi, however, had a talent for exploiting this kind of creative edge and they also recognized the food revolution of the 1980s.

Internationally, people were experimenting with new authentic regional foods and pasta, which, although always widely enjoyed, required specialist cooking equipment.

Morozzi's set consists of a multi-purpose boiling unit and steamer, a colander with handles and a lid with a hollow knob for steam to escape. Not only did it succeed in cooking large quantities of pasta efficiently – it also made a stylish contribution to the new "designer kitchen" of the 1980s.

Michael Graves is one of the leading theorists and architects of Postmodernism, a movement in architecture and design that has sought to invest buildings and objects with a narrative content. Implicit within the movement's ideas is a critique of the international style and the sober and allegedly impersonal character of Modernism.

Graves studied architecture at Harvard University and has taught at Princeton since 1962. Although he has designed relatively few objects and his architectural output remains small, he has become an influential spokesman for an approach to design that advocates bold use of colour and pattern and witty references to popular culture. In this respect he broke away from his original allegiance to Modernism and it is significant that when the Italian Memphis group produced their first collection in 1982 it featured the work of only one American: Graves. This brought him to the attention of Alessi.

The Graves kettle was one of Alessi's first, and most successful, experiments with Postmodernism. With its simple form and restrained use of materials, the kettle is essentially a straightforward modern piece of design. However, Graves gives it a humorous twist with the addition of a blue plastic bird mounted on the spout that sings when the water boils.

Whistling Kettle 9093

DATE: 1985

DESIGNER: Michael Graves (born 1934)

MATERIAL: steel with polyamide handle

MANUFACTURER: Alessi, Crusinallo, Italy

Arizona Carpet

DATE: 1984

DESIGNER: Nathalie du Pasquier (born 1957)

MATERIAL: wool

MANUFACTURER: Memphis, Milan, Italy

Nathalie du Pasquier was part of the Memphis group working in Milan in the early 1980s that helped to change the design map. The Postmodernist agenda, which had been gaining ground throughout the 1970s, had reintroduced colour and decoration as important themes in architecture. However, in the world of design, the dominant taste remained for classic simple shapes in neutral colours. Memphis was part of a radical change that brought bright colour and patterns back into fashion, echoing the Pop aesthetic of the 1960s. The Arizona carpet illustrated here is typical of these designs.

Trained as a painter, du Pasquier was still a young woman when she joined Memphis. Her early designs for laminates, fabrics and carpets created a tremendous impact. Her use of bold form and a palette of the brightest colours helped to establish pattern as a priority for interiors in the 1980s.

Du Pasquier worked in collaboration with her partner and fellow founder member of Memphis, George Sowden. Together they produced a whole series of patterns designed for carpets, wallpapers and textiles called Progetto Decorazione. One successful commercial project was the laminate designs produced by the Italian company Abet Laminati.

Ginevra Carafe

DATE: 1997

DESIGNER: Ettore Sottsass
(born 1917)

MATERIAL: glass

MANUFACTURER: Alessi,
Crusinallo, Italy

Ettore Sottsass is the grand
old man of Italian design. His work
spans over forty years and in each
decade he has produced a fresh and
original vision that manages to
express the period. The Ginevra
range of glasses and carafe is no
exception. It fits perfectly into a
1990s direction for simple classic
shapes in which Sottsass cast his
master's eye for balance and detail.
Sottsass has worked in glass over
many decades. In a series of famous
experiments for Memphis in the
1980s, he took a traditional Italian
craft and used glass as a plastic
material combining bright colours
with simple forms reminiscent of a
child's play with plasticine. Sotsass'
versatility in glass is illustrated here
by his superb redefinition of the
classic carafe.

I Petali

DATE: 1997

DESIGNER: Michele de Lucchi
(born 1951)

MATERIAL: ceramics with
metal handle

MANUFACTURER: Produzione
Privata, Milan, Italy

Michele de Lucchi first came to public attention with his work for the Italian Memphis company in the 1980s. He has since established himself as one of Italy's leading designers working with leading furniture and design companies throughout the world. Produzione Privata is a new venture that reflects a 1990s concern with re-use but develops the recurring twentieth-century theme of the found object. De Lucchi assembles ordinary objects in an unexpected way, rediscovering the potential of the ordinary and everyday. I Petali uses white plates to create a traditional table centrepiece while other items in the range use industrial glass, anonymous drink containers and forks (see p. 162).

Jasper Morrison is a young British designer best known for his stylish, minimalist furniture, but he has also produced a series of objects for the home, including this new version of the wine rack. Previous designs had relied on traditional vernacular form, with wood and metal supports, sometimes scaled down for kitchen work surfaces. Jasper Morrison took the simple but obvious step of producing the wine rack in plastic. Using simple geometric forms he made it an accessory for the modern home, producing it in flat pack form in a series of bright modern colours.

Wine Rack

DATE: 1994

DESIGNER: Jasper Morrison (born 1959)

MATERIAL: plastic

MANUFACTURER: Magis, Treviso, Italy

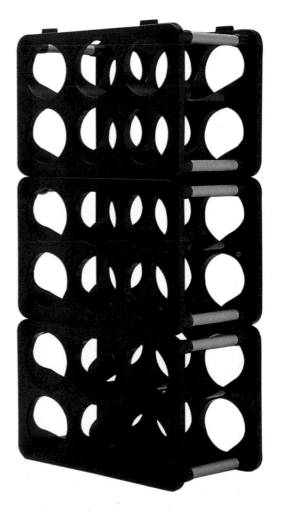

products

SWISS ARMY KNIFE

BRUTON ELECTRIC FIRE

THIS SECTION, CALLED PRODUCTS, deals with machines for the home, including washing machines, fridges, irons and vacuum cleaners. The domestic appliance industry is unique in that the pace of its growth was not governed so much by consumer demand as by the increasing availability of utilities in the home. With the widespread introduction of gas and plumbing in the nineteenth century, to be followed later by electricity, the character of the domestic house and domestic products was radically changed. The Victorian home contained many appliances, indeed there were countless and ingenious task-specific items on the market, including machines for the preparation of marmalade and meat mincers; however, they were hand-operated. The key domestic tasks of the nineteenth-century middle-class household – washing, ironing, cooking and the preservation of food – had relied on the availability of a cheap servant class. By the beginning of World War One, domestic service was no longer the only option in the job market for working-class men and women, so the attraction of new electrical appliances was obvious.

The development of electrical domestic appliances started from the 1880s, with simple basic items such as immersion heaters and flat irons. More importantly, they relied on electricity, which in Britain was made more widely available following the Electricity (Supply) Act of 1926, when the Central Electricity Board was empowered

PYRAMID FRIDGE

to create the first National Grid to connect supplies throughout the country. The appliance industries evolved from engineering plants but they relied on individual experimentation and development from pioneer individuals and companies. Manufacturers faced the problem of new methods of production, which required parts for machines that were standardized and interchangeable in order to make available goods for the mass market. Companies were driven by the need of consumers for products that would offer practical, functional solutions to the new lifestyles of the century. Bringing these products to a wider market was a slow process, with the creation of ever-smaller electrical motors to drive washing machines and food mixers and heat elements in kettles and irons. One important pioneer in this context was the designer Peter Behrens. His work from 1907, for the then most powerful electrical appliance company in the world, Germany's AEG, set a precedent. Under Behrens, AEG produced electrical goods that created a range of easy to use, simple and rational products that established the aesthetic for such items. It was Behrens' pioneering work that proved an inspiration to the Modern Movement's quest for the house as a machine for living in. The kitchen, for example, was now viewed as a laboratory where scientific principles could be applied to the organization of domestic tasks, including areas for the preparation and cleaning of food. Walls were often tiled, cookers were now made of enamel for easy cleaning and aluminium cooking pans replaced the old tradition of copper pots. The Bauhaus and its designers were quick to respond to these changes producing, for example, laboratory-like heat-resistant glass containers like the Kubus range that is featured in the homeware section. In the field of products, however, the world's most powerful economic power, America, led the way. Under the leadership of designers such as Norman Bel Geddes, Raymond Loewy and Walter Dorwin Teague, the profession of the industrial designer began to take shape and they quickly turned its attention to domestic appliances. These men set up professional offices that were modelled on those of the architect and the solicitor rather than the independent artist. They introduced the attractive idea of redefining the market using design. For them design meant restyling, providing a streamlined and modern outer casing for products whose engineering and machine function was already established but whose appearance was often antiquated and outdated. The Coldspot fridge is such an example; previously the fridge had been offered to consumers as a traditional larder with the cumbersome freezing equipment placed on top; now Loewy's Coldspot offered a sleek elegant form that could take its place with pride in the new kitchen. Irons, cookers and weighing scales quickly followed suit, using new materials and sculptural form to give these utilitarian objects a sense of quality and prestige.

SURFLINE IRON

The Modernist rationale was continued in the postwar period by the German company Braun. It produced electrical goods for the home and used its business to foster an overall design strategy that stressed simple geometric shapes, no decoration and no colour, using white for the majority of products. From 1960, the Braun approach dominated the international styling of domestic products. Challenges to Braun's domination did come. During the 1960s pioneer companies like the Italian Brionvega promoted a vision of objects that used wit and humour more in keeping with the prevailing Pop aesthetic. Nonetheless the majority of electrical products could be placed in the category of the white box.

MOKA EXPRESS

The early 1980s signalled an important shift in attitude. There had always been a market for products that used colour and decoration, but these had often been relegated by design purists to the category of bad taste. Now, influenced by the new attitudes of Postmodernism, manufacturers started to explore organic shapes while other companies like Zanussi introduced quirky detailing and colour into products such as fridges.

In the 1990s the product designer has increasingly been involved in more and more technically advanced products for the home. Function remains the key approach but increasingly the consumer wants design as an element put back into these machines for the home.

DYSON

Hoover
Junior

DATE: 1907

DESIGNER: unknown

MATERIAL: metal alloy
and plastic

MANUFACTURER: Hoover
Limited, United Kingdom

In 1907 the Hoover company
developed its first simple vacuum
cleaner and quickly established an
international market for the
company's products. In 1919 the first
Hoovers came to Britain, where they
soon proved popular. Hoover
pioneered new retailing methods
and by the mid-1930s their
vacuum cleaners, such as the model
shown here, were regularly
demonstrated in the home by
travelling salesmen. Mass
production methods made them
cheaper to buy: by 1935 cleaners
were a third of the price they had
been in the 1920s and by 1949 forty
per cent of British households
owned one. Sales in the UK were so
buoyant that the company decided
to invest in a British manufacturing
plant and in 1932 they built their
flamboyant Art Deco factory in
Perivale, West London. Designed by
Wallis, Gilbert and Partners, it was
intended to consolidate their
modern image. The Hoover Junior
was a cheaper version of the Hoover
Senior. Both machines united all the
working parts together under one
covered section, making a neater,
more streamlined design and
thereby creating an association with
progress and hygiene.

THE
HOOVER
REG. TRADE MARK IT BEATS
AS IT SWEEPS
AS IT CLEANS

Electrolux Vacuum Cleaner

DATE: c.1945

DESIGNER: Sixten Sason (1912–69)

MANUFACTURER: Electrolux, Sweden

First produced in 1915, the cylinder vacuum cleaner, which travelled horizontally across the floor, was produced by Electrolux, a Swedish company dedicated to good design. As part of the company's policy of hiring renowned designers, Sixten Sason was engaged by Electrolux as a design consultant and produced the more refined, sleek torpedo-like form for the cleaner. Although a silversmith by training, Sixten Sason went on to design some of the most distinctive industrial products of the century, including the first Hasselblad cameras and Saab 96 and 99 cars.

Dyson Dual Cyclone

DATE: 1983

DESIGNER: James Dyson
(born 1947)

MATERIAL: moulded plastics

MANUFACTURER: Dyson
Appliances, United Kingdom

Since it was first produced for the mass market in 1993 the Dual Cyclone, which combines unconventional styling with technical innovation, has become a best-selling vacuum cleaner in the United Kingdom. Conventional cleaners use a filter bag, which traps dirt and dust while allowing clean air to re-enter the room. The effectiveness of such cleaners gradually reduces as the bag fills up, because the pores in the bag clog up with microscopic dust particles. James Dyson's cyclonic system, which uses the principle of centrifugal force, sucks up air and revolves it at eight hundred miles per hour through two cyclone chambers until the dust and dirt drop to the bottom of the transparent cylinder.

Dyson spent five years and over five thousand prototypes developing his first cleaner, a very Postmodern pink and lavender machine called the G-Force. At first he found little enthusiasm for it among European and American manufacturers, but in 1984 a Japanese company put it into limited production. In 1991 he sold his licence interests to the Japanese, which enabled him to fund the manufacture and marketing of the cleaner in Britain. He now manufactures the Cyclone in his own research centre and factory in the UK and has a multi-million pound business worldwide. The later Absolute model uses a bacteria-killing screen to pick up viruses and pollen in the air.

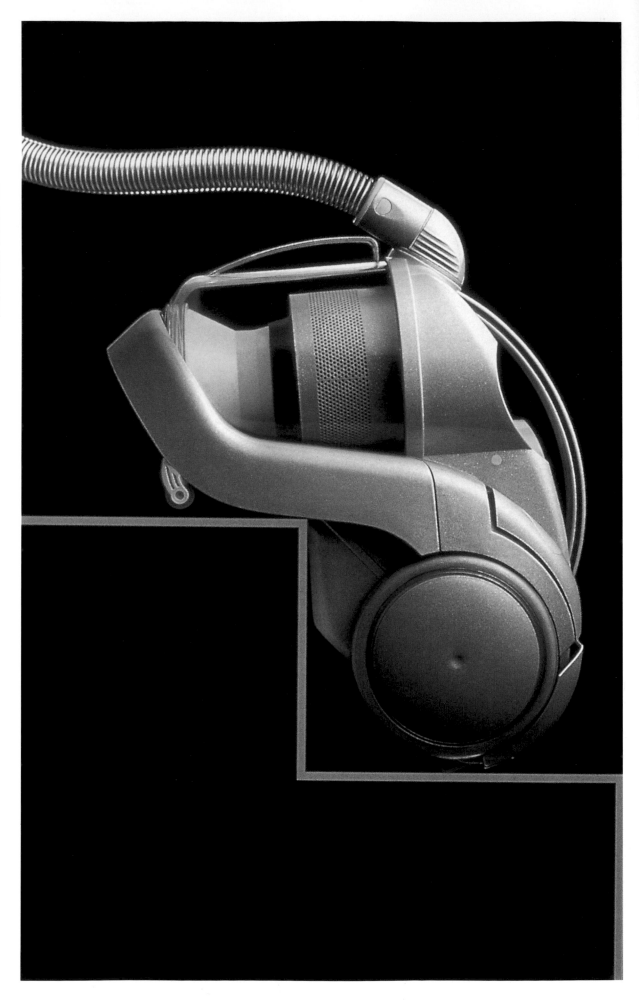

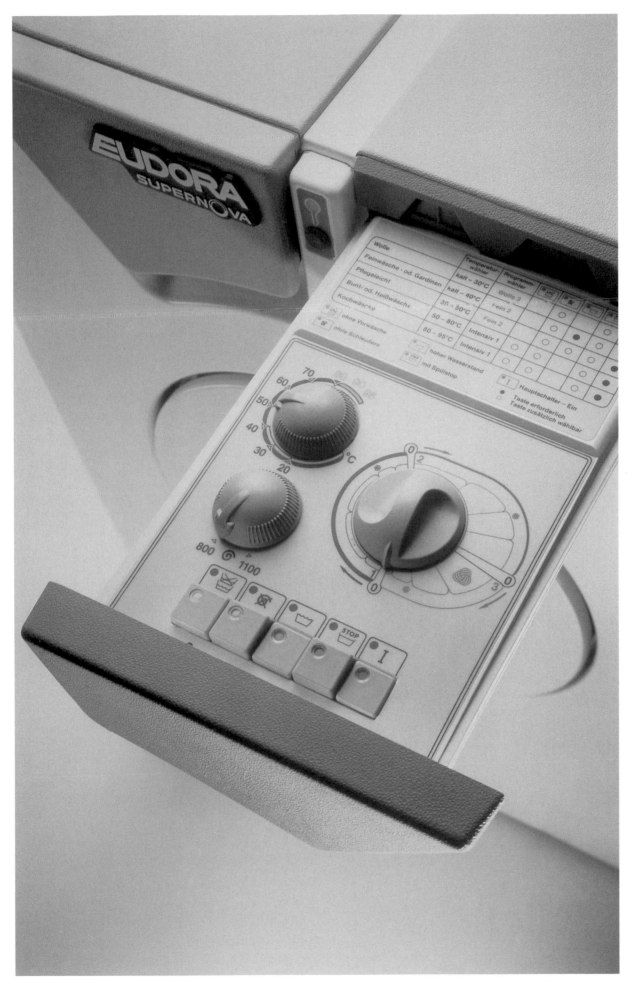

Supernova Washing Machine

DATE: 1989

DESIGNER: Porsche Design, GmbH, Austria

MATERIAL: steel and plastic

MANUFACTURER: Eudora, Austria

This domestic product defies the ubiquitous form of most large kitchen appliances commonly described as "white goods". Within two months of its launch the Supernova became the fourth best-selling washing machine in Austria. The traditional "TV screen" was replaced here by an operational control ring. The controls are housed in the right-hand panel of the machine, which mirrors the adjacent soap dispensing compartment, and the drawer principle protects the controls from soap and water. Heavy duty plastic panels protect the top surface from scratching. The product also includes an automatic sensor which recognizes the size of the wash load and supplies the precise amount of water required, saving electricity, detergent and water. Such ecosystems have now become a standard feature of washing machines in the 1990s.

Coldspot Super Six Refrigerator

DATE: 1934

DESIGNER: Raymond Loewy (1893–1986)

MANUFACTURER: Sears Roebuck Company, Chicago, USA

Raymond Loewy remains America's best-known industrial designer. Gifted with a legendary talent for self-promotion, his definition of good design was an upwards sales curve. In the 1930s this was appealing for manufacturers battling against the worst ever US recession. Loewy used design to produce distinctive modern objects for the home. He was famous for restyling, often providing a totally new casing concept for an existing machine. The Coldspot fridge is a classic example of this approach and remains one of Raymond Loewy's most enduring designs. It was commissioned for Sears Roebuck, a company that revolutionized mail-order retailing in the United States. Customers could simply order products by post and also benefit from attractive extended credit terms. The Coldspot was one of the first consumer products to use the sculptural lines of streamlining to market household goods. The fridge was no longer just a machine, but a thing of beauty, a piece of modern design. The Coldspot was one of the most enduring demonstrations of Loewy's prime concern with styling. It employs all the most sophisticated metal forming techniques, with rustproof aluminium shelving and a handle that responded to the lightest touch, and features a distinctive blue logo. It was a turning point in consumer products and signalled the beginning of the "objects of desire" trend.

Pyramid Fridge

DATE: 1987

DESIGNER: Roberto Pezzetta (born 1946)

MANUFACTURER: Zanussi, Italy

In the 1980s Zanussi introduced this fridge to challenge the prevailing dominance of white as the colour for domestic products in the kitchen. Colour is now established as a theme for the kitchen, giving "white goods" a front-rank presence and turning them into a point of reference in the home and the equal of furniture.

This decidedly Postmodern fridge, designed by Zanussi's in-house head of design, was not commercially successful, since its dramatic shape did not lend itself to the space constraints of modern kitchens.

Aga, New Standard Stove

DATE: 1922

DESIGNER: Gustaf Dalen
(1869–1937)

MANUFACTURER: Aga Heat
Limited, Sweden

For many, the Aga oven conjures up the definitive image of domesticity. The stove typifies values, preferably rural, that allow time for cooking and keep the kitchen at the heart of family life. Interestingly, when the Aga was first designed it was seen as leading-edge Modernist styling and technology. It was illustrated in many 1930s books that explored modern design, such as the important English critic Herbert Read's *Art and Industry* (1936).

The Aga was invented in 1922 by Gustaf Dalen, who, in 1912, had won the Nobel Prize for Physics for his Sun Valve. The Aga was not, however, put into production until the early 1930s, when it was licensed for manufacture in Britain. It offered a simple but highly effective solution to the rather unpredictable performance of the then widely used kitchen range. The design consisted of a cleverly insulated iron box with two ovens of constant temperature. It worked on the principle of heat storage with preset cooking plates for boiling and simmering, topped by the Aga's distinctive hinged plates.

Originally only available in classic cream, in the 1960s and 1970s the colour range was widened to include primary colours and dark blues and greens. Although the design has been modified and most models now work on electricity, the Aga remains true to its original cooking principles and as such maintains its appeal for the traditional consumer.

During the 1930s American industrial designers published key books that set out their design agenda and also acted as a form of self-publicity. In 1932 Bel Geddes published *Horizons*, a classic of the period in which he published an image of the Oriole cooker. It was his object lesson in the principle of "form following function". To make it easy to clean, the burners were covered with flat panels, the oven doors were flush and corners were rounded. The material was vitreous white enamel, which, when dirty, could simply be wiped down. With an eye on new technology, Bel Geddes borrowed a device from the skyscraper construction industry, building a chassis of steel onto which the enamel panels could be clipped after installation, thus minimizing the problem of chipping the enamel surface. Standard Gas had an immediate success on their hands, with sales doubling and copycat versions appearing from rival companies.

The Oriole made large manufacturing corporations sit up and recognize the power of design to increase sales. Manufacturers of washers, fridges, vacuum cleaners and irons quickly followed suit with new products that were to transform the visual appearance of the home.

Oriole Electric Stove

DATE: 1931

DESIGNER: Norman Bel Geddes (1893–1958)

MATERIAL: vitreous enamel

MANUFACTURER: Standard Gas Equipment Corporation, USA

ORIOLE

Bruton Reflective Electric Fire

DATE: 1939

MATERIAL: chrome plate

MANUFACTURER: HMV, London, England

To symbolize its qualities of modernity and efficiency, the designers of electrical products in the 1930s looked to reproduce features derived from Art Deco and streamlined automobile styling. The Bruton electric fire was typical of many designs of the period in that the extensive use of chrome had connotations of contemporary car styling. In addition, its use of a double parabola also improved the heat distribution and thus the efficiency of the fire.

The introduction of electric fires into the domestic market offered consumers their first experience of instant and portable heating in the home, and, although relatively expensive to run, were extremely popular supplements to coal fires, which were the standard form of heating before the widespread introduction of central heating in the postwar period.

Electric irons became the most successful of the early twentieth-century appliances. Early technology, in the form of an electric element, was quite simple: irons were quick to heat and easy to keep hot, clean and free of fumes and smell.

Nothing did more than the iron to increase the early demand for convenient electricity supplies to the home and irons became the century's best-selling electric appliance. In the postwar period it was basic equipment for virtually every home. As a product,

its development centred on the additions of technical extras, more reliable thermostat control, water spray devices for steam and the styling of the product casing.

The German company Rowenta has looked carefully at this market and positioned its recent range, the Surfline, very successfully. The iron combines the latest technology and lightweight metal alloys with a non-stick plate, but its success relies on the distinctive turquoise-blue plastic casing. This

design feature gives the iron a contemporary Postmodern feel, which fits in with the taste for colour in the design of domestic products. It transforms an ordinary, dull, utilitarian product into a stylish design object for the home. In addition the casing colour fulfils a useful function in that it evokes the fresh and clean feel of the ocean, and the housewife – statistics reveal that women still do most of the ironing in the home – can easily see if the water level is sufficient.

Surfline

DATE: 1994

MATERIAL: metal and plastic

MANUFACTURER: Rowenta, Germany

Philips Toaster

DATE: 1996

DESIGNER: Philips Corporate Design with Alessandro Mendini (born 1931) /Alessi

MANUFACTURER: Philips, Eindhoven, The Netherlands

Philips is a world leader in the production of kitchen appliances and electronic technology. In 1995 they launched a series of products in collaboration with Alessi, a small, Italian, design-led company that manufactures kitchen and household products. The range included a coffee maker, juice extractor, kettle and toaster, all using distinctive plastic sculptural forms and in a range of contemporary colours from green to pink and cream. The toaster uses a sensor system that gives accurate control for light to dark brown toasting. The bread carrier can be raised high enough to take out the smallest piece of bread.

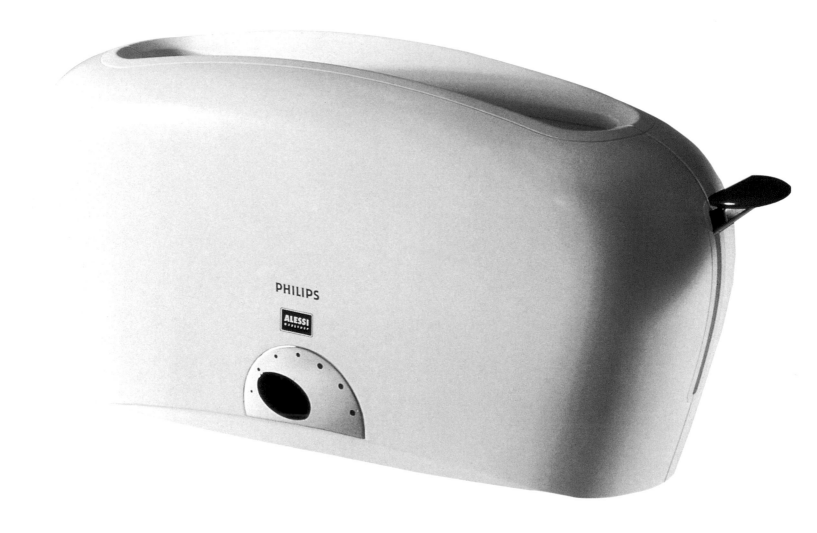

Combination Cutlery

DATE: 1978

DESIGNER: Ergonomi
Design Gruppen

MANUFACTURER: RFSU Rehab
AB, Stockholm, Sweden

Design for the handicapped community has usually been given low priority among manufacturers and designers. The result has often been unattractive equipment to address the problems of those, whether young or old, who cannot cope with ordinary implements and products.

The Swedish company RFSU Rehab, along with the designers Maria Benktzon and Sven-Eric Juhlin of the Erogonomi Design Group, have succeeded in providing the same level of design and detailing for its products as for those for the mainstream commercial sector. Sweden has enjoyed an unshakeable record for its humane concern for groups with special needs.

This range of cutlery is designed to help those with a limited ability in their hands. It functions as a knife and fork or a knife and spoon in one. A supporting surface ensures that the cutlery is easy to hold firmly for cutting and the knife edge is straight and parallel with the handle, making cutting work easier. The combispoon is designed for persons with grave disabilities as it is easier to pick up food using a spoon. The bowl of the spoon has a double-sided serration and is deeper than normal.

Moka
Express

DATE: 1930

DESIGNER: Alfonso Bialetti

MANUFACTURER: Moka, Italy

The Moka Express is a simple coffee-making machine for the stove. It unscrews in the centre, water is placed in the bottom, coffee in the centre compartment and it is then heated until the boiling water and superheated steam are forced up through the coffee grounds and freshly made coffee collects in the top compartment. Designed in 1930, the styling is classic Art Deco with its geometric facets, shiny metal and Bakelite surfaces. The Moka was also attractive enough to be placed straight from the cooker onto the table. In the 1930s it was an expensive, avant-garde object in limited production. After the Second World War it was put into mass production and became a best-seller. Easy to use and inexpensive, it was exported all over the world and came to represent the elegance and style of Italy.

For the baby boom generation of the 1950s, two objects came to symbolize the new aesthetic of postwar Italian design: the Vespa scooter and the celebrated chrome espresso coffee machine, designed by Gio Ponti in 1947 for La Pavoni. Its sleek engineering styling was no accident. During the 1930s, Ponti was a rare Italian example of a product designer working for industry. He studied architecture in Milan and graduated in 1921. His early work was built within the constraints of Italian Fascism but after the war Ponti became one of Italy's most respected figures, not only because of his original vision but also because of his key role at the heart of the Italian design establishment. He was an important force behind the creation of the Milan Triennale and an influential writer and educator. In 1928, he became the founding editor of *Domus* which he edited for fifty years, transforming the magazine into a publication of international importance.

For many years Ponti taught at the Milan Polytechnic and helped shape the intellectual ideas underlying the best of Italian design. He was respected by, and generous to, several generations of young designers.

La Pavoni exported its coffee machine all over the world but it was particularly important in London, forever associated with the new teenage lifestyle of coffee bars. It represented an important stylistic shift away from American dominance to an emphasis on things European and became part of a new outlook revealed in films like *The Ipcress File* and novels such as *Absolute Beginners*.

La Pavoni Coffee Machine

DATE: 1947

DESIGNER: Gio Ponti
(1891–1979)

MANUFACTURER: La Pavoni,
San Giuliano, Italy

Mirella Sewing Machine

DATE: 1956

DESIGNER: Marcello Nizzoli (1895–1969)

MATERIAL: steel, aluminium

MANUFACTURER: Necchi, Pavia, Italy

Marcello Nizzoli worked across most of the design disciplines during the course of his career, most notably the design of office equipment and typewriters for Olivetti.

In the 1950s Necchi was typical of many Italian manufacturing companies in engaging a consultant designer to work on their products and give them an individual signature in order to compete better in the domestic and export markets. In the 1950s Italy, supported by American financial aid, experienced an economic boom because of the great demand for electrical household appliances such as refrigerators, washing machines and sewing machines. Italy's steel industry flourished and the results of the techniques developed, such as die-casting, which enabled the production of sophisticated outer casings, can be seen here. In common with other Italian products of this period, the Mirella sewing machine demonstrates a preoccupation with form. The Necchi sewing machines that Nizzoli designed concentrate on strongly organic outline shapes made to disguise and house the machinery. The Mirella was also important in design terms because of the careful placing and detailing of the machine and its controls.

Braun
Shaver

DATE: 1951

DESIGNER: Dieter Rams
(born 1932)

MANUFACTURER: Max Braun,
Frankfurt, Germany

Through his work for the German
company, Braun, Dieter Rams has
established himself as one of the
most influential product designers of
the postwar era. His approach to
design follows the principle of
functionalism – that design should
use simple, undecorated forms
which express the object's use.
Colour was not encouraged and
Braun products were famous for
their use of either white or black.
Rams represents an unbroken line
of Modernism that stretches back to
the Bauhaus through to his own
education at the Ulm school. So
powerful has the Braun aesthetic
been that even the challenge of
Postmodernism has not altered the
Braun design philosophy. Every
product the company manufactures
reveals its trademark of simplicity
and function, including the razor
illustrated here.

The electric razor made it
possible to dispense with shaving
creams and soap. The first
prototype electric razors were
designed in the 1930s but not put
into production until after the
Second World War. The Braun
company pioneered the electric
razor and, in 1951, launched a
prototype of the product, using a
simple outer case and an oscillating
motor, which used rechargeable
batteries. It established a design for
the razor that has altered little.

Kitchen Machine

DATE: 1957

DESIGNER: Gerd Alfred Muller (born 1932)

MATERIAL: metal and polystryol plastic

MANUFACTURER: Max Braun, Frankfurt, Germany

Before the 1920s, kitchen gadgets for the preparation of food were operated by hand. The invention of the electric motor changed this situation and heralded the advent of electric food mixers and processors. But it wasn't until the 1930s that such motors were small enough to operate successfully in the kitchen. At first, the early food mixers looked more like workshop tools than kitchen equipment but the USA pioneered a more streamlined and attractive look to the casing, which concealed the motor. It was a German company, however, that integrated these developments and produced a new and directional product: the Braun Kitchen Machine.

Since its establishment in the 1950s, Braun has stuck to a firm design ideology, that products should be functional, elegant, and simple, using only neutral colours. It was an aesthetic derived from the Bauhaus, and continued at Germany's new design school at Ulm. Braun worked with a number of teachers and designers from Ulm, including Hans Gugelot, the professor of Industrial Design. Muller, who worked on the Braun design team in the late 1950s, was also inspired by the idea of formal purity, the use of geometric shapes and truth to materials. His mixer was one of the first to be fabricated predominantly in plastic, with the joins in the casing treated as clean, black lines.

The Kitchen Machine established the approach to design not only for Braun, but was widely imitated by other manufacturing companies all over the world for the next twenty years.

In 1960 Kenneth Grange redesigned the famous Kenwood Chef, which had first been launched in 1950. Grange was strongly influenced by the discreet, smooth styling employed by the German firm Braun. He produced the design for this archetypal domestic appliance in just four days. Kenneth Grange has worked continuously over the past forty years as Kenwood's external design consultant. Over that period the Kenwood Chef has been regularly updated by him and stands in pride of place in many British kitchens.

Kenwood Chef

DATE: 1960

DESIGNER: Kenneth Grange (born 1929)

MANUFACTURER: Kenwood, United Kingdom

NEW Kenwood CHEF

does so much more than mixing ✳

For you . . . Kenwood presents the *new* Chef! With the Kenwood *Sheer Look* . . . beautifully designed. And beautifully easy to use! Now, attachments simply 'click in, click out' . . . beaters slide in and lock with only one movement . . . a push-button lifts the beater-head effortlessly from the bowl . . . the spill-proof bowl is double-lipped for easy pouring. Yes, Kenwood is the first in the world to bring you these—and many other advantages. Plus, of course, all the time-saving, cook-aiding jobs *only* the Chef can do!

We'll gladly send you a leaflet explaining all about them. Show it to your husband . . . he'll see the sense of investing in a new Chef. Particularly as you can own one for only 5 9d. a week!

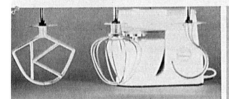

✳ New Kenwood Chef with its dozen wonderful attachments
(FIVE OF THEM ARE SHOWN HERE)

A NEW KENWOOD CHEF, complete with mixing bowl, K-beater, whisk, dough hook, spatula, big recipe and instruction book (over 100 pages) and its own protective cover is yours for only £2.14.6 down and 24 monthly payments of £1.2.6 (cash price 26 gns, tax paid).

MIXES · LIQUIDISES · MINCES · PEELS POTATOES · WHIPS · BLENDS CUTS · SLICES · SHREDS · SIEVES · STRAINS · JUICES · PURÉES SHELLS PEAS AND SLICES BEANS · OPENS CANS · GRINDS COFFEE
. . . it's the most versatile food preparing machine in the world!

Write today for free literature
ABOUT THE EXCITING NEW KENWOOD CHEF, AND NAME AND ADDRESS OF YOUR LOCAL DEALER

K *Kenwood*
your servant in the kitchen

NAME..............

ADDRESS..............

....

NC/IH/2

KENWOOD MANUFACTURING CO. LTD · OLD WOKING · SURREY

K2 Kettle

DATE: 1959

DESIGNER: W.M. Russell

MANUFACTURER: Russell Hobbs, United Kingdom

Designed in 1959, the K2 was an advance on an earlier kettle of 1954, the K1, and part of a range that Russell Hobbs then called "Forgettable" because they included an automatic cut-off switch. This proved to be an extremely popular feature, because prior to its introduction, if the user forgot to turn off the kettle it simply filled the room with steam and burnt out the element. Other technical innovations included a powerful element that could bring the water to the boil in seconds and an indicator lever in the handle that automatically snapped back when it was turned off. The handle and lid knob were always cool to the touch. The K2 came in a variety of finishes from brushed and polished stainless steel to copper and chrome. In a market now dominated by the upright, electric plastic jug kettle the Russell Hobbs remains the leading metal kettle and has established itself as a classic.

Peter Behrens is the best-known of the group of designers who established the Deutsche Werkbund in 1906 as an organization to promote good design. They believed in standardization and the idea that product design should reflect abstract form. Behrens carried these ideas into industry when, in 1906, he was invited to design the publicity for AEG (Allgemeine Elektrizitäts-Gesellschaft, the General Electric Company) including the advertisement shown here. In 1907 he was appointed coordinating architect to AEG and in that capacity designed not only factory buildings, shop fronts and advertising, but also electric lighting systems, fans, kettles, ovens, clocks and typefaces. This radical work continued for AEG until the outbreak of World War Two.

The wide range of electrical products that Behrens designed for the firm included three different shapes of kettle, including a model with the first immersed element. The element was built into the body of the kettle rather than in a separate compartment and the design incorporated interchangeable parts. New standardization techniques facilitated production and reduced costs. Each kettle shape was available in different materials and in different finishes and sizes.

AEG Electric Kettle

DATE: 1908–09

DESIGNER: Peter Behrens (1869–1940)

MANUFACTURER: AEG, Berlin, Germany

ELEKTRISCHE TEE- UND WASSERKESSEL
NACH ENTWÜRFEN VON PROF. PETER BEHRENS

Messing glatt, matt achteckige Form				Kupfer flockig gehämmert achteckige Form				Messing vernickelt, glatt achteckige Form			
PL Nr	Inhalt ca. l	Gewicht ca. kg	Preis Mk.	PL Nr	Inhalt ca. l	Gewicht ca. kg	Preis Mk.	PL Nr	Inhalt ca. l	Gewicht ca. kg	Preis Mk.
3588	0,75	1,75	20,—	3589	0,75	0,75	22,—	3587	0,75	0,75	19,—
3598	1,25	1,0	22,—	3599	1,25	1,0	24,—	3597	1,25	1,0	22,—
3608	1,75	1,1	24,—	3690	1,75	1,1	26,—	3607	1,75	1,1	23,—

ALLGEMEINE ELEKTRICITÄTS-GESELLSCHAFT
ABT. HEIZAPPARATE

Swiss Army Knife

DATE: 1891

DESIGNERS: Carl and Victoria Elsener

MANUFACTURER: The Elsener Family, Switzerland

Every schoolboy's dream, the Swiss Army Knife was first manufactured in the late nineteenth century. With its characteristic bright red body bearing the hallmark white cross, the knife is more than a simple pen-knife: it is a compact household tool kit. Carl and Victoria Elsener manufactured their own high-quality cutlery at their small factory in the Swiss Alps. Their reputation quickly developed and in 1891 they were offered a contract by Switzerland's tiny army to provide a sturdy knife for soldiers. The simple design was well received and the following year they won a second contract. This time they developed the elegant, multi-purpose "Officer's Knife" – the first version of the Swiss Army knife that would sell by the million. Four generations of the family have now produced the legendary knives, based on the three original principles – high quality, versatility and design excellence. Although produced in many forms, the fundamental knife remained the same. The basic model is little more than a variety of foldaway blades, while models like the monster "SwissChamp" include a corkscrew, can and bottle openers, nail file, screwdrivers, wood saw, pliers, scissors, toothpick and chisel. The knife's long-standing appeal with scouts, campers, travellers, explorers and fans of compact gadgetry is due to its simple premise – a miniature toolbox that folds away and fits into the palm of your hand.

Swatch

DATE: 1983

MANUFACTURER: Swatch, Switzerland

The watch market has been transformed by Swatch during the last two decades. The combination of Swiss technology, design and low price has meant that the Swatch became the fashion accessory of the 1980s. Its first watch, with a black plastic strap and plain watch face, has become the classic style. Adopting the marketing principles of the fashion industry, the company produces collections every season, limited editions for dedicated collectors, and a range of classic designs that are kept in production. Throughout the twentieth century, watch design has always reflected fashion, but over the last fifteen years the company has produced a range of styles and colours that have turned the company into a world leader. Early prototypes were designed by three engineers, Ernst Thonke, Jacques Muller and Elmar Mock. They developed the first integrated watch, in which the action was not a separate element. Then came the quartz Swatch, which overcame the association of plastic with unreliability, by offering the consumer the latest technology. Composed of fifty-one pieces as opposed to over ninety in traditional watches, Swatch also made a virtue of these workings by producing a transparent version, in which the components were fully visible.

Corinthian 180 U Inset Panel Heater

DATE: 1963

DESIGNER: D. M. R. Bruton (born 1938)

MANUFACTURER: Belling and Company Limited, United Kingdom

Belling was a family firm founded in 1913 and pioneered the production of early electrical appliances in Britain. This three-kilowat inset panel heater, which gave out convected heat, won a British Design Council Award in 1963 for its simple, streamlined and functional shape. To enable a radiant heater to be mounted or built into a wall fireplace, the manufacturers offered inset versions with a panel mounting. During the 1960s the trend was to rip out old Victorian fireplaces and replace them with more modern forms of heating. Heaters such as the Corinthian, using restrained colour and detailing, were normally specified by an architect rather than bought by the general public.

Cactus Radiator

DATE: 1994

DESIGNER: Paul Priestman
(born 1961)

MANUFACTURER: Priestman
Goode, London, England

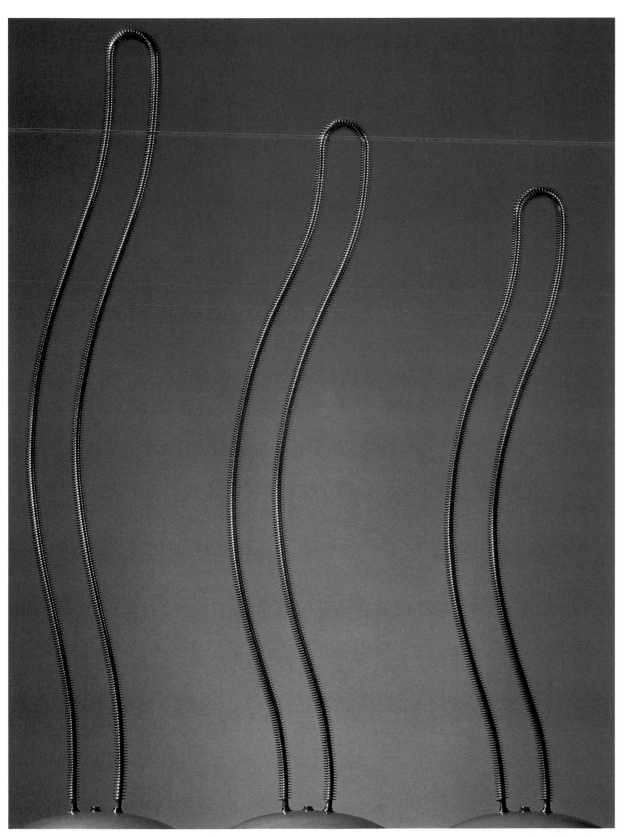

Paul Priestman was a star graduate of London's Royal College of Art in 1985 with his design for a portable radiator system. Since then he has established his own design consultancy with Nigel Goode. Together, they have worked on a series of heaters including a Belling Stove and, in 1994, the Cactus heater. Priestman identified a gap in the design market: since the 1960s the design of central heating radiators have altered very little, the flat design of traditional radiators began to look very outdated in the new designer homes of the 1980s. Priestman took the simple idea of redesigning the appearance of the radiator from scratch. Although he has faced the usual problems of persuading manufacturers to take up his ideas in mass production, it is surely a question of time before alternatives begin to find their way into the construction industry and the consumer market. In 1996, the humble ring binder suggested yet another design for a radiator. "Hot Springs" used a spiral coil, made rigid by a back pipe that holds the fitting to the wall, making a tubular radiator in an economical way. It was available in a series of bright, fresh colours.

Serie B Bathroom Range

DATE: 1953

DESIGNER: Gio Ponti
(1891–1979)

MATERIAL: porcelain

MANUFACTURER: Ideal
Standard, Milan, Italy

It is typical of the Italian approach to design that one of the country's greatest postwar talents, Gio Ponti, should turn his attention to essential products for the home – bathroom and toilet fittings. Before the 1950s these were generally seen as unexciting trade items, although the introduction of colour and Art Deco architectural motifs had made an appearance in 1930s homes. Ponti, however, turned them into strikingly original sculptural forms. They were not a success and the following year Ideal Standard launched the more commercial Zeta range by Ponti.

The Kyomi suite from Ideal Standard continues the company's ongoing commitment to modern design within the bathroom industry. In this case, the creative talent was Robin Levien, Royal Designer for Industry and a partner of the well-known ceramic design partnership Queensberry Hunt Levien who also designed the Studio range for Ideal Standard in the early 1980s, one of the company's most successful products.

The philosophy behind Kyomi was to combine good design with function; this is manifested in the basin, with its elegant rim that catches any splashes; the turned up flush lever for ease of use and the wall-mounted toilet roll holder and towel ring, which have shelves on top.

Kyomi includes eleven vitreous china pieces. These include back-to-wall and free-standing toilets and four washbasin models with options for a free-standing pedestal or wall mounted semi-pedestals, which keep the floor clear for easy cleaning and a lighter look. The oval bath is made from Idealcast, the modern alternative to cast iron, which is thick, solid and warm to the touch.

The Kyomi Arc bath, made from Idealform, a highly rigid acrylic material, fits within a standard recess yet offers a very roomy interior with its curvaceous bow front. The quarter turn handles in translucent matt green resemble fragments of bottle glass you find on the beach.

Kyomi Bathroom Range

DATE: 1997

DESIGNER: Robin Levien (born 1952)

MANUFACTURER: Ideal Standard, Hull, England

A7–1700 Kitchen Unit

DATE: 1996

DESIGNER: Balthaup In-House Design Team

MATERIAL: aluminium and steel

MANUFACTURER: Balthaup Gmbh, Aich, Germany

Balthaup is a German-based company founded in 1949 by Martin Balthaup. The company developed from manufacturing kitchen buffets to the specialist supply of system furniture for kitchens, bathrooms and laboratories. Since the 1980s the company has concentrated on the kitchen. In 1982, Balthaup commissioned the German designer Otl Aicher (born 1922), to produce a book called *The Kitchen as a Place to Cook*. Aicher was at the heart of postwar German modern design. He studied at Ulm under Max Bill and worked for Braun, a company whose design creed was based on functionalism and simple forms. Aicher's

aesthetic for Balthaup was first expressed in the company's development of a "butcher's block", a robust table of solid wood placed in the middle of the room. This became a trademark of the Balthaup kitchen with a simple stainless steel workbench that could be used independently or integrated into a range of units, cupboards, and appliances Balthaup supplied. In 1989, this simple and functional design won a number of awards and Balthaup went on to develop new products including a new kitchen extractor system in 1991. Balthaup, with their emphasis on design, high quality materials and

construction, quickly became the designer's choice of kitchen. In 1992, they called their range System 25, a series of multi-functional working areas, using units and surfaces designed in wood, aluminium, and stainless steel. Balthaup pioneered the idea that the kitchen was the most important room in the house and that the money, time and effort spent here should reflect this. Balthaup continue to remain leaders in new technology and manufacturing techniques. In 1994, their product and research division developed technologically advanced water-based coatings for wood surfaces in the furniture industry.

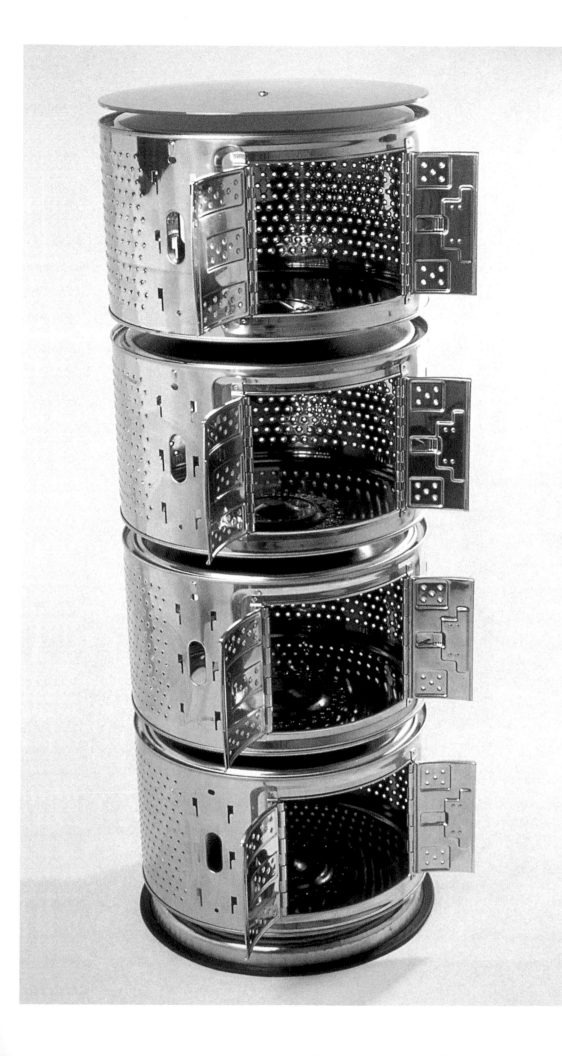

Robo-Stacker

DATE: 1994

MATERIAL: recycled washing machine drums, glass

MANUFACTURER: Jam, London, England

Astrid Zala, Jamie Ankey and Matthieu Paillard, three young designers with backgrounds in architecture and fine art, established Jam in London in 1994. The nature and outcome of their collaborative design work has been diverse and they describe their mission as "focused on the creative utilization of the material and technological innovations of today." In terms of product design, this means a recycling reuse agenda. The Robo-Stacker uses washing machine drums supplied by Whirlpool to make attractive general purpose storage units for the home. Jam collaborate with large companies. Whirlpool supply them with drums that have not passed quality control while Sony provided projectors and sound systems for a bed featured in a recent Crafts Council exhibition called Flexible Furniture. These companies enjoy the association with young leading-edge talent and the implications of recycling and reuse of products in another very different context. This has led to other commissions, including an installation made out of old television sets for the foyer of the Independent Advertising Association in London and a Chelsea bar for the Evian drinks company, where the decorative surface in the serving area is formed from bottle tops.

PART 8

transport

QUEEN MARY OCEAN LINER

IF THE NINETEENTH CENTURY was the century of the safety bicycle, the railway engine and the steam powered ship, the twentieth century is the century of mass and personal transport, of mass car ownership, supersonic jets, and space travel.

Urban public transport systems have been rapidly expanding since the Metropolitan underground train line opened in London in 1863, heralding an entirely new breed of worker: the commuter. The early years of this

DREYFUS TRAIN

century were to see bus, tram and underground train networks, although essentially products of the nineteenth century, expand into the streets and suburbs of every major industrialized city. The close of the century is now witnessing mass transport increase to ever greater proportions, with the new generation of "Jumbo" jets, including the Boeing-777, and the creation of new super airports at Chek Lap Kok, on Hong Kong's Lantau Island and Kansai in Japan.

In 1883 Gottlieb Daimler produced a single-cylinder engine mounted onto a bicycle. In 1903 the Wright brothers undertook their pioneering first air flight. These two events, alongside Frank Whittle's patent for the jet engine in 1930, were to pave the way for the most significant developments in twentieth-century transport: the birth of the mass-produced car and the creation of the civilian airline.

VESPA

Following swiftly on from Daimler's motorized bicycle of 1883, the German Karl Benz was to complete a three-wheel vehicle with a four-cylinder engine in 1885. This and other "horseless carriages:" were essentially toys for a wealthy elite. Their interiors were lavishly upholstered and the carriages employed the styling and construction techniques of nineteenth-century coachbuilders. Gradually, however, the desire to expand the market for the motor car took hold. New means were sought by which to produce a level of standardization into the production process in order to lower the end cost to the consumer. Just before the advent of World War One, the revolutionary process of manufacturing sheet and then pressed steel opened up new avenues for car production. But it was the ambitious plans of one man in particular that were to change not only the system of automobile production, but the whole basis of industrial design and mass production. At his factory in Detroit, Henry Ford changed the system of production, not only for transport but for the whole of industry and design. Ford developed assembly-line production systems that soon became known all over the world as Fordism. One important factor in its success was the organization of separate operations in the assembly, each car had hundreds of components in which workers followed a strictly controlled sequence of machining operations to achieve high levels of production and quality control. These techniques enabled Ford to turn out 3,000 Model T vehicles a day and to drop the sales price from over $1,000 in 1908 to under $300 by 1928.

The Model T established international production standards for the motor industry. In 1919, the first European mass produced car, the Citroën A was produced in France and by the 1920s, new forms of transport had captured the imagination of designers and public alike.

From the 1930s onwards, such seminal designers as Ferdinand Porsche in Austria and Germany, Dante Giacosa in Italy, Pierre Boulanger in France and Alec Issigonis in Britain were to create the successors to Henry Ford's Model T in a range of "people's cars" that ranged from the Volkswagen of 1937 to the famous Mini of 1959. These vehicles were all designed to meet the needs of a Europe "on the move". They were essentially utilitarian products, advocating radically new design solutions to meet the huge needs of the postwar era.

On the other side of the Atlantic, where the market for the motor car was both larger and more mature, the services of the industrial designer were called upon in a rather different fashion: to shape, style, adorn, and "package" the automobile or railway train. In 1930 the industrial designer Harley Earl established the first styling research centre at General Motors and, together with his compatriots, Raymond Loewy and Henry Dreyfuss, went on to transform the US transport system: from gas stations to Greyhound coaches, railway locomotives and automobiles, reaching a zenith in the the notorious excesses of late 1950s "planned obsolescence".

Road and air travel have not only revolutionized our social and working patterns, but have had a radical impact on urban planning, changing forever the landscape of both urban and rural areas. With the increased freedom of mobility offered by the car and the plane has come the high price of environmental pollution, the erosion of rural communities and a loss of agricultural land and natural wilderness. These consequences of industrialization were forecast at the turn of the century by such "prophets" as John Ruskin and William Morris, but none could have foreseen the speed and scale of such developments.

LAND ROVER

In the 1980s and 1990s, with one major oil crisis behind them and increasing pressure from Governments to reduce car ownership, car manufacturers have now turned their attention to reducing the emissions from car engines to meet strict new criteria imposed in Europe and the US; designers have reduced the weight of vehicles through an increased use of plastics and an experimentation with alloys, including aluminium; manufacturers, including General Motors, have tested electrically powered vehicles as an alternative to the petrol or diesel engine. Mass transport, all analysts agree, will reach saturation point by the end of this century if car ownership continues to rise at its present rate. Western economies, once again, will be looking for new solutions to mass transport: and a return to the rail networks, safety bicycles and tram systems first proposed in the nineteenth century are, ironically, once again being considered by Western governments.

APOLLO 11

SPACE SHUTTLE

Ford Model T

DATE: 1908

DESIGNER: Henry Ford (1863–1947)

MANUFACTURER: Ford Motor Company, Detroit, USA

When Henry Ford began building his first car by hand in 1893 there were only four petrol-powered automobiles in the United States. By the time of his death in 1947 more than sixty per cent of American families owned a motor car. This enormous growth in car ownership can largely be credited to Henry Ford's introduction of mass production techniques for the Model T in 1913.

The Ford Motor Company was established in 1903 and in 1908 Henry Ford launched a small and affordable car called the Model T. In 1913 Ford introduced the world's first moving assembly line for car construction. This was accompanied by a radical standardization of components, which

allowed Ford to cut his costs dramatically by ordering materials in tremendous bulk.

By 1915 the Ford factory in Detroit could build a thousand vehicles per day. As a result of this high productivity Ford was able to lower the price of the Model T from $950 in 1908 to $360 in 1915, double his employees' wages and shorten the working day. He used the complete standardization of his car to launch a self-mocking advertising campaign, announcing that "you can buy a Ford in any colour as long as it's black."

By the early 1920s, when this photograph was taken, Ford had captured half of the American car

market and in 1925 he began assembling Model Ts in Berlin. When production of the Model T was halted in 1927 after nineteen years, fifteen and a half million examples of the car had been built. This was to remain the world's longest and largest production run of a single model of car until 1972 when the record was broken by the Volkswagen "Beetle".

In America the car has dictated many aspects of business and culture, influencing urban planning, architecture and people's lifestyles to a far greater extent than in any other country. Henry Ford's impact on American life has been greater than that of any other industrialist of the twentieth century.

When the Deux Chevaux, or "two horsepower", was launched at the Paris Automobile Salon in 1948 it was met with a degree of ridicule suffered by no other car before or since. Produced to compete with the Volkswagen Beetle and the rival French "Auto du Peuple", the Renault 4CV, it was really contending to replace the horse and cart, which remained the dominant form of transport in a largely rural France.

When Boulanger set out to design a car for the agricultural market in 1939, he was given a demanding brief. The 2CV had to be capable of carrying a man wearing a top hat and carrying a basket full of eggs across a field without breaking any of his fragile cargo. Less fancifully, it had to provide good head-room, excellent suspension and comfort, but in a truly small car that would be inexpensive to build and maintain.

The simplified, geometric bodywork facilitated minimum use of materials and ease of assembly in the immediate postwar period when resources were scarce. The lightweight hammock-style seats could be removed to provide additional storage space and the retractable canvas roof allowed the vehicle to accommodate long or bulky objects.

Despite its many detractors and the numerous insults it has collected, the 2CV has become a cult favourite. With a production run between 1948 and 1990 of more than five million units, it remains one of the most successful French cars ever.

Citroën 2CV

DATE: 1939

DESIGNER: Pierre Boulanger (1886–1950)

MANUFACTURER: Citroën, France

Queen Mary Ocean Liner

The *Queen Mary* is one of the largest sea-going vessels ever constructed and has had a romantic and illustrious history. The formidable task of building what was to be one of the largest and most luxurious ocean liners was given to John Brown and Company, which commenced construction of Job No.534, as the ship was originally called, in 1931. Later that year work was halted due to the Depression and it was not until March 1934 that building was recommenced. The new Cunard ship was finally launched in September 1934 by Her Majesty Queen Mary, who gave her name to the vessel.

With the outbreak of World War Two the *Queen Mary* was forced to cease service for the Cunard Steamship Company as a transatlantic passenger liner and was refitted in Sydney, Australia, as a troopship. She became known the "Grey Ghost", acting as an essential troop carrier. In 1943 she carried 16,683 people on one voyage, the largest number ever conveyed on a ship. The *Queen Mary* is now a floating hotel and tourist attraction in Long Beach, Los Angeles, where she has been berthed for the last thirty years.

DATE: 1934

CONSTRUCTED BY: John Brown and Company, Clydebank, Scotland

In the interwar years designers and architects in Europe and America were gripped by the possibilities of speed and power afforded by modern technology. Fast cars, aeroplanes and powerful locomotives became potent symbols of the "Machine Age" and the dizzying pace of urban life.

Ever increasing speed became an end in itself and designers began to look to the scientific principles of aerodynamics to decrease the wind resistance and thus increase the efficiency of vehicles. Streamlining, the practice of shaping an object to reduce drag, found its greatest expression in Henry Dreyfuss' locomotive for the New York Central Railroad.

Dreyfuss began as a set and costume designer for theatre and opened his own industrial design bureau in 1929. He would quickly become one of the leading exponents of a rational and functional approach to design that was characterized by clean lines and bold, undecorated statements in form.

During the 1930s in America streamlining developed into a superficial style as the sleek, rounded forms which served a genuine aerodynamic function in high-speed vehicles were applied to house-hold objects as diverse as cameras, vacuum cleaners and refrigerators. This cosmetic styling of objects was often nothing more than a cynical marketing ploy designed to dress up old products as new.

Unlike his contemporaries, Raymond Loewy and Walter Dorwin Teague, Dreyfuss was largely opposed to this practice, which he considered a rejection of pure functionalism and ergonomic or anthropometric design. His measured and integral approach resulted in some of the most enduring classics of twentieth-century product design such as his telephone for the American Bell Company in 1933 that defined the basic shape of the modern telephone for more than fifty years.

Hudson J-3a

DATE: 1938

DESIGNER: Henry Dreyfuss (1903–72)

MANUFACTURER: New York Central Railroad, USA

Greyhound Bus

DATE: 1940

**DESIGNER: Raymond Loewy
(1893–1986)**

**MANUFACTURER: Greyhound
Corporation, USA**

In a country dominated by the ethos of individuality and with the highest percentage of private car ownership in the world, the Greyhound Bus system is a potent symbol of the democratizing force of affordable and accessible public transport. In novels, films and advertising it has become synonymous with freedom, escape and the pursuit of adventure across America's vast expanses.

The company began modestly in Minnesota in 1914, when a Swedish immigrant called Carl Wickmann set up an inexpensive transport service for mine workers. By 1921 the service could offer intercity connections and had its own fleet of buses, which were dubbed "Greyhounds" because of their sleek design and distinctive grey colouring.

Wickmann merged with Orville Swann Caesar in 1926, acquiring many smaller bus companies to become The Greyhound Corporation in 1930. The familiar "running dog" trademark was adopted and remains the company's logo to this day.

In the 1940s Greyhound employed one of the great pioneers of American industrial design and styling, Raymond Loewy, to redesign the fleet of buses, producing a vehicle which with its reflective and fluted aluminium bodywork is one of the greatest essays in American streamlining.

The Routemaster, the classic red London bus, has become a symbol of Britain's capital throughout the world, along with the black taxi and Giles Gilbert-Scott's K2 telephone box.

Designed in 1954 to replace the existing trolley-buses, the Routemaster remains a familiar sight on London's streets. Its ungainly appearance attracted criticism from many sceptics and almost as soon as it entered service in 1959, its design was seen to be outdated, as legislation introduced in 1961 permitted buses of up to thirty feet in length. However, the Routemaster's basic design proved to be endlessly adaptable and extremely popular with Londoners. Early in its history there were already plans to phase out the Routemaster in favour of a crewless vehicle, and by the 1970s London Transport's "Reshaping Plan" set out a timetable for the elimination of all but the new driver-only buses. However, this project proved to be both inefficient and unpopular, and as a result the Routemaster remains a part of London's cityscape after nearly forty years of service.

Routemaster Bus

DATE: 1954

DESIGNERS: A.A.M. Durrant (1898–1984), Douglas Scott (1913–90)

MANUFACTURER: London Transport, London, England

Dursley-Pedersen Bicycle

DATE: 1893

DESIGNER: Mikael Pedersen (1855–1929)

The turn of the century saw some of the greatest innovations in the design of the bicycle, which was fast becoming a universal means of personal transport. At the forefront of these developments was Mikael Pedersen, a Dane living in Dursley in England.

Pedersen's bicycle was a masterpiece of sophisticated engineering, which relied upon an ingenious frame structure, as shown below, to the right, held by the woman cyclist. The frame was constructed of fourteen separate thin hollow tubes, connected at fifty-seven points to produce twenty-one triangles. This structure, the "space frame", afforded great strength with relative lightness. The saddle consisted of a leather "hammock" strung between the top part of the frame and the handlebars, giving a high degree of suspension and so providing a relatively comfortable ride on primitive roads and lanes at the turn of the century.

Many of Pedersen's pioneering developments have been taken up in recent years, especially in the field of frame design.

Like the black leather jacket, the Harley-Davidson motorbike is synonymous with non-conformity, rebellion and danger. More than any other brand of motorbike, the Harley symbolizes the association of speed and power with independence and sexual prowess.

The original Harley-Davidson was born at the turn of the century when two childhood friends, William Harley and Arthur Davidson, attempted to build a motorized bicycle. Working on the project in their spare time, they were soon joined by Davidson's brothers Walter and William, the latter of whom was a skilled toolmaker. In 1903 the four men constructed their first single-cylinder, three-horsepower bike, and happy with their creation set about building two more. Another three followed in 1904 and the Harley-Davidson Motor Company was born.

Their reputation for building resilient vehicles quickly spread and by 1910 their sales were guaranteed by a network of dealerships. The success of their bikes was primarily due to their reliability. By 1913 the first bike they built had covered an astonishing 100,000 miles without the need to replace any of its main components.

The growth of motorcycle racing in the 1920s and 1930s (this model is 1939) and the use of their vehicles by the military in virtually every continent during World War Two ensured that Harley-Davidson has become a household name.

Harley-Davidson Motorbike

DATE: 1903

DESIGNERS:
William Harley (1871–1937),
Arthur Davidson (1881–1950),
Walter Davidson (1876–1942),
William Davidson (1880–1943)

MANUFACTURER: Harley Davidson Motor Company, USA

Vespa

DATE: 1945

DESIGNER: Corradino
d'Ascanio (1891–1981)

MANUFACTURER: Piaggio, Italy

The Vespa has become one of the greatest symbols of postwar Italian reconstruction. At the close of World War Two, like most European countries, Italy faced a transport crisis. During the war the entire Italian automotive industry had been converted to military production and had subsequently been reduced to rubble by the Allies. With raw materials such as metal and fuel in short supply and with a greatly lowered standard of living, a cost-effective and modern means of personal transport was required.

The Piaggio company had begun constructing aeroplanes in 1915; however during World War Two the factory was bombed. The company's president Enrico Piaggio decided to replace aeronautic production with building a vehicle that was cheap, reliable, easy to maintain and easy to drive in order to get the Italian nation back to work. Piaggio's chief engineer Corradino d'Ascanio set about designing a scooter that would be launched in 1946 as the Vespa, which is Italian for "wasp".

D'Ascanio brought his experience and

knowledge of helicopter and aircraft engine design to bear on the Vespa's development. His design incorporated "stress-skin" technology with body and frame fused into a unified whole. This monocoque design, now a staple of the automotive industry, was virtually unique in civilian vehicle design in 1945.

As this 1960s photo demonstrates, the Vespa's surprising and stylish looks have made it an enduring favourite with young people, and have established it as one of the most successful vehicles of the postwar period.

Ducati Motorbike

Renowned throughout the world as producers of some of the best high-performance motorbikes, the Ducati family business began in Bologna in 1926 as a manufacturer of components for the fledgling radio industry. Adriano Ducati's patents in this field quickly gained the company an international reputation.

Like those of so many other Italian companies, Ducati's factories were destroyed during World War Two and in the restructuring that followed, the company was compelled to broaden its product range. At a Milan Fair, Ducati presented a small auxiliary motor designed to be fitted to bicycles. This design laid the foundations for the company's move into motorcycle production, and with the launch of the 175cc Cruiser in 1952, Ducati was firmly established as one of the world's leading manufacturers in the field.

In 1955 the company was joined by Fabio Taglioni who went on to produce some of the company's legendary designs, which were pushed to their limits in endurance races. Since then Ducati has continued to apply the engineering lessons of its racing successes to consistently innovative road bikes.

The M900 Monster, designed in 1993 by the Argentinian designer, Fabio Taglioni, has ushered in a new era of top-class Ducati bikes. Its remarkably minimal bodywork gives full attention to its powerful engine and its lightweight trellis construction tubular frame.

DATE: 1993

DESIGNER: Fabio Taglioni (born 1920)

MANUFACTURER: Ducati Motor S.p.A., Italy

Porsche 356

DATE: 1948

DESIGNERS: Ferdinand
Porsche (1875–1951),
Ferry Porsche (born 1909)
and Erwin Komenda
(1904–66)

MANUFACTURER: Porsche,
Gmund/Stuttgart, Germany

Ferdinand Porsche was one of the greatest pioneers of automotive engineering and design. His first car, designed in 1900 for the Austrian manufacturer Lohner, was an electric vehicle driven by hub-mounted motors. The most important of his countless innovations include torsion-bar suspension and the rear-mounted air-cooled engine.

Before establishing his own automotive design consultancy in Stuttgart in 1930, Porsche had acted as chief engineer and designer for Austro-Daimler, Mercedes-Benz and Steyr, for whom he produced some of the most celebrated cars of the prewar period. During the 1930s his energies were split between the development of the Volkswagen and the design of revolutionary Grand Prix racing cars for Auto Union.

World War Two found Porsche and his son Ferry designing military vehicles including an amphibious version of the Volkswagen and tanks such as the Tiger and the Maus.

The 356 was the first car to be manufactured by the Porsche family under its own name and was the fulfilment of Porsche's dream to build a sports version of the Volkswagen. Using many components from the "People's Car", including the rear-mounted air-cooled engine developed by Franz Xavier Reimspiess, the 356 established the pattern of engineering excellence and aesthetic elegance that the Porsche company maintains to this day.

When the 356 won its class at the twenty-four hour endurance race at Le Mans in 1951, it initiated a run of spectacular racing victories that few other marques have rivalled. Production of the 356 ceased in 1965 after the introduction in 1963 of the Porsche 911, designed by Porsche's grandson Butzi, which many see as the ultimate expression of the Porsche design ethos.

Cadillac

DATE: 1959

DESIGNER: Harley Earl
(1893–1969)

MANUFACTURER: General
Motors, USA

Few products have been so heavily invested with the aspirations and dreams of a nation as the 1950s Cadillac and few designers have been so willing to pander to an entire generation's lust for superficial extravagance as Harley Earl.

Earl was born into a family of coach-builders in California that specialized in customized cars for Hollywood's first generation of affluent film stars. Early in his career Earl pioneered the now-universal practice of modelling a car's exterior form in clay, a technique that allowed for great sculptural freedom.

By the late 1920s, when Henry Ford's Model T had brought motoring to the majority of America's population, stylistic differentiation between car models was an important factor in attracting new buyers. In 1928 Earl was invited to head General Motors' newly formed Art and Colour section, to develop the styling of the company's vehicles. The age of the "dream car" was born and the success of Earl's Buicks, Cadillacs, Chevrolets, Oldsmobiles and Pontiacs soon established him as the most influential designer in the American car industry.

By the time he retired in 1959, more than fifty million cars had been produced to his designs. The Cadillac demonstrates his fascination with aeroplane design. With its elongated body, extended fins, rocket-like tail-lights and masses of chrome, it is the ultimate expression of the self-confidence and power of America in the 1950s.

From Great Achievements...An Inspiring Tradition!

Cadillac's many and varied contributions to the cause of automotive progress have, over the years, represented one of the most important and inspiring traditions in all motordom. And certainly, that list of Cadillac's achievements has become all the more meaningful in the light of the current year. For in styling, in design and in engineering, this latest "car of cars" has added dramatic emphasis to the fact of Cadillac leadership. If you have not yet inspected its magnificent new Fleetwood coachcrafting—or experienced its brilliant new performance—you should do so soon. Your dealer will be happy to introduce you to all the new models, including the distinguished Eldorado Brougham.
CADILLAC MOTOR CAR DIVISION • GENERAL MOTORS CORPORATION
Every Window of Every Cadillac is Safety-Plate Glass

Standard of the World for more than half a century

Series II Land Rover

DATE: 1955

DESIGNER: David Bache
(born 1926)

MANUFACTURER: Rover,
Coventry, England

The Land Rover was developed in response to the Willys-Overland Jeep which, since its launch in 1940, had proved enormously successful as both an agricultural and military vehicle throughout the world.

The Land Rover was first unveiled to the public at the Amsterdam Car Show in 1948. Initially seen as a sturdy four-wheel drive vehicle to replace the horse and cart, the Land Rover was quickly adapted for use in the desert, the jungle, on Safari and in mountainous regions.

The vehicle has a steel frame chassis onto which can be bolted a variety of aluminium body panels to produce a car that is suited to a particular terrain. The body work has a simple form and is designed to be stripped with only the aid of a screwdriver and wrench.

Soon after joining Rover in 1954, David Bache set about redesigning the body work of the Land Rover and with his design of the Range Rover in 1970, he took the language of the large four-wheel drive vehicle a stage further, adding the attributes of luxury and style to that of rugged reliability.

David Bache was one of the few British car designers, along with Alec Issigonis, to achieve an international reputation and to exert a powerful influence on a generation of automotive designers – his Rover P10 of 1975 can be seen as the point of departure for Uwe Bahnsen's foresighted design of the Ford Sierra in 1982.

Like the skirt of the same name, the Mini has come to be seen as a cultural icon of the 1960s, a decade that saw a process of radical democratization in British social life, spurred largely by the growth of a new class of young, financially independent people. The resulting dramatic increase in car ownership led to the need for a small, dependable and modern car that conveyed an urbane and youthful image.

Alec Issigonis had already gone some way to revolutionizing the British motor car with his Morris Minor of 1948, but this car still owed much to the automotive styling of the 1930s and was in many ways similar to the Volkswagen Beetle and the Renault 4CV.

The Mini represented a radical departure from all previous car design and owed nothing to prevailing ideas in American or European engineering and styling. Issigonis produced an extremely small car that could comfortably seat four adults and was ideally suited to busy city streets. The large amount of space in the car's minimal interior was achieved by Issigonis installing the engine transversely, or sideways, a departure that was to influence much automotive design of the 1960s and 1970s.

With various modifications and new models, such as the Mini Cooper, shown here starring in the film *The Italian Job* (on the Fiat factory roof), the Mini has been in production for over thirty-five years. It is Britain's most successful and best-loved car, mainly due to its reliability and classic, timeless shape.

Mini

DATE: 1959

DESIGNER: Alec Issigonis (1906–88)

MANUFACTURER: Morris (British Motor Corporation), United Kingdom

Douglas DC-3

DATE: 1935

DESIGNER: Donald Wills
Douglas (1892–1981)

The DC-3 ushered in the era of modern mass air travel and remains to this day the most successful commercial aircraft of all time. One of the first services to fly the craft was American Airlines, and within five years of the DC-3's launch in 1935 more than four hundred models were being used by over a hundred airlines around the world. By 1939 it was carrying ninety per cent of the world's air traffic. During World War Two the planes were put into service by the American air force. These military versions, known as the C-47 and the Dakota, accounted for 10,123 of the total 10,929 machines that were built. After the war many of these military craft were refitted for civilian transport. Production of the aircraft ceased in 1946, but the DC-3 remained in service with some smaller airlines until the 1970s.

The DC-3's designer Donald Douglas received his technical training at the US Naval Academy and as chief civilian engineer to the US Signal Corps before founding the Douglas Company in 1920. His pioneering designs laid the foundations for all future commercial aeroplane design.

Developed jointly by British Airways and Air France, Concorde was the first and remains the only supersonic civilian aircraft to be put into commercial service. Designing an aeroplane that could propel passengers at speeds exceeding that of sound involved surmounting thousands of individual technological and physical problems and resulted in a machine that looked more like a military aircraft than a civilian one.

Concorde has a novel shape, consisting of a needle-shaped nose and a "delta wing", both responses to the aerodynamic problems of flight at such high speeds. The distinctive wing shape combines great length and a minimum relative thickness which is well suited to supersonic flight as well as the lower speeds for take-off and landing. It also contributes great structural rigidity to the slim fuselage, and allows Concorde to be the only commercial aircraft that does not require stabilizing rudders. The long, pointed nose assures maximum air penetration. During take-off and landing Concorde is at a much more pronounced angle to the ground than other aircraft. To provide greater visibility for the pilot, the nose can be lowered independently of the rest of the craft.

The first test flights of the British and French prototypes began in 1969, but it was not until 1976 that commercial flights were introduced. In 1972 an American study suggested that Concorde would have a lifespan of no longer than seven years due to the stress caused to the fuselage by dramatic variations in temperature. Concorde has shown itself to be more resilient, but will probably cease flights in 2005. A replacement craft, called Alliance, is planned.

Concorde

DATE: 1967

DESIGNERS: Sir Archibald Russell (1904–95), Dr William J. Strang (born 1921), Pierre Satre (born 1909) and Lucien Servanty (born 1909)

Apollo Spacecraft

DATE: 1961

DESIGNER: NASA/Werner von Braun (1912–77)

In 1961, the then US president, John Fitzgerald Kennedy, declared that by the end of that decade the United States would have achieved the goal of "landing a man on the moon and returning him safely to Earth." On July 20, 1969, the crew of Apollo 11 achieved this goal. Apollo 11 marked the pinnacle of the space race, a technological battle that mirrored the Cold War between the USA and USSR.

The Apollo Spacecraft was fired by the massive Saturn V rocket, which stood 111 metres (363 foot) high and at the time was the most powerful rocket ever built. The Apollo craft itself consisted of the tiny command and service module, which housed the craft's instruments and the equipment with which the astronauts controlled the craft. The service module also contained the bug-like lunar module, which was designed for use only on the moon. Looking impossibly fragile, unlike the rest of the Apollo spacecraft, the lunar module did not need to be designed with aerodynamics in mind, hence its peculiar shape.

On later Apollo missions the lunar rover was implemented. The four-wheel drive vehicle folded out from the lunar module, and had a top speed of 11 kilometres per hour (7 miles per hour).

US Space Shuttle

DATE: 1981

DESIGNER: NASA

Consisting of three main sections, the orbiter, the solid rocket boosters and the external tank, the Space Shuttle is the only reusable space craft in operation today. Launched by a thrust of 2.7 million kilograms (6 million pounds), the two solid rocket boosters burn out and fall away from the orbiter after two minutes, followed six minutes later by the massive external tank. Once in orbit, the Shuttle is controlled using the Orbital Manoeuvering System. The Shuttle can house up to ten people and is used for scientific experiments and launching satellites.

When a mission has ended the Shuttle re-enters the atmosphere. The underside of the craft, where the heat is at its most extreme, is covered with approximately 23,000 heat-resistant ceramic-coated tiles to protect the craft during re-entry. With its engines off, the Shuttle glides back down to land like an aeroplane.

Specialized Stump-jumper

DATE: 1981

DESIGNER: Mike Sinyard
(born 1949)

MANUFACTURER: Specialized,
Morgan Hill, California, USA

Since the mid-1970s the introduction of mountain and all-terrain bikes has brought about the greatest number of technological and design innovations in cycling history. The search for bicycles capable of greater speeds, combined with enormous strength and lightness, has created a thriving industry of companies devoted to producing specialized gears, pedals, tyres and above all highly sophisticated frames. It is particularly in the design of frames that materials technology has advanced at an astonishing rate, as designers have experimented with the use of carbon fibres, ultra-light alloys and metals such as aluminium and titanium.

The Specialized company was founded in 1974 by Mike Sinyard and by the late 1970s had established a reputation as one of the most innovative producers of mountain bikes. In 1981 following scores of impressive developments, particularly in the field of tyre technology, Specialized launched the Stumpjumper, the world's first mass-produced mountain bike.

In 1983 Specialized created the first professional mountain bike racing team and has achieved many successes. The lessons Specialized has learned in racing have contributed to countless innovations in its production of bicycles and accessories including helmets and water bottles.

Electric Car

DATE: 1994

MANUFACTURER: Kewet
Industri, Hadsund, Denmark

Concern for the environment
has increasingly focused on car
usage. The mixture of gases emitted
from petrol and diesel cars has
contributed to the deterioration of
the atmosphere, so more and more
manufacturers are looking for an
economical, effective alternative to
traditional fuel.

One option is to construct
electric cars. The model shown
here, the Kewet El-Jet, which was
developed in Denmark, provides
up to 65 kilometres (40 miles) of
pollution-free driving on a single
six-hour battery charge. Its
maximum speed is 70 kilometres
an hour (about 45 miles per hour),
and its running costs are mimimal
compared to those for petrol-
powered cars. The El-Jet is only two
and a half metres (eight feet) long,
has a powerful 7.5 kilowatt motor
with an electronically controlled
gear system and can be fitted with
long-range nickel cadmium batteries
or solar panels. The cabin is
constructed from galvanized steel
and the body from glass fibre. Extra
luggage can be accommodated by
removing the passenger seat.

type

MERZ MAGAZINE

EMIGRÉ MAGAZINE

THANKS TO DESKTOP DIGITAL TECHNOLOGY, TYPE has placed itself at the centre of design and its future. It was the first design discipline to be revolutionized by computers. Once a deeply unfashionable subject, type now provokes discussion on important issues concerning design: the nature of creativity, the survival of craft skills and the vexed question of originality. Nowadays type designers are no longer anonymous technicians, but well-known designers in their own right. And it is not only designers who have rediscovered typography; ordinary people are exploring typography via their home computers. Now ten years into this techno-revolution, the Apple Macintosh computer has opened up type design possibilities for us all.

Over the twentieth century typographic design has seen many changes of style, from the clarity of the International Style to the druggy expressionism of psychedelia. The common thread has always been the search to articulate new ideas, with each typeface having a character and expression of its own. In the early years of the century type design like architecture and furniture sought to throw off the nineteenth century with its decorated forms. In a fine-art context, type was often used in Cubist paintings or in the Dada experiments with poetry. In terms of new type design in the 1920s, Bauhaus designers such as Herbert Bayer introduced simple sans

MUSEUM POSTER

serif letter forms that expressed the new age. Similar experiments were taking place internationally: Edward Johnston in England, Paul Rand in the USA and Adrian Frutiger in Switzerland.

In the postwar years the single most important new European direction in typography came from Basel, and so came to be known as the Swiss School. Their intellectual response was to look back to the Bauhaus and to take a rational approach to the problem of developing typography for the new era. It can be seen as a search for order, reason and peace. After the chaos of the war it is hardly surprising, however, that many European type designers looked to order and unity as a vision of the way forward. These designers truly believed that they were setting universal and unchanging typographic standards. Other countries also went in search of the new. America saw a period which established a powerful and new creative identity and in this context type design was to play its part with the work of Herb Lubalin and Saul Bass.

Far from being on the peripheries of change, type design has come to reflect key technological shifts and carry with it resonances that helped define the postwar cultural revolution. In this context the culture of type design underwent a fundamental change in the 1960s with the arrival of Pop Design and its challenge to the traditions of Modernism. The priorities of Pop Design,

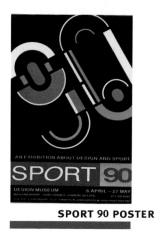

that it was instant and expendable, witty and ironic, found expression in type experiments of the early 1960s. In California, a number of people, often not trained as designers, created posters for bands that were a conscious reaction to the "boring" Swiss-influenced design around them. Based in the Haight Ashbury district of San Francisco, and active participants in the emerging counter-culture movement, designers such as Stanley Mouse, Rick Griffin, Victor Moscoso and Alton Kelley created posters with bright, clashing colours inspired by psychedelic drugs and Indian mysticism. They were free to break all the rules about legibility, clarity and communication. Influenced by the decorative letter forms of the Vienna Secession, they created complex, organic lettering, in which legibility took second place to the overall shape of the word.

Mainstream American type design was dominated by designers like Aaron Burns and Herb Lubalin whose International Type Company was known as ITC. They pioneered the use of close letter spacing, packed layouts, highly condensed and heavy serifed typefaces, which became the all-pervasive American and international style of the mid 1970s. Inevitably challenges came in the late 1970s from designers in Britain, West Coast America and Holland. Within the climate of Postmodernism they started to upturn traditional rules by mixing and layering typefaces and by using and retrieving imagery from

virtually any source. But the single and most important change to type design was technology led.

In the mid 1980s the type industry was revolutionized by the introduction of the independent typesetting software PostScript. This invention by the Californian company Adobe Systems meant that pages of type could now be printed on any output capable of reading that language. PostScript typesetting software's influence grew as the industry standard overturned the traditional role of the type designer forever. In the last decade of the century, typography is about to undergo its most profound upheaval since the invention of the printing press. New technology creates not just new means of production, but changes the way cultural messages are received and sent. The computer has dramatically altered the way that we design, use, and think about the visual expression of language. In a period when traditional type culture is under threat, it was inevitable that type designers would fight back and offer different, as well as traditional, solutions for the way forward. In this they are part of a wider twentieth-century concern that mechanization would lead to a fall in standards and the disappearance of long-established typographic rules. Many important graphic designers moved closer to the world of fine art than design, integrating typography, lettering and image-making. Their work reminds us of the importance of traditional skills alongside the new, but no one can stop the force of the new computer revolution.

THIS IS
DRONE

FOR TEXT
WITHOUT
CONTENT

The Deer Cry

DATE: 1916

DESIGNER: Archibald Knox
(1864–1933)

It is not hard to see the links
between Knox's brightly coloured
hand-drawn type and the freeform
experiments in hand-drawn lettering
associated with psychedelia in the
1960s. What also makes this work
so extraordinary is the direction
Knox took towards abstraction in
the letterforms, a direction that ran
against the contemporary trend in
the 1920s towards simplification.

Archibald Knox is an Arts and
Crafts architect–designer best known
for his work for the London
department store Liberty's for whom
he produced a distinctive range of
metalware. Less familiar is his work
as an illustrator and calligrapher.
The best surviving collection of his
work can be found in the museum
of his home town Douglas in the
Isle of Man. All of Knox's designs
were inspired by Celtic art and
nature, as is visible in this
illustration for *The Deer Cry* from
1916. In his calligraphy this
produced linear interlaced motifs
and ornamentation. During the
1920s Knox produced a range of
graphic work including illustrated
books and greeting cards, based on
his considerable first-hand
knowledge of Celtic ornamentation.
One of his techniques was to draw
the outline of the letter forms in
pencil and then fill in the shapes
with watercolour.

In about 1910 the new ideas emerging from art and architecture began to have an inevitable effect on type and design. Just as architecture challenged the idea that buildings should refer to historical sources, type designers also experimented with new forms. Important here were the Italian Futurists who saw new type design as a way to "redouble the force of expressive words". Kurt Schwitters was a leading force behind another art movement – Dada. Using type he put together a series of famous collages employing the principle of random choice. In doing so Schwitters placed type within a fine art context and opened up the possibility that type was not only concerned with function and legibility.

Merz Magazine

DATE: 1920

DESIGNER: Kurt Schwitters (1887–1948)

Million Mark Note

DATE: 1923

DESIGNER: Herbert Bayer
(1900–85)

The Bauhaus has become the most famous design school of the twentieth century. It was always a small school and during its fourteen-year life only trained 1,250 students. It has, however, come to represent the century's new Modernist approach to design and industry. In 1923 one of its successes was to win a commission from the State bank of Thuringia to design a series of emergency banknotes. The production of banknotes was an expanding industry in Germany's Weimar Republic at this time, due to an ever-increasing inflation rate.

Herbert Bayer, then a young student, was asked to design notes in denominations of one million, two million and two billion. By the time they were issued on September 1, 1923, the German economy was in a state of collapse and even higher denominations were required. Bayer's designs reflect the ideology of hardline Modern Movement graphics – direct and simple typography, no decoration, and strong horizontals and verticals. For banknotes they are highly individual, with an experimental approach made possible by the unique economic circumstances of their era.

Edward Johnston is responsible for one of the most famous corporate identity programmes in the world for London's Underground system. Based on a font he had designed in 1916 for Frank Pick, London Transport's design manager, it was also Britain's first Modernist typeface using clean, geometric forms

that proved easy to read and immensely popular with the public. Arguably it was the first sans serif face of the twentieth century and was deeply influential on British graphic design in general and in particular on Johnston's pupil, the famous sculptor and typeface designer Eric Gill (1882–1940). London's

Underground system expanded rapidly after World War One and provided the British public with their first, sometimes only, opportunity to see modern architecture and design. In the 1980s the type was redrawn by Banks and Miles to meet the more complex applications of the 1990s.

Railway Type

DATE: **1916**

DESIGNER: **Edward Johnston**
(1872–1944)

Penguin Book Covers

DATE: 1946–49

DESIGNER: Jan Tschichold
(1902–74)

Tschichold was born in Leipzig in Germany but emigrated to Switzerland in 1933 and became a Swiss citizen in 1942. He became one of the twentieth-century's most renowned typographers and his achievement was to lead the new postwar developments in typography while remaining firmly committed to traditional Modernist principles. In 1923 he saw an exhibition of work from the Weimar Bauhaus and was converted to the principles of the Modern Movement.

Tschichold's best-known work remains his designs for Penguin paperback books in the 1940s, and his achievement was to apply the theories of Modernism to the requirements of book production. One of his most successful innovations was the use of colour coding for different subject categories. Although he only worked for the publisher for three years, he introduced new standards of text layout and design that influenced the whole of British postwar graphic design.

Tschichold was also a dedicated historian and writer, with over twenty books to his credit, on subjects ranging from Chinese calligraphy to polemics on design. In the 1960s he worked as a freelance consultant to numerous Swiss and German publishers. In 1968 he retired to Locano, where he died six years later.

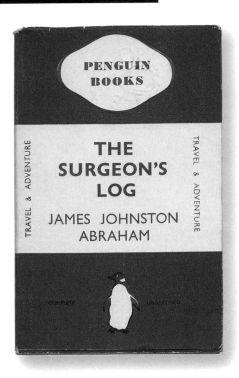

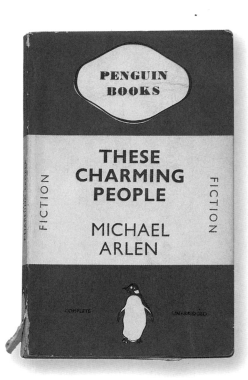

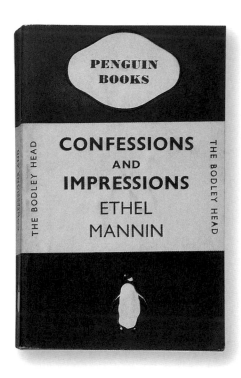

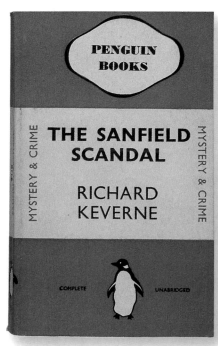

Univers

DATE: 1954–55

DESIGNER: Adrian Frutiger (born 1928)

Univers Medium

ABCDEFGHIJKLMNOPQRSTUV
WXYZ 1234567890
abcdefghijklmnopqrstuvwxyz
(&.:;!?"'%£)

Univers Medium Italic

ABCDEFGHIJKLMNOPQRSTUV
WXYZ 1234567890
abcdefghijklmnopqrstuvwxyz
(&.:;!?"'%£)

Univers Bold

ABCDEFGHIJKLMNOPQRSTU
VWXYZ 1234567890
abcdefghijklmnopqrstuvwxyz
(&.:;!?"%£)

Univers Bold Italic

ABCDEFGHIJKLMNOPQRSTU
VWXYZ 1234567890
abcdefghijklmnopqrstuvwxyz
(&.:;!?"'%£)

After the chaos of the war it is hardly surprising that many European type designers looked to order and unity as a vision of the way forward. Their intellectual response was to look back to the Bauhaus and take a rational approach to the problem of developing typography for the new era. Nowhere was this new spirit more clearly expressed than in the development of the International, or Swiss Style, which was pioneered at the Zurich School of Applied Art, the Kunstgewerbeschule. The designers there believed that they were setting universal and unchanging typographic standards.

Their aim was to make typography as objective as possible, believing that the design and typography should be "neutral", so that the information contained in the text would not be clouded by the form the text took. As the Swiss style, with its insistence on the use of sans serif faces, became more influential, a whole series of new fonts reflecting this influence were created. One of the most important of these was Univers, designed by Adrian Frutiger who, as a young man, was appointed artistic director of one of Europe's most famous type companies, Deberny. Created as a "universal" typeface, it was drawn in twenty-one variations – combinations of italicized, condensed and bold versions, as well as a range of weights – so that the one face could be used for any application.

Mother and Child

DATE: 1966

DESIGNER: Herb Lubalin
(1918–81)

In the postwar years, New York City became the world's cultural capital and one of the city's achievement's was the emergence of a distinctly American school of typography. It was not until the 1950s that a new group of graphic designers including Milton Glaser and Saul Bass established an original American approach. Arguably the most talented type designer of his generation was Herb Lubalin.

If European typography was theoretical and structured then American typography was intuitive and informal, with a more open, direct presentation. Herb Lubalin's decorative and hand-drawn lettering appeared in marked contrast to the formal mechanical Swiss and German Schools of typography and reflected the unique economic affluence and cultural confidence of 1950s America.

Born in New York City of immigrant Russian and German parents Lubalin studied typography at the Cooper Union School of Architecture. He led the way in manipulating typography to express an idea; letter forms became objects and images, and his figurative typography allowed visual properties a new freedom and importance. One of his most famous inventions was a new genre called the "typogram", a kind of brief visual poem. Perhaps the best-known example of this expressive typography is a masthead, designed in 1966, for a magazine called *Mother and Child* in which the ampersand evokes the image of the womb complete with foetus. These experiments, using what Lubalin called "the typographic image", were widely imitated in advertising. Designers realized the possibilities of using typography to create a "word picture" that allowed them a new creative potential. It was Lubalin's achievement to pack an idea into a single, convincing piece of typography.

Bass is an American graphic designer best known for his innovative work for the film makers Otto Preminger and Alfred Hitchcock. A native New Yorker, Saul Bass studied graphic design at night school in Brooklyn College between 1944–45, while practising as a freelance graphic designer. In 1946 he moved to Los Angeles and founded Saul Bass and Associates. Bass designed more than sixty graphic symbols for films and more than forty motion picture title sequences. He is particularly well known for his work with the director Otto Preminger, for whom he designed the symbols and opening titles for *The Man with the Golden Arm* (1955), *Bonjour Tristesse* (1956) and *Anatomy of a Murder* (1959) and for his working relationship with Alfred Hitchcock, designing the opening credits and, some suggest, directing the shower sequence, from *Psycho* (1960).

From Hollywood's earliest days until the mid-1950s, credits to mainstream American movies had been set in virtually uniform templates and superimposed over an unchanging static image or the film's introductory scene. Bass used animation and, later, live action to create graphically considered title sequences that attracted the attention of audiences and critics and were soon widely imitated.

Bass designed relatively few film credit sequences after the early 1970s, although he created the opening titles for the remake of *Cape Fear* (1991) at the request of the film's director, Martin Scorsese.

Anatomy of a Murder

DATE: 1959

DESIGNER: Saul Bass (1920–96)

IBM Logo

DATE: 1956

DESIGNER: Paul Rand
(1914–96)

Paul Rand was America's most respected graphic designer. Born in New York City, he began his career as assistant designer in George Switzer's studio, and became art director of *Esquire* and *Apparel Arts* magazines from 1937 to 1941. During the 1940s and early 1950s he was creative director at William H. Weintraub advertising agency, and from 1955 went freelance, working as a consultant to companies such as Cummins Engine Company, Westinghouse Electric Corporation and IBM.

One of Rand's achievements was to secure the influence of modernist art movements such as Cubism, Constructivism, De Stijl and the Bauhaus to overthrow traditional American graphic design – with its symmetrical, isolated elements and narrative illustrations. He also began to work with the visual space as a whole, integrating copy, art and typography. Rand understood the expressive potential of colour, texture and collage and used these to develop his style. His work for IBM is seen as seminal in the development of corporate graphic identity, notably his use of abstract and pictographic symbols, which he saw as a common language linking artistic expression and its audience.

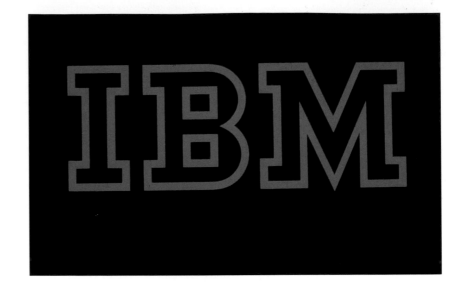

Galt was an established British furniture company that moved into children's toys in 1961. At the time, they invited Ken Garland to create their graphic identity and the result remains one of the most successful and distinctive corporate identity schemes of the 1960s.

Garland was typical of the generation of designers who allied themselves to Modernism. To his generation of designers the International Style, with its emphasis on the minimalism of clean lines and rational systems, seemed much more relevant to planning a Britain of the future than the gentle humour, whimsy and nostalgia that had informed much 1950s graphic work. Garland combined a knowledge of technology and basic practice with an ability to deal with ideas and communicate information. An early publication, *The 1966 Graphics Handbook,* was typical of Garland and the British School. It focused on the practicalities of being a professional graphic designer. Solid and practical, it dealt with type, letter-spacing, print technology and so forth, but also emphasized less obvious communication skills such as the importance of knowing how to answer the telephone and take notes!

Catalogue: Galt Toys

DATE: 1963–64

DESIGNER: Ken Garland (born 1929)

Festival of Britain Logo

DATE: 1948

DESIGNER: Abram Games
(1914–97)

Abram Games was part of a generation of British graphic designers who injected new life into their profession. These designers succeeded in developing a distinctively English visual identity, often displaying gentle humour and an illustrative, decorative style that was popular in the austere postwar years. The most famous example was the 1951 Festival of Britain logo with its stylized head of Britannia, half circle of waving flags in red, white and blue, and use of Victorian numbers, a link back to the 1851 Great Exhibition.

Born in Whitechapel, London, Abram Games was the son of an immigrant Latvian photographer, and from him learnt techniques such as airbrushing. When, in 1936, he won a poster competition he attracted the attention of the legendary art director Ashley Havinden and started to build up a client list that included forward-looking companies such as Shell and London Transport. In 1940 Games enlisted in the army and it was during the Second World War that his reputation as one of Britain's leading poster artists was established. In 1942 he was appointed Official War Poster Designer, often using Surrealist imagery to create powerful propaganda images, as in his famous "Careless Talk Costs Lives" series. This willingness to use the graphics language of the twentieth century avant-garde makes his work of lasting interest.

Roger Excoffon's typography has become an integral part of postwar French culture. Throughout France you can still see examples of his work and during the 1950s Excoffon, with a group of his contemporaries including Raymond Savignac, revitalized French graphic design.

Excoffon was born in Marseilles in the Southern region of Provence, in 1910. During his career he developed and designed a total of nine typefaces, largely for use in advertising, in addition to working on posters, corporate identity projects and advertising campaigns. Excoffon had originally studied law but persuaded his parents to let him go to Paris to study as an art student. After World War Two he established himself as a graphic designer, opening his own studio in 1947 and working as the Art Director for the Paris based advertising agency Urbi et Orbi. That same year Excoffon joined a family business in Marseilles, to become Art Director of a small type foundry called the Fonderie Olive. It quickly became one of France's leading type foundries, its appeal largely due to the commercial success of Excoffon's type designs.

During the 1950s, at the Fonderie Olive, Excoffon designed and produced several decorative scriptfaces, all based on calligraphy, that reflected a stylish and confident approach to French typography as well as expressing the new spirit of postwar optimism. These typefaces were Banco (1951), Mistral (1953), Diane (1956) and Calypso (1958). As well as being attractive these typefaces were technically excellent and soon became popular with the printing trade and widely available, for that very reason.

Excoffon based the best-known of these typefaces, Mistral, on his own handwriting. It was an immediate worldwide success. It took him several years work on Mistral to convert the spontaneity of handwriting into a usable hot metal type. Excoffon himself went on to use these typefaces in a body of work that gave French graphic design in the 1950s a new life and a new freshness and intelligence.

However by the 1970s Excoffon's reputation had been eclipsed. Different influences appeared that made Excoffon appear rather isolated and out-of-date. in the last years of his career Excoffon shifted away from designing towards writing and lecturing and until his death in 1983 remained an important establishment figure in the world of international typography.

Mistral

DATE: 1953

DESIGNER: Roger Excoffon (1910–83)

triomphante aux bornes d'un

triomphante aux bornes d'un

Biba

DATE: 1960s

DESIGNER: John McConnell
(born 1939)

John McConnell was responsible for the design of the famous Biba logo. Biba as a concept marked a change in direction for the brightly coloured geometry of Pop design. McConnell's use of Art Nouveau and, in particular, Celtic imagery reflected a new interest in the rich decorative tradition of type design.

Biba also introduced a range of products alongside its famous clothes. Barbara Hulanicki, Biba's founder, virtually invented the idea that it was possible to recreate a way of living through shopping, inspiring the idea of the designer lifestyle. It was the first time a distinctive designer logo appeared on all kinds of products

from perfume and make-up to baked beans and soap powder. As a styling concept it was ahead of its time and only became part of the mainstream in the 1980s. McConnell went on, in 1979, to join Pentagram, where his talent for effective design solutions found an outlet in work for publishers Faber and Faber.

Perhaps the nearest that Britain came to accepting the International Style was in its road sign system, designed in 1964 by Jock Kinneir and Margaret Calvert. The Government had commissioned the *Worboys Report* to report on overall road signage, which they wanted to bring in line with the Continental conventions established in the 1930s. With the advent of the motorway age the rationalization of signage systems for both motorways and other roads became a priority and the Ministry of Transport commissioned a team including Jock Kinneir, who had previously worked in the 1950s on the signage system for Gatwick Airport. Kinneir and Calvert adapted a standard type from the Bertold foundry but introduced some quirky and very British elements, such as the stroke on the lower case "l", taken from Edward Johnston's London Underground type of 1916, and the design of the lower case "a", borrowed from an Eric Gill typeface. When the designs were published many people wanted more conventional roman letters for the capitals rather than a sans serif upper and lower case. With its reliance on sans serif type, a hierarchical structure for ordering information and its colour coding, the motorway signs follow many of the principles of Modernism. At the same time the signage avoids the almost expressionless clarity of true Swiss Style and its inherent Britishness is so pervasive that it has been called the corporate identity of Britain.

Motorway Signage System

DATE: 1964

DESIGNERS: Jock Kinneir (1917–74) and Margaret Calvert (born c.1935)

Museum
Poster

DATE: 1982

DESIGNER: Wolfgang
Weingart (born 1941)

In the 1970s, the first serious
experiments using the new
Postmodernist aesthetic for type
came from surprising sources. One
of these was the work of Wolfgang
Weingart in Basel, then the centre of
formal Swiss Style type design. His
work sought to subvert the
formalism of International Style and
in doing so breathed new life into
new type design. Weingart's
approach was expressive, intuitive
and experimental. Typical of his
work is this poster for Basel's
Gewerbe Museum in which he
played around with word and letter
spacing, contrasted weights and the
layering of images. These devices
were widely imitated and were to
become the clichés of Postmodernist
graphics in the 1980s.

Weingart still teaches at the
Kunstgewerbeschule in Basel where
he trained as a student. It has been
his influence as a teacher, rather
than as a practitioner, that has been
paramount. Particularly influential
was his period as a visiting
professor at the Cranbrook Academy,
near Detroit, where he inspired a
whole generation of graphic
designers to experiment with a new
approach to type design. One of
Weingart's best-known students is
the West Coast designer April
Greiman and, via her, Weingart's
influence has filtered through to a
new wave of Californian design.

DATE: 1960s

DESIGNER: Rick Griffin
(1944–91)

As a teenager Rick Griffin's roots
were in 1950s California surfer
culture, with its own unique music
and clothes. Griffin went on to study
for a short time at the CalArts
school in Los Angeles. However he
took an immediate dislike to simple
modern type and good taste and
took off, moving in 1965 to San
Francisco where he designed
posters for rock 'n' roll bands at the
city's legendary Fillmore Auditorium
and the Avalon Ballroom.

Griffin was an enthusiastic
participant in the new drug culture
and had taken part in the writer
Ken Kesey's experimental counter
culture gatherings. The influence of
these experiences is reflected in one
of the hallmarks of his style; the
use of weird imagery, snakes, skulls,
insects, bizarre science fiction
creatures and Hell's Angels motifs.
The effect of LSD on Griffin's work
was in his use of luminous and
intense colours that were balanced
but chromatically opposite. In the
1960s Griffin reclaimed colour as a
valid means of graphic expression.
The new pop poster became the
perfect expression of the new drug
culture.

Griffin's work also epitomized the
psychedelic rejection of legible
typography. The copy on his posters
took legibility to the limit, working
on the premise that if the image
was exciting enough people would
not only take the trouble to
decipher the information but also
enjoy the process of decoding.

Berlin Underground Signage

DATE: 1990

DESIGNER: Erik Spiekermann
(born 1947)/MetaDesign

The tradition of Modernism in type design did not disappear in the 1980s but ran alongside the new experiments with technology. The rational work for the Berlin underground system by Erik Spiekermann is an example of this continuing tradition. After the fall of the Berlin Wall public transport in the city needed new passenger information and Meta was asked to look at the redesign of the corporate symbol and logotype to signage and maps. The work was so successful that BVG asked MetaDesign to undertake a complete corporate design programme. They are currently working on the design of fully interactive information kiosks to help the traveller.

Erik Spiekermann trained as an art historian at Berlin's Free University in West Germany in the late 1960s, where he established a small press. During the 1970s he worked in England, but in 1983 he returned to Berlin and set up his own studio, MetaDesign. MetaDesign attracted some of Europe's most talented young designers, including Jan van Toorn and Max Kisman, and it became something of a catalyst for new ideas. Spiekermann is well known as a writer on type and typography; his best known book, *Rhyme & Reason: A Typographical Novel*, is a handbook for typographic designers. MetaDesign specializes in

corporate identity for clients such as H.Berthold AG, the Deutsche Bundespost, Apple Computers and in 1991 a timetable for the Berlin Transport Authority. Spiekermann's approach to type design combines a respect for history and tradition with a commitment to new technology.

In 1988 Spiekermann, with his wife Joan, set up a company called the Fontshop to market typefaces. The company has become a key outlet for both radical work and more commercial typefaces including Spiekermann's Meta, now one of the most popular electronic fonts, widely used for signing systems and for magazine design.

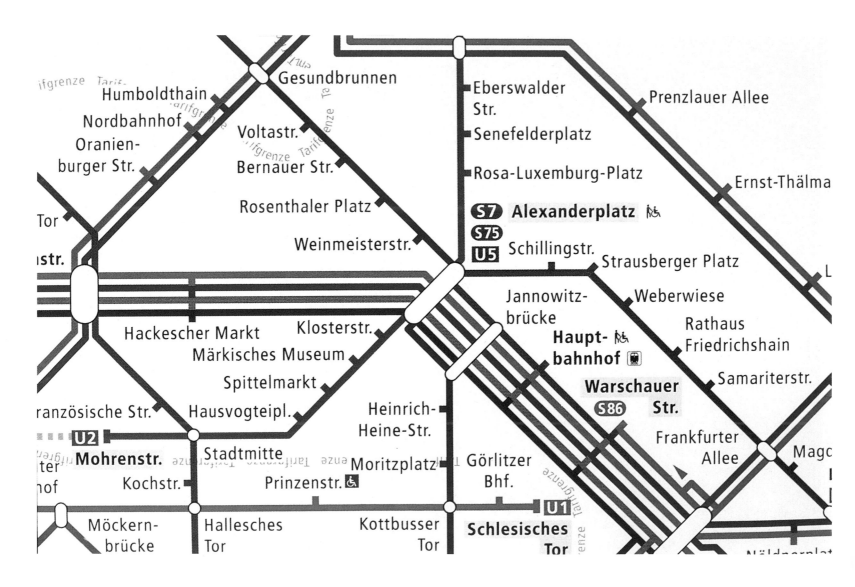

Cranbrook School of Art Poster

DATE: 1985

DESIGNER: Katherine McCoy (born 1945)

CLIENT: Cranbrook School of Art, Michigan, USA

Katherine McCoy is not only a designer; she has also come to represent a new attitude to typography and graphic design, expressed in the work of the staff and students at a small American design school called the Cranbrook Academy of Art in Michigan. Cranbrook has established itself as one of the world's most influential design schools, attempting in the sphere of graphics to introduce an intellectual rigour and environment of experimentation to the discipline.

In 1971, Katherine and Michael McCoy, a husband and wife team, were invited to take over the department. They set up a course with an emphasis on theory and analysis and which concentrated "on the purely syntactic aspect of typography on structure and form – with semantic exploration and analysis." During the 1970s the theoretical basis of Postmodernism began to interact with graphic design. These research ideas and the range of critical writing within Postmodernism offered a rationale for a new language of form within graphic design. Semiotics, for example, and the work of Claude Levi-Strauss provided a theoretical base for graphic design. At Cranbrook these theories encouraged an approach to type which produced layers of imagery and text, an approach to the subject disseminated by leading graduates of Cranbrook who included April Greiman and Jeffrey Keedy.

Punk Fanzine: Sniffin' Glue

DATE: 1977

DESIGNER: Mark Perry

One of the new directions that British Punk pioneered in the 1970s was the aesthetic of do-it-yourself. The idea that design was the sole prerogative of designers and design practices was challenged by a new approach to music, fashion and design that questioned the establishment. One of these experiments was the appearance of a range of fanzines which were produced using simple techniques such as cut and paste, hand-drawn lettering, crude marks, cropped images and photocopying. Hundreds of the these fanzines appeared of which *Sniffin' Glue* was the best known. They had a small circulation and a short life but their influence spread into mainstream publishing. One small fanzine, *i-D*, produced by the art director Terry Jones made the transition from a fanzine into a huge publishing success in the 1980s. In doing so, *i-D* placed these techniques into the international spotlight where they were translated and used by designers all over the world.

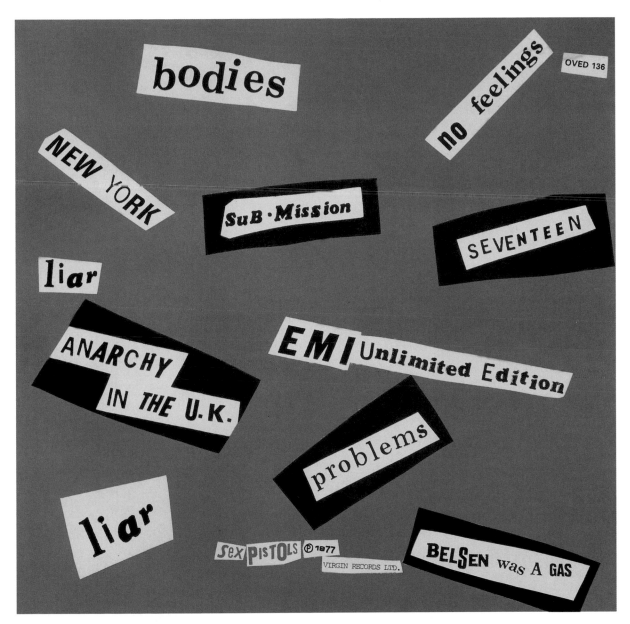

Sex Pistols Record Sleeve

DATE: 1977

DESIGNER: Jamie Reid
(born 1940)

Perhaps the most immediate visible result of British Punk culture in the 1970s was the cut-and-paste mayhem of Jamie Reid's designs for the Sex Pistols' record sleeves and posters. All of his work had – and still has – a political subtext. It carried with it an analytical edge that was transferred to the hugely influential type experiments for The Sex Pistols.

In 1970 Reid set up a community paper called *Suburban Press* in Croydon and integrated into the design and copy ideas he had picked up from his interest in the French Situationist movement which, in the 1960s, had used political slogans and art to subvert the status quo. These experiences were to influence his work as Art Director for the Sex Pistols from 1975. Reid's graphics, using cut-out blackmail letters, clashing colours and political slogans created the perfect visual expression for British Punk. Although his style was used for record sleeves it gradually influenced mainstream graphics in a profound way, establishing visual images that have come to stand for the cultural revolution Punk championed in the late 1970s.

Emigré Magazine

DATE: 1986

DESIGNER: Zuzana Licko (born 1961) and Rudy VanderLans (born 1955)

Zuzana Licko is a type designer whose work has pioneered the use of typefaces designed on, and for, the Apple Macintosh. Born in Bratislava in Slovakia, her family emigrated to America in 1968. While at college she met the Dutch designer Rudy VanderLans, whom she married in 1983. In 1986, she set up the design consultancy Emigré with VanderLans and together they designed and produced the cult magazine of the same name, a journal for experimental graphic design. They bought their first Apple Mac in order to produce their arts magazine but soon realized that they could use the Mac to create typefaces. These faces started as an attempt to overcome the ugly bitmapping which occurred when traditional faces were transposed onto the then low-resolution machine. As the machine became more sophisticated, so did their typeface design, and, realizing that they could easily copy and sell their designs, they began to publish their typefaces as well as the *Emigré* magazine. In 1986 Licko and VanderLans set up Emigré Fonts, to market digital typefaces designed for low-resolution systems, including Emigré, Emperor and Universal.

The Face

DATE: 1986

DESIGNER: Neville Brody
(born 1957)

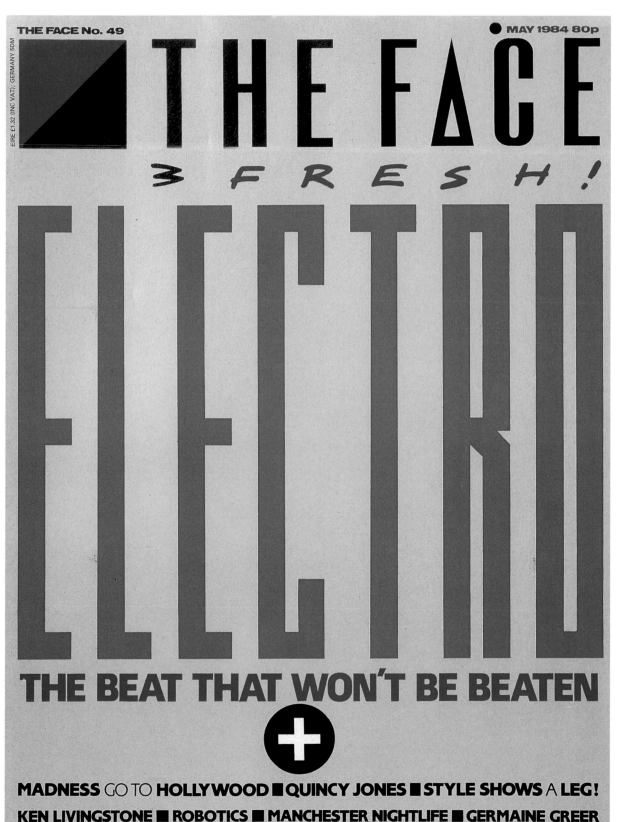

THE FACE No. 49

EIRE £1.32 (INC VAT); GERMANY 5DM

● MAY 1984 80p

THE FACE

≥FRESH!

ELECTRO

THE BEAT THAT WON'T BE BEATEN

✚

MADNESS GO TO HOLLYWOOD ■ QUINCY JONES ■ STYLE SHOWS A LEG!
KEN LIVINGSTONE ■ ROBOTICS ■ MANCHESTER NIGHTLIFE ■ GERMAINE GREER

Neville Brody is Britain's best-known designer and his work, in particular his Brody font, defined the graphic style of the 1980s, not only in this country but internationally. Brody was born in Southgate, North London and in 1976 went to study graphic design at the London College of Printing (LCP). The LCP then enjoyed a reputation as an institution dedicated to a disciplined, vocational training based on the prevailing Swiss Modernist orthodoxy of the 1970s. It was not an educational culture that Brody enjoyed, teaching – in his words – "the traditional type rule book by rote". By 1979, the year he graduated, the Punk revolution was in full swing and Brody gravitated towards the clubs and magazine scene of London.

In the early 1980s, if you wanted to know what was happening in terms of new style trends you simply read two magazines, *i-D*, designed by Terry Jones, and from 1981 *The Face*, which was originally designed by Brody. These two magazines were read by enthusiasts from Tokyo to New York and beyond. From the first early designs for *The Face*, Brody attracted a cult following. His ideas of page layout and type design seemed fresh, radical and innovative. He developed certain distinctive trademarks, using, for example, symbols and logo-type almost as road signs to guide the reader through the pages. Brody created a vocabulary for magazine design of the period using handwriting marks and type that ran sideways. This cover of *The Face* is the only issue that used only type and no cover photograph.

Uck N Pretty Typeface

DATE: 1992

DESIGNER: Rick Valicenti
(born 1958)

Uck N Pretty is a decorative typeface designed for issue 4 of *Fuse* magazine in 1992 by Rick Valicenti. Valicenti has been described as a Deconstructionist. Educated at Bowling Green State University, New York, he graduated in painting in 1973 and then took a Masters course in photography at the University of Iowa in 1975. In 1988 he launched his company Thirst, or 3st, in Chicago, a group he describes as devoted to the creation of Art With Function. In the 1990s, Thirst has enjoyed a high profile in US graphic design.

Valicenti works with Ark Rattin, who graduated with a degree in visual communications from Northern Illinois University in 1988 and a Masters in photography in 1990. Their approach, using witty word constructions and layering text and imagery, has more humour and irony than that of most of their contemporaries. Clients include the Japanese cosmetic company Shiseido, the Museum of Science and Industry, Chicago, and the Lyric Opera, Chicago.

NEW AND USED
100% RECYCLED CULTURE
WORK FROM THE CUSTOMIZED TERROR & SYNAESTHESIA
EXHIBITIONS NEW YORK CITY 1995
CUSTOMIZED TERROR CURATED BY RONALD JONES

Customized Terror

THE DESIGNERS REPUBLIC
@THE FORUM SHEFFIELD
NOV.21/95 - JAN.28/96
THE FORUM DEVONSHIRE QUARTER SHEFFIELD S3 7SB
INFORMATION 0114 276 7454

the designers republic.   the workstation unit 415 paternoster row sheffield s1 2bx.   0114 275 4982. 0114 275 9127.
+44 114

Exhibition Poster

DATE: 1995

DESIGNER: Designers Republic, Sheffield, England

Designers Republic is a British graphic design practice based in the northern town of Sheffield and specializing in work for the music industry. It was established in 1986 by Ian Anderson (born 1961), who had had no formal training in graphic design, graduating in philosophy from Sheffield University in 1982. Anderson had worked in the music industry as a club promoter and DJ, and as a band manager, so the shift into designing album covers seemed a natural progression. The original team included Nick Philips, Helen Betnay, Dave Smith, Nick Bax, John Crossland and Bette Anderson and now consists of Michael Place (born 1967), Roger Coe (born 1969) and Vanessa Swetman (born 1965). All published work from the studio is, however, simply signed Designers Republic. Clients include Pop Will Eat Itself, Age Of Chance, Cabaret Voltaire, Guerrilla Records and Chakk. Their anarchic approach to practice and to imagery, which this offset lithograph illustrates, is reflected in their press release, which suggests the company's positioning: "Auto Martyrs on the Wheels of Steel City Say it Loud" or "Sanyo – Go! Dynamo Designers Republic – The Clash of the Bulletproof Icon-titans. The Designers Republic: a new and used taste of paradise."

Their work has been exhibited at the Boymans van Beuningen Museum in Rotterdam and the Victoria and Albert Museum in London. In spring 1993 the Mappin Art Gallery in Sheffield mounted a retrospective of their work called "Designers Republic: New and Used".

Sport 90 Exhibition Poster

DATE: 1990

DESIGNER: Malcolm Garrett
(born 1956)

In the 1980s Malcolm Garrett's name was increasingly linked with Peter Saville and Neville Brody as one of the three British designers who had done most to introduce new directions in graphics. An early computer enthusiast, Garrett became increasingly excited by challenges offered by interactive media and electronic publishing. Sport 90 was a turning point. To complete this exhibition project, which included catalogue, posters, captions and an interactive guide, Garrett introduced himself to new digital software: QuarkXpress for page layout, Adobe Illustrator to draw lettering and Apple's HyperCard to build the interactive exhibition guide. The poster's number type suggests a running track. The aim was to combine sport's recreational and more competitive, technological image.

Born in Northwich, Cheshire, Garrett studied typography and psychology at Reading University and graphic design at Manchester Polytechnic. He then formed the design group Assorted Images and was joined in 1983 by his partner Kasper de Graaf. In 1977 he worked on packaging and promotion for the Manchester Punk band Buzzcocks. Garrett's work includes graphic identity, exhibition and television design, and design for literature of all kinds, as well as respected music industry work for well-known artists. In 1997 he was appointed professor by the London Institute.

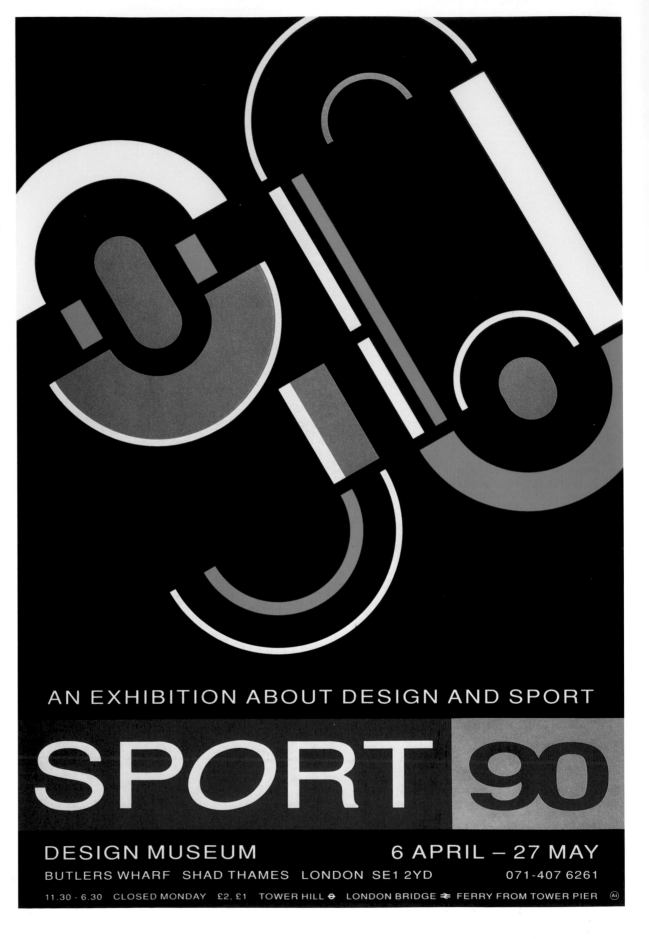

AN EXHIBITION ABOUT DESIGN AND SPORT

SPORT 90

DESIGN MUSEUM   6 APRIL – 27 MAY
BUTLERS WHARF   SHAD THAMES   LONDON SE1 2YD   071-407 6261
11.30 - 6.30   CLOSED MONDAY   £2, £1   TOWER HILL ⊖   LONDON BRIDGE ⇌ FERRY FROM TOWER PIER

The American David Carson has become one of California's best-known graphic designers. His use of type and imagery and his work for *Ray Gun* magazine, which established his reputation, became highly influential in the 1990s. Carson is a self-taught graphic designer who originally studied sociology at university. Part of the Californian new wave, his work is based on magazine design, starting with *Beach Culture*, which has won over 100 awards worldwide for its innovative design. The American magazine *i-D* selected Carson as one of the US's most innovative designers and he has maintained this profile with his more recent work for *Ray Gun*. This magazine for the visual arts rapidly achieved cult status for young graphic designers all over the world.

Carson no longer designs the magazine and has established his own design studio. His clients include Nike, Pepsi, whose 1994 campaign used a Carson type design, MTV, David Byrne, Kentucky Fried Chicken and Sony. Carson also works with Tony Kaye Films as a commercial and video director. He lectures worldwide on typography.

Ray Gun

DATE: 1990s

DESIGNER: David Carson
(born 1958)

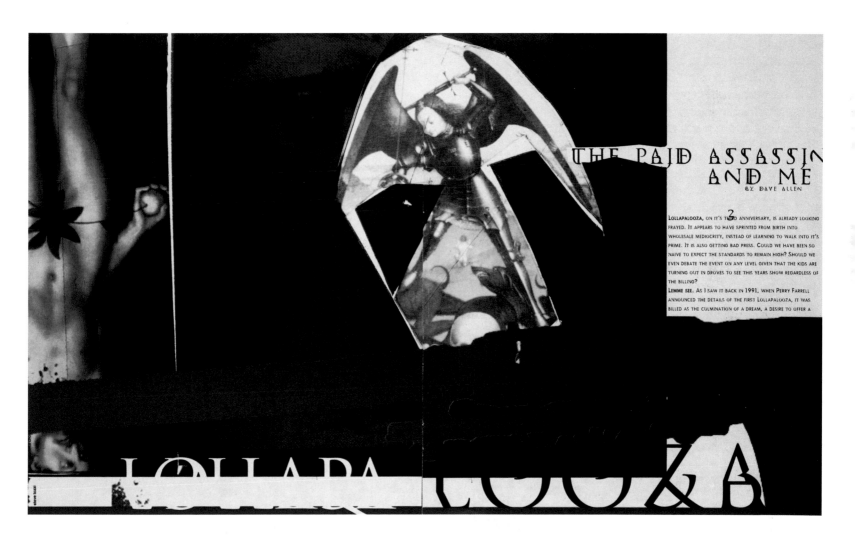

FloMotion
and
Niwida

DATE: FloMotion 1990
DESIGNER: Peter Saville
(born 1955)

DATE: Niwida 1991
DESIGNER: Erik van Blokland
(born 1967)

In the summer of 1990 Neville Brody and writer Jon Wozencroft developed the concept for a new digital magazine, called *Fuse*. Each issue set out to challenge the current state of digital language and communication, and invited four designers to produce a new font. *Fuse* magazine has opened up the debate about the direction and function of type design in the post-digital era. Its revolutionary approach attracted the young movers and shakers in type design to create typefaces for the next generation.

Fuse provided a forum and a dialogue for the new type revolution. More importantly, it was a disk containing copyright-free screen fonts, such as those illustrated here, so the user could experiment with the minimum of technical equipment, for example the basic Apple Macintosh Classic. The only restraint was disk memory. *Fuse* created an experimental outlet for designers and design students to push manufacturers to consider the applications of what they are doing. It set out to chart the changes to language in the post-electronic age and open up the possibilities of what the computer keyboard could do.

FloMotion

ABCDEFGHIJKLMN
OPQRSTUVWXYZ
abcdefghijklmnopqrst
uvwxyz (::!'')

Niwida

THIS IS DRONE

NO 666

FOR TEXT

WITHOUT

CONTENT

NO 90210

TYPEFACES BASED ON PRIMITIVE
HISPANIC CATHOLIC LETTERING

DATE: 1995

DESIGNER: Jonathan
Barnbrook (born 1966)

Jonathan Barnbrook is one of the
few individual designers producing
typefaces for the digital age in a
tradition more akin to the lone
artist than the font companies
operating in the industry such as
Fuse and *Emigré*. His fonts include
Bastard and Manson, a classically
proportioned font based on his
drawings of churches. It was used in
a diluted form on the condom
campaign for Femidom. Since then
Barnbrook's distinctive typefaces
have been used in a number of
advertisements and have made a
unique contribution to contemporary
advertising. Barnbrook studied
between 1985 and 1988 at
St Martin's School of Art in London,
before completing a Masters degree
at the Royal College of Art. While
still a student, Barnbrook worked in
collaboration with Why Not
Associates on the Next mail-order
catalogue, using an experimental
approach to deconstructing
typefaces.

Barnbrook's decorative typefaces
have been widely used in
contemporary graphic design. In the
future they will come to represent
the 1990s in the same way that
Charles Rennie Mackintosh
letterforms represent the 1890s.

Radio Scotland Television Advert

Tomato, founded in February 1991, are recognized as the innovators in their field. The group of ten designers form a loose but highly cooperative affiliation whose professed aim is to "blur" and transgress boundaries of response and method. Members have included John Warwicker (born 1955), Simon Taylor (born 1965), Dylan Kendle (born 1971), Dirk van Dooren (born 1959), Graham Wood (born 1965), Jason Kedgley (born 1969), Greg Rood, Karl Hyde, Steve Baker and Richard Smith. Tomato's iconoclastic approach polarizes opinion, yet continues to gain the respect and commercial commitment of leading clients such as Pepsi, MTV and Nike. Their insistence on extending their range of references beyond those normally employed in typographic design means that their conceptual language is one that is not open to easy absorption by competitors.

For this project Tomato had to attract listeners to Radio Scotland via a television advertisement. They ingeniously combined spoken words – snatches of the programmes – with moving type as subtitles.

DATE: 1993

DESIGNER: Tomato, United Kingdom

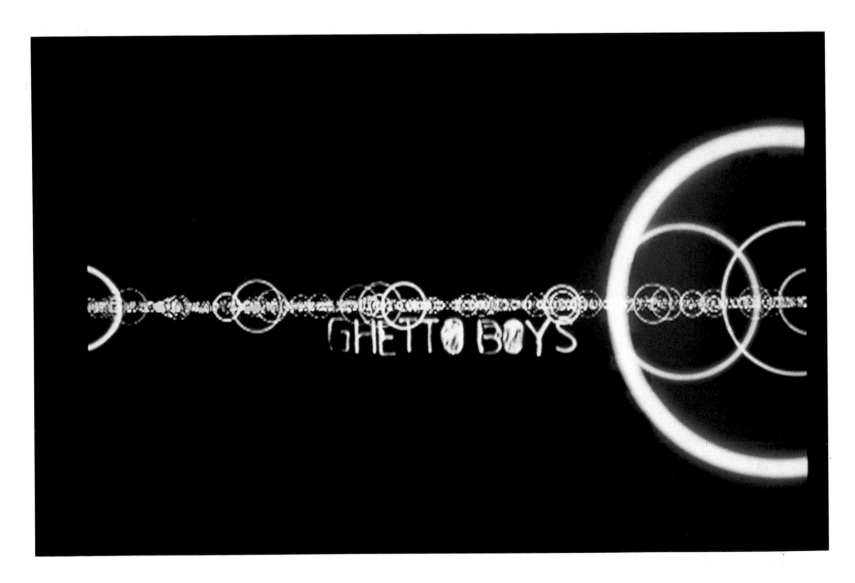

In 1997, eleven million world businesses use email and the number of private users with Internet access is sixty million. By 2000, the predicted number of people who will communicate using the Internet will be four hundred and fifty million. The introduction of the World Wide Web raised the problem of on-screen design and many Web sites are unattractive and visually confusing. Web site designs are usually dominated by visual images and the organization of clear, well-designed type is often ignored. There are, however, some exceptions and the Web site of New York's Museum of Modern Art (MOMA) is one example. MOMA is a world-famous museum, which celebrates twentieth-century art and design. Its Web site raises the important issue of the relationship between type information and image for museums in general. The museum tradition is object centred but, with the advent of the Internet, curators now have an opportunity to place their collections in the wider context of social and cultural history and to broaden access to their collections. Museums can only display a fraction of their collections, with small information captions. The Internet can, in theory, break through these limitations. It can link objects to others in the collection and provide background information to the ideas and theories that influenced their production. The Internet makes it possible to bring a museum collection to the desktop in homes all over the world.

At the present time, however, most museum Web sites are still digital brochures listing the collection, opening hours and offering a mail order service to the gift shop. The real potential of Web sites is in their ability to make available sights which would otherwise be unseeable and break down barriers between object and information. Museums can now offer a rich alternative experience, if a visit to the "real" museum is not possible.

Web Site

DATE: 1997

DESIGNER: Museum of Modern Art, New York City, USA, www.moma.org

packaging

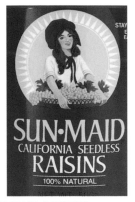

SUN MAID RAISINS

EGG BOX

TROPICANA TETRA PAK

PACKAGING IS A VITAL ELEMENT in all our lives. In the twentieth century, packaging has made available to the Western consumer food and goods in near perfect condition. It is worth pointing out that in Western Europe and the USA the wastage figure for food is under three per cent, a figure that should be compared to that of less developed countries where up to half of all food is spoilt before it reaches the consumer. Good packaging can also help to keep prices down, by reducing the cost of transport, distribution, storage and wastage. During the twentieth century, alongside its functional purpose, packaging has also produced some highly creative designs to protect goods and also to increase sales. Packaging is more than merely the outer container we bring food and everyday items home in. It is also the box and the tray that groups products together during distribution, and the container that collates the groups into larger loads for transport. Finally, packaging plays a vital social role – packaging for gifts is part of the way we form relationships and express love and affection. In some countries such as Japan, it is also an important social and status indicator, which marks out a strict formal code of behaviour and helps to define Japanese culture.

The history of modern packaging can be traced back to the inventions of the nineteenth century. It was in France that the first experiments in canning took place with the preservation of meat, vegetables and fruit in glass airtight containers. During the 1850s, a mechanical means of manufacturing tin cans was discovered, and an immediate market opportunity was apparent – feeding the army; after which, canned food quickly became a convenience food used in the home. In the USA the fishing industry led the field, building their own canning plants, and by the 1850s all kinds of fruit and vegetables were sold in cans. Manufacturers quickly learnt that any attractive label or distinctive container attracted higher sales and from this period derive many examples of classic labels and packs, including companies such as Lea and Perrins, Colman's Mustard, Campbell's Soups, Quaker Oats and Kellogg's Corn Flakes.

One new twentieth-century material that influenced the history of packaging was the introduction of plastics, which are now used more than any other material. Plastics have the advantage of being extremely light and can easily be moulded into intricate shapes using bright colours. More recently, a number of different finishes have been developed to challenge the premium status of the glass container. Another major advantage of plastic packs is that they can be squeezed: toothpaste is the traditional example, but more recently the market has been extended to include tomato sauce, cheese and savoury products. Due to the innovation of the designers who work with plastics, such containers have now become a familiar and essential part of household requirements, for toothpastes, cleaning materials, toiletries, foods and so on. Other plastic innovations include the new plastic

MATES CONDOM PACK

polymer PET bottle, which revolutionized the fizzy drinks market from the 1970s. More recently another plastic polymer PEN, suitable for hot fillings, is undergoing trials. Other new packaging materials include aluminium foil for snack products and the new technology of modlfied atmosphere packaging. This places meat, for example, under a plastic film in air with increased nitrogen and decreased oxygen content. This means that the product lasts not just for a few days but for up to two weeks. The same technology is also used for film bags for salads.

In the latter part of the twentieth century new technology, computer aided-design, new materials, demographic changes and changing consumer needs have continually altered packaging. The growing trend of people living alone has encouraged the development of single portion food, while the traditional family meal has been replaced by prepared food. This throwaway culture has come under direct attack from the ecology lobby. Nonetheless changes in eating habits, and the food revolution of the 1980s, has influenced the packaging of many luxury foods such as olive oil, pasta and sauces. In some cases their presentation has become as elaborate as that of an expensive luxury item like perfume.

One of the greatest challenges now facing the packaging designer is the challenge of the green movement which points out the unsustainable levels of waste that packaging generates. Some of the more recent changes include the introduction of refill systems, a concept that is not new in the United Kingdom where many still enjoy the survival of doorstep delivery of milk or in France where some wines are sold in refillable bottles. In addition, companies like the Body Shop have pioneered the idea of refillable bottles for shampoo and cosmetics. One new idea, however, is the availability of refilling at home. This can be seen in the reduction of packaging sizes for detergents and fabric conditioners, allowing them to be used in concentrated form. Leading detergent companies now produce these products in two different types, one strong, one more light-

ARTLANTIC WINE LABELS

weight, typically saving up to seventy per cent of material. Consumers now buy one strong container and then refill at home using liquid detergent or powder from a thin pouch. Other products using this system include baby wipes, where the refill pack uses eighty percent less material than the parent pack. Packaging reduction has also affected the amount of materials used for other products. Toothpaste tubes, formerly made in metal, are now designed in plastic, and are able to be shelved standing on their caps, to save up to a third of previous packaging requirements. Flow pack film for chocolate bars is another example of saving materials by reducing the amount of packaging.

DAZ DETERGENT POUCH

Sun Maid Raisins

DATE: this example 1990s

The Sun Maid brand of Californian raisins uses an obvious yet appealing visual pun, linking the appeal of a natural sun-made product with the eponymous and suitably wholesome sun maid. This traditional illustration style has remained popular throughout the twentieth century and is firmly linked in the mind of the consumer to the values of tradition and quality. The continued success of the brand can also be attributed to the adaptation of the packaging to changing consumer lifestyles. This can be seen in the mini-packets introduced for children's lunchboxes and in the adaptation of Marvin Gaye's hit song "I Heard It Through the Grapevine", complete with cartoon dancing raisins to tap into the juvenile market. Its distinctive packaging is difficult to copy and has also allowed it to compete well with the rise of supermarket own-brand labels.

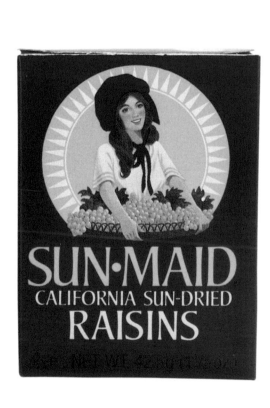

There is some packaging that has become so closely identified with a product that it has come to represent the food itself. Colman's Mustard is one such example. The Norwich firm of J. and J. Colman was founded in 1823. The use of mustard yellow, coupled with the distinctive bull's head trademark on the mustard's packaging, ensured that the brand became an immediate success.

Colman's understood a fundamental principle of pack design – the vital role that colour always plays in customer identification of the product. Using the vivid yellow meant that Colman's customers recognized the product before they even registered the bull's head design. The consistent use of the latter has meant that Colman's has maintained its place in the market over the years.

Colman's Mustard

DATE: this example c.1905

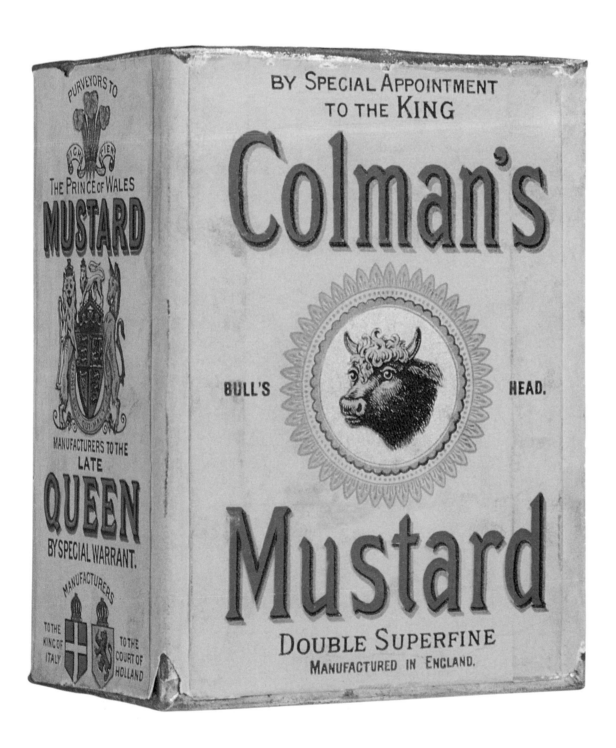

PURVEYORS TO

THE PRINCE OF WALES

MUSTARD

MANUFACTURERS TO THE LATE

QUEEN

BY SPECIAL WARRANT.

MANUFACTURERS

TO THE KING OF ITALY

TO THE COURT OF HOLLAND

BY SPECIAL APPOINTMENT TO THE KING

Colman's

BULL'S   HEAD.

Mustard

DOUBLE SUPERFINE

MANUFACTURED IN ENGLAND.

Quaker Oats

DATE: this example 1920s

The Quaker Mill Company of Ohio, USA, first produced their now-famous Quaker Oats, complete with the instantly recognizable Quaker emblem, in 1877. For Americans the now familiar image of the patriarchal Quaker carried an important message. In a country that prided itself as the refuge for non-conformist religious groups, the Quakers were seen to uphold the values of honesty and fair trading. With this powerful brand image it is not surprising that when in 1890 Quaker Oats was sold to the American Cereal Company, it became their biggest-selling brand, leading in 1900 to a name change: the Quaker Oats Company. One of the interesting marketing innovations the company introduced was the tradition of free gifts with cereal packs. During the early years of the century the company attracted prospective customers with offers that included free cereal bowls for the required number of pack coupons and this strategy proved such a success that it inspired many trade copycats. By 1904 Quaker Oats was offering a variety of special offers on household and personal items if the purchaser sent off the required number of trademark logos.

Kellogg's Corn Flakes

DATE: this example 1930s

Corn Flakes hailed the beginning of a food empire that has dominated the twentieth-century invention of the instant breakfast. In 1894 Dr John Kellogg introduced his first dried maize flakes as an invalid food, a light, dry breakfast that was felt to be easily digested by the sick. He was, however, quick to spot the product's potential for a wider market. Along with his younger brother Will, with whom he joined forces in 1898, he began in 1906 to sell Kellogg's Toasted Corn Flakes complete with the legend "None genuine without this signature". The distinctive W.K. Kellogg signature on the packaging was presented as a guarantee. This was enhanced by the simple packaging informing the consumer of the quality of the contents.

Kellogg's sold their cereal in cardboard boxes. The demand for cardboard boxes had increased steadily in the late nineteenth century and it was not long before cheap, mass-produced cartons became available. The design solution was simple and effective, using a folding carton that meant a complete box could be made by cutting and creasing a single sheet of card, which stored flat and took up little storage space. With the packaging and design of the logo in place, Kellogg's looked to expand their business empire and the range of products. The company set up in Britain in 1924 and was a particular success, the popularity of the cereals changing British breakfast habits. Other Kellogg's brands followed, including Rice Krispies in 1928 and in 1952 Sugar Frosted Flakes, the first sugar-coated cereal.

Ajax Scouring Powder

DATE: this example 1970

The design of the Ajax tube originated in the nineteenth century when several food manufacturers began experimenting with the idea of airtight tins, particularly for perishable products such as biscuits and tobacco. When this technical problem was solved not only could manufacturers increase sales in the domestic market, but expand their business overseas. Some early tins were cylindrical and opened with a revolving lid, which had an in-built cutter designed to pierce the airtight inner foil. In the postwar period the Ajax tube, effective in keeping the contents dry, represented the epitome of modern packaging technology and efficiency to the consumer.

Although the scouring powder itself has now been replaced in the home with creams and cleaning sprays, the spirally wound cardboard tube lives on. Its combination of rigidity, low weight and reduced shelfspace makes it particularly effective for the packaging of snacks.

"No effort, no waste, no rags, no powder". It was with this snappy slogan that the Brillo Manufacturing Company of New York introduced its new scouring pad in 1913. Brillo was intended as a cleaning agent for a complete range of difficult household jobs from pans to stove tops. The product used a steel wool pad containing soap, which produced a lather and had a vigorous scouring effect. Originally Brillo was marketed in a green-coloured pack; it was changed to red in the 1950s. Along with the Campbells soup can, Brillo's transit shipping carton was reproduced by Andy Warhol as a famous icon of Pop Art in the 1960s.

Brillo
Scouring
Pads

DATE: this example 1950s

Campbell's Soup Can

DATE: this example 1930s

Joseph Campbell first began to can foods in 1869, in his factory in New Jersey. In 1898, he launched his canned soups with their characteristic red and white label. Campbell's were not the first company to use coloured labels on canned products; by the end of the nineteenth century they were used extensively in the USA. However, the design of the Campbell's can has endured, the soups were instantly popular and are still dominant in the American canned-soup market today. In fact they proved such an ubiquitous American product that in the 1960s Andy Warhol used the cans as a theme for a series of famous Pop Art paintings. Through his use of the product, packaging gained an important place in the history of twentieth-century art.

Named after the infamous eighteenth-century gentlemen's drinking club, the Kit Kat chocolate wafer was originally produced by the Quaker Rowntree family company in 1935, having initially been known as Chocolate Crisp. Rowntrees had been established in the 1880s and produced crystallized gums and boxed chocolates. The name Kit Kat, although it had historical connotations, also evoked the Jazz Age. It has since become the most popular chocolate bar in the United Kingdom and is exported all over the world.

The success of Kit Kat is inextricably linked to the innovation of its packaging – the chocolate wrapped in foil with a separate paper wrapper cover – and the fact that this distinctive wrapping has remained unchanged for more than sixty years.

KitKat

DATE: this example 1937

Egg Box

DATE: this example 1997

The pressed paper-board egg box is one of the most familiar generic forms of packaging of the twentieth century. It provided a simple but effective solution to marketing a fragile food that could then be stored compactly in the home larder or fridge. Although plastic versions are now widely available, they do not provide the same quality of protection for the eggs, as they still need some extra protection from damage in the form of bubble wrap. The success of the cardboard version is proven by the fact that a successor to this low-tech product has not been found.

Milk Bottle

DATE: this example 1950s

Many British households still enjoy one of the world's most successful packaging recycling schemes – the doorstep delivery made possible by the milkman's round. First thing in the morning, milk is delivered in traditional glass bottles and the empty bottles are simply picked up, washed and reused. Originally the bottles were sealed with card, but these were replaced by aluminium tops during the 1930s. The bottle itself has evolved from a tall-necked vessel, shown here, to today's more compact and stocky bottle. Over the years the weight of the bottle has been steadily decreased without loss of strength, making a substantial saving in materials and energy.

Because the bottles are recycled and reused, the glass used to construct them must be capable of withstanding repeated use. The glass milk bottle is more than just packaging – it is linked to a valuable consumer service. Unfortunately the future of the traditional milk bottle is under threat, with increased use of supermarket plastic bottles and Tetra Paks.

HOLE'S & DAVIGDO DAIRIES

Toilet Duck

DATE: this example 1985

Increasingly, manufacturers seek to differentiate their brands by commissioning unique outer package shapes that can be legally protected in the same way as brand names or logos. Plastic, in particular, lends itself to this aspect of the designer's task. Containers made from plastics are extremely light and can be moulded into any number of shapes, sizes and colours. This versatility has led to many innovative forms of packaging. One famous example is the angled toilet jet made famous by Toilet Duck. Manufactured by Johnson Wax, the bottle is shaped to fit the hand and the angle of the neck is moulded for ease of use. More recently, designers have devised a number of different finishes for plastics, to counter the challenge from the glass manufacturers that plastics packs can never project a high-quality image.

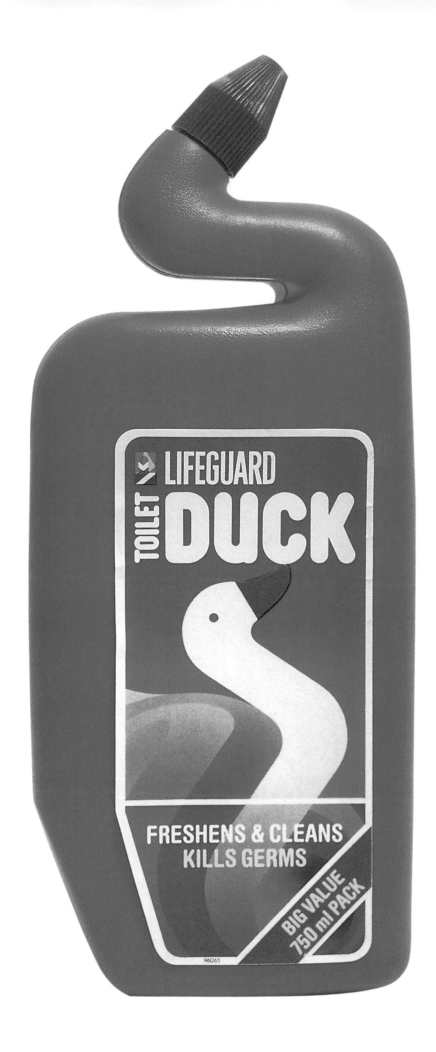

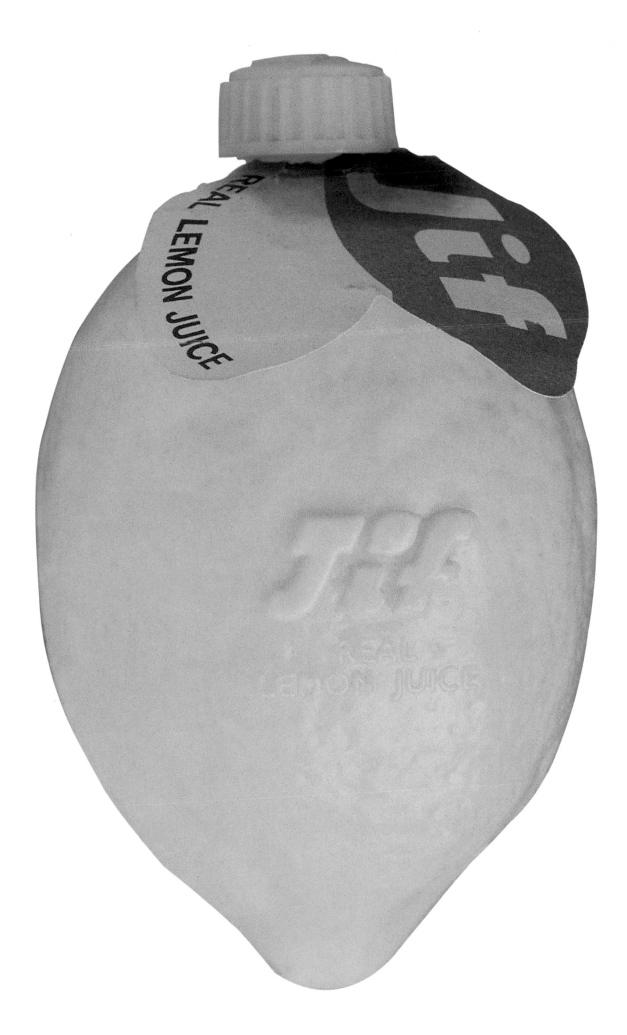

Jif Lemon

DATE: this example 1954

DESIGNER: W.A.G. Pugh

For many people, the Jif lemon is the definitive pack design: functional, easy to use and highly distinctive. In the United Kingdom no Shrovetide was complete without the distinctive "Jif" lemon to help complement the annual pancake and golden syrup treat. The lemon was designed by W.A.G. Pugh and launched by Colman's in 1956. The obvious shape and its "squeezability" ensured that the Jif lemon was a huge success. It was one of the earliest food applications for blow-moulded polythene, replacing glass bottles for lemon juice.

By the 1950s plastic packaging offered new possibilities for shape and innovation, such as the toothpaste tube. A particular favourite with the consumer is the squeezable plastic bottle, which is used for a wide variety of products. The Jif lemon design has remained virtually unchanged for over forty years.

Coca-Cola Bottle

DATE: this example 1915

Many manufacturers believe that shape is often the greatest competitive edge a product can have. It identifies products on the shelf and it is easy to advertise a memorable shape that is not just another tall, slim bottle, or yet another rectangular box. Perhaps the most famous pack shape of all time that has become synonymous with a product is the Coca-Cola bottle. Even though the bulk of Coke is now sold in cans and plastic bottles, Coca-Cola always features the bottle in TV advertisements. Its sinuous contours continue to identify the product embodied in the white wisps used on the cans and on plastic bottle labels.

In 1886, Dr John Pemberton, a pharmacist in Atlanta, Georgia, invented the Coca-Cola formula and a year later Willis Venables, an Atlanta drugstore barman, first mixed Coca-Cola syrup with carbonated water at five cents a glass. Three years later all rights to the product had been bought by Asa Chandler, owner of a pharmaceutical company. At first mainly sold at soda fountains, Coca-Cola was first bottled in 1894, and legend has it that Pemberton asked his book-keeper to create the famous handwritten trademark.

The classic Coca-Cola bottle evolved from 1915, when a Swedish engineer, Alex Samuelson of the Root Glass Company of Terre Haute, Indiana, based the curved shape on an illustration of a cocoa bean found in a copy of the *Encyclopedia Britannica*. In 1920 the final version of this design, made of German green glass and slimmed down to use existing bottling machinery, was patented and put into production.

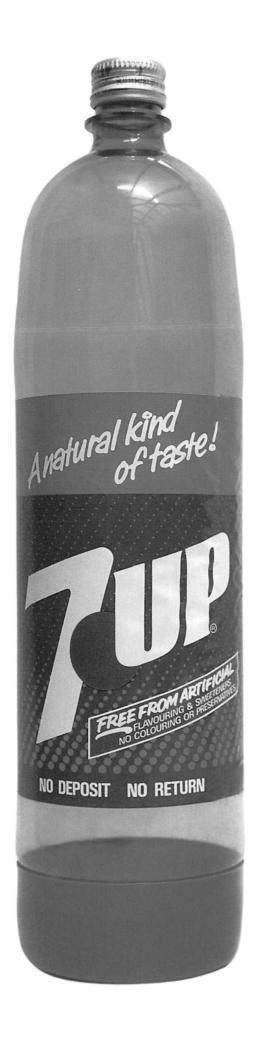

7up Plastic Bottle

DATE: this example 1985

Polyethylene was first used to manufacture plastic bottles in the 1960s. In the 1970s this use was extended with the creation of the cheaper polyethylene terephthalate (PET) bottles for carbonated drinks.

Before the advent of PET plastic bottles, fizzy drinks had only been available in more expensive glass bottles and small cans. One immediate result of PET bottles was the increase of home sales for fizzy drinks such as 7UP, as the consumer was able to buy larger quantities more cheaply for the home.

More recently this trend has been set alongside companies producing small PET bottles to imitate their more expensive rivals, for example, the Coca-Cola PET bottle, which is shaped like the classic glass container.

Budweiser
Beer
Bottle

DATE: **this example 1990s**

The biggest beer brand in the world owed its success in America to the early adoption of refrigeration. This allowed Budweiser to be sold far from the brewery site and establish itself as a national American brand. Budweiser itself was launched in 1876, named after the town of Budweis, in Bohemia, from which the brewery's founding Anheuser and Busch families originated. The red, white and blue label evolved throughout the twentieth century, although the elaborate Victorian style remains.

The "long-neck" bottle shown was originally used in the local Texas market but with the success of similarly shaped Mexican import brands, the "long-neck" was increasingly used in other markets.

Lucky Strike Cigarette Pack

DATE: this example 1942

DESIGNER: Raymond Loewy (1893–1986)

The majority of pack designs are not attributable to a single individual. Lucky Strike cigarettes is one exception. Raymond Loewy is an example of a famous designer working in the field of pack design. The brand was established in 1917 by the American Tobacco Company, founded by James Buchanan Duke. The red bull's-eye motif originated on the packaging of Lucky Strike Tobacco, which was already an established brand. In 1942 Loewy was commissioned to change the pack, his brief being to increase sales. He did this by introducing a white background (it was previously green). This strengthened and defined the pack's distinctive logo. The word "cigarettes" was placed in an Art Deco-style typeface, running across the bottom.

LUCKY STRIKE

"IT'S TOASTED"

CIGARETTES

Planters Peanut Packaging

DATE: this example 1990s

Because they are so light and flexible, foils are an essential material in the modern packaging of food. Aluminium foils have been used as packaging since the 1960s, when sachets of powdered soup and coffee were first produced. In the 1980s the development of high quality printing effects on aluminium foil introduced new designs onto the supermarket shelves. These designs lent added value to several luxury snack items which appeared on the market as part of the increasing diversification of foods available. Planter's Peanuts were not marketed as any ordinary peanuts – they used special roasting techniques– and seasonings to increase their flavour and consequently their price. Although aluminium was initially used to manufacture these packs, most metallic laminates now use a foil effect.

Tropicana Tetra Pak

DATE: this example 1990s

The Tetra Pak was developed by a Swedish firm in the 1950s. Originally used to package milk, the revolutionary pack was constructed from a paper tube, which was pinched together at regular intervals to create a pyramid-shaped container. The user could then simply cut a corner off the package to pour the liquid.

During the 1950s and 1960s use of the Tetra Pak grew, eventually evolving into a more traditional rectangular shape. Through the 1970s, 80s and 90s it has become a hugely popular vessel for milk, providing a serious challenge to the traditional glass milk bottle, and other liquids such as the fruit juice shown here. Tetra Paks are also used for liquid foods such as sauces and soups, and as refillable containers for products such as fabric conditioner for washing machines.

The Tropicana package utilizes the Tetra Pak to promote the contents by depicting their natural ingredients whole and in vibrant colours. Here the packaging offers a fresh, healthy and colourful image of a refreshing drink.

FedEx Mailing Packages

DATE: this example 1995

DESIGNER: Lindon Gray Leader (born 1949)

Federal Express is America's best-known courier company, dispatching mail order purchases and important documents all over the world. In Europe and the USA, where mail order is well established in all retail sectors, packaging for Federal Express is largely concerned with protective boxes, envelopes and resealable plastic sacks. Their packaging has to project the image of efficiency, security and speed to the customer. The use of a distinctive logo is the key to success.

In 1994 Federal Express commissioned the San Francisco-based consultancy Landor Associates to redesign their packs. Lindon Gray Leader's new look for Federal Express's public image canonized a phrase from everyday speech: he cut the company's name down to FedEx, capitalizing on the international slang that had, through popular use, begun to replace the company's proper name. In contrast with the dramatically shaped and angled letters the company had used since the 1970s, the new logotype employs upright roman letters.

Founded in 1955 in the US, McDonald's is the international chain of fast food hamburger restaurants. Their product is available in most modern cities – twenty-six million people eat in McDonald's every day. McDonald's have manufactured food as an industrialized product. Their aim is standardization and quality, and the packaging is integral to their success. The French fries pack is a typical example of the company approach. The cardboard scoop container is designed to appear overloaded but in fact it holds an exact quantity of fries. This prevents the server wasting or spilling any of the product, which would affect quantity control and profits. The bright red and yellow corporate colours reinforce McDonald's branding and add value to what would otherwise be a commodity product.

McDonald's Fast Food Pack

DATE: this example 1990s

Contraceptive Pill

DATE: this example 1960s

In the 1960s the first contraceptive pills appeared, but on prescription rather than on the open market. "The pill" offered the first reliable method by which women could control their own fertility. In this context the contraceptive pill represented much more than a pharmaceutical advance – it triggered a social and economic revolution. Manufacturers designed their packs as accurate dispensers, not just containers, with pills to be taken in sequence using the new technology of blister packs. The technological aspect is softened, however, by the almost personal diary-like abbreviations. The cardboard pack shows further deference to the female market, using pink as a colour felt to appeal to women and to make the pill more user-friendly.

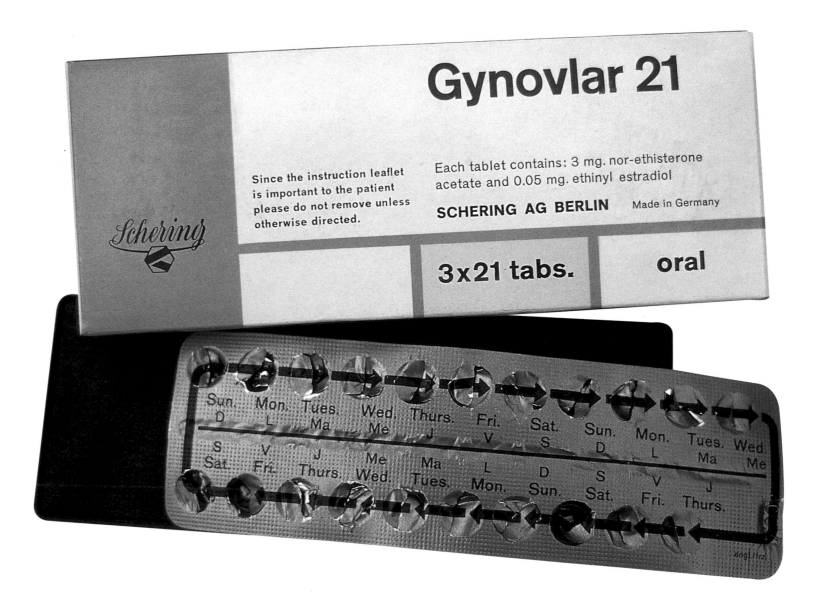

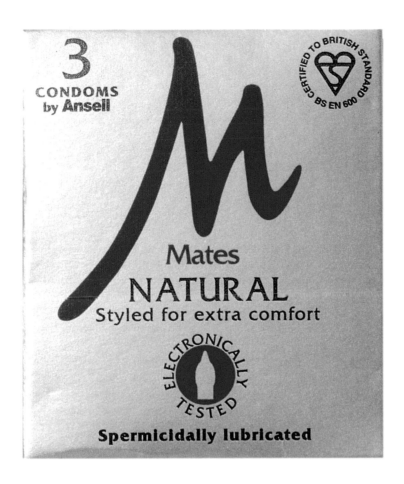

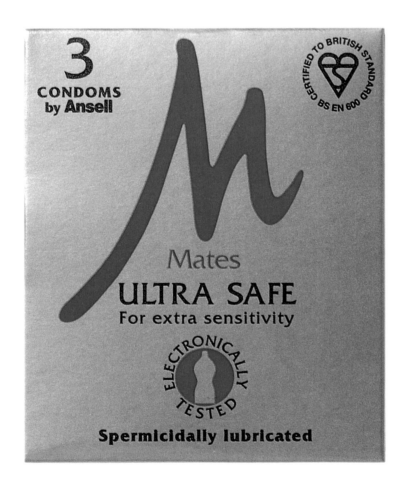

Mates Condom Pack

DATE: this example 1990s

Until the 1980s condoms were a contraceptive device you bought over the chemist's counter, at the barber shop or from a slot machine in the lavatory. This product placement made its purchase if not difficult, then certainly restrictive.

Ansell's Mates were one result of a general move to open up the accessibility of condoms in the light of international concern about Aids. The name and typeface move the product category away from that implied by serious medical names and seek to make Mates a kind of accessory for the young club-goer. This was one product emanating from Richard Branson's Virgin Group that did not carry the Virgin name.

Chanel No.5 Perfume Bottle

DATE: this example 1921

Coco Chanel was already an established figure on the Parisian fashion scene when she launched her exclusive Chanel No.5 perfume in 1921. Although other couturières had marketed their own scents, they were generally based on easily identifiable floral fragrances. Coco Chanel was the first fashion designer to create a completely artificial perfume, with a complex aroma that smelled only of itself. Her aim was to present an independent perfume for the modern woman – a timeless, classic scent to match her clothes.

The idea came about when she was told that a rare sixteenth-century manuscript had been unearthed that was purported to be written by René the Florentine – personal perfume-maker to Queen Catherine de Medici. The creation was a collaboration between Chanel and a perfumier named Ernest Baux, whom she had first met a few years earlier. Baux's legendary concoction combined some eighty different organic chemical ingredients. Like Chanel's dresses, the perfume's presentation was designed to look elegant, simple and expensive – the hallmark of classic chic. The bottle is almost severe in its clear-glass design. The package is free from decoration, with only the words "No.5", "CHANEL" and "Paris". Chanel No.5 has been the biggest selling perfume range in the world. Even though – unlike Chanel clothing – it is priced at a level that most people can reasonably afford, it has managed to retain an air of exclusivity.

L'Eau d'Issey Perfume Bottle

DATE: this example 1997

The perfume industry provides a major opportunity for fashion designers to franchise their names and diversify into new product areas. It is a luxury, exclusive yet highly fragmented market where packaging is the vital means of maintaining image and differentiating fragrances. Glass is still widely used because of its high quality image, crystal clarity and jewel-like appearance. The strong, sculptural Issey Miyake perfume bottle is enhanced by etched glass in a dramatic pyramid form, slightly curved to accommodate the hand. The thick heavy base is finished with a large silver collar topped with a small circle, which is intended to evoke a drop of dew. This individual and minimalist approach reinforces the Miyake company's unique Japanese approach to fashion and styling.

Ty Nant
Water
Bottle

DATE: this example 1989

In 1988 a new technique for colouring glass was introduced by a division of UK company British Foods under licence from an Australian research company, and in 1989 the stylish blue Ty Nant bottle appeared. Ty Nant was the first modern packaged brand to use a distinctive colour of glass to add value and distinction in the highly competitive table water market. The company is one of the few manufacturers in the world that have successfully trademarked a colour–shape combination. The rich blue colour is similar to that of the "Bristol" blue glass introduced in the seventeenth century. Intended as a designer accessory, to be placed alongside the wine bottle in homes and restaurants, the Ty Nant bottle, with its extremely sensuous shape based on burgundy and champagne bottles, looked expensive and exclusive.

The distinctive style and strength of colour enables the consumer to immediately identify a product that would otherwise be inseparable from its contemporaries. In 1989 the bottle won the British Glass Award for Design Excellence. It has been marketed internationally and has proved very popular in the Arab States as well as Italy and Japan.

Sapporo Beer Can

DATE: this example 1988

Sapporo was launched in 1876, and is the oldest surviving Japanese beer on the market. The Sapporo beer can was launched in the UK in 1988 and quickly became the choice of the design-conscious consumer. The can was distinctive in three ways. First, it reflected the minimalist aesthetics of Japanese culture to great effect with its use of black graphics and a tiny red star printed directly onto the natural silver coloured can. Second, the can had a waisted shape, a development that moved it away from a simple functional container towards a shape that evoked a more elegant drinking vessel. Finally, to complete the vessel effect, the can was given a specially constructed lid which could be entirely removed to allow the drinker to use it as if it were a glass.

Harvey Nichols Olive Oil Bottle

DATE: this example 1992

DESIGNER: Michael Nash Associates, London, England

Harvey Nichols is one of London's most famous department stores and justifiably proud of its reputation for retailing some of the world's finest designed products. In the early 1990s it developed its own restaurant and food supermarket and wanted to market the food revolution affecting all of our lives. Harvey Nichols took advantage of the growing fashion for designer foods to package some of the items of the new lifestyle such as virgin olive oil, sun-dried tomatoes and handmade pasta, and present them with the same care and attention to detail as the cosmetics industry applied to creams and perfumes. Here the glass uses 3-D abstract effects to package extra virgin olive oil like fine wine, an approach to detail reflected in the quality of the label graphics and design.

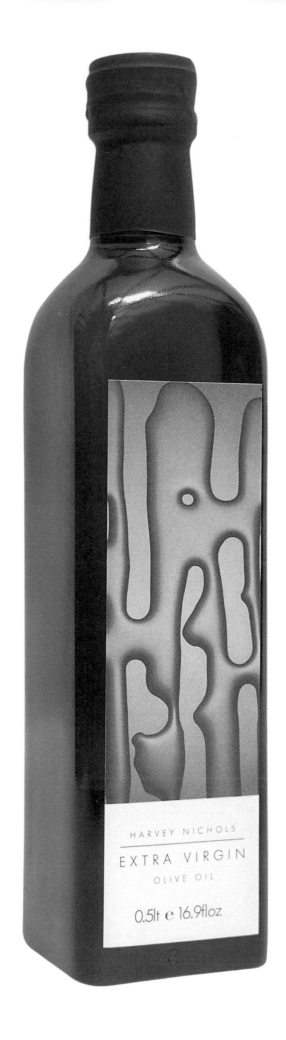

HARVEY NICHOLS

EXTRA VIRGIN

OLIVE OIL

0.5lt e 16.9floz

Artlantic Wine Label

DATE: **this example 1995**

Manufacturers have always recognized the potential of the label to give their product a unique shelf presence. The 1980s saw a move to raise the status of the label into a work of art in its own right as leading artists and illustrators were commissioned to present their work in this form. One well-known example was a series of limited-edition beer labels by the German company Becks, which included images by Gilbert and George. Supermarkets also followed this lead; Waitrose used the work of the illustrator Christopher Wormell for a series of soup cans. The idea was taken a step further by a project called Artlantic.

Oliver Peyton is part of the new revolution in bars and restaurants that have opened in London in the 1990s. His stylish Atlantic Bar and Grill produced a selection of wines each with a special edition label, commissioned from well-known artists including Damien Hirst, the Japanese sculptor Tatsuo Mijajima and Sarah Lucas. The Atlantic company offered these wines for sale in the restaurant or to buy to take away. Atlantic described the project as "a new concept in portable, consumable art". The idea, however, reflects a more widespread move to place contemporary art in these popular bars and restaurants, giving the consumer an opportunity not only to socialize, but to view the latest work of leading artists. In this way, a new generation of restaurants are challenging the idea that art can only be seen in conventional places such as galleries and they point the way forward for a new approach to integrating art and design into the experience of everyday life.

Body Shop Cosmetics

DATE: this example 1990s

"No glossy advertising, no wild promises, no products tested on animals, only minimal packaging and products which have minimal impact on the environment." This quote, taken from the Body Shop's official website, perfectly encapsulates the philosophy of the company. The Body Shop was founded in 1976 by Anita Roddick. Originally just one small retail outlet in Brighton, it is now an internationally successful company.

With environmental concerns now at the forefront of public concern, emphasis has been placed on excessive consumption, which relates directly to packaging and its possible waste of natural resources. The Body Shop, with its green image, has tapped in to the public conscience, with its minimal packaging – no excess packaging is used – and policy of recycling and refilling. The distinctive labels are generally green and white, colours that themselves evoke the company's ecological and environmental standpoint.

Daz Detergent Pouch

DATE: this example 1990s

Some of the more recent and important changes in packaging include the introduction of refill systems, and with concerns about the wastage of natural resources high on political and social agendas these developments have the important effect of reducing the amount of materials used. Refill is nothing new in itself. In the United Kingdom many still enjoy the survival of doorstep delivery of milk and in France some wines are sold in refillable bottles. A new idea is the availability of refilling at home. This can be seen in the reduction of packaging sizes for detergents such as Daz, allowing them to be used in concentrated form. In addition shops now sell these products in two different packages: a strong metal or cardboard box and in lightweight pouches, which typically save seventy per cent of the material. Customers first buy the stronger containers, then the pouches as refills. The packaging of liquid detergent in thin pouches that can easily be taken home is now a popular trend. Although detergent is the best example such packaging has also been introduced for shampoo, while Germany has seen experiments in pouch packaging for food products such as jam.

PART 11

advertising

SALON DES CENT POSTER

DUTCH POST OFFICE

VOLKSWAGEN

THE ADVERTISING INDUSTRY had its modern origins in the development of the Industrial Revolution and the concept of a modern consumer culture, but it can be traced back even to Roman times: images on walls advertising goods and services survive at Pompeii. In the late eighteenth century pioneer manufacturers, such as Josiah Wedgwood, recognized an important fact – simply producing goods was not enough: in order to become a commercial success you had to market and advertise your products. From the 1760s Wedgwood did this by placing simple notices in the press and by launching the first catalogue of his products, which enabled people to peruse and select his ceramics from the comfort of their own home.

In the nineteenth century manufacturers were quick to realize the potential of the single striking image, and signs painted on buildings to advertise products became commonplace. These were followed by temporary paper posters and then purpose-built billboards, which appeared on major roadsides and city junctions. By the end of the nineteenth century the use of press and magazine advertisements had become a key element in marketing campaigns: the commercial world of advertising had come into being. In the early years of the twentieth century many commentators wrote with disapproval about the sheer amount of commercial visual imagery that had started to appeared in the modern city. Manufacturers had always exploited the power of the visual image and recruited well-known artists as well as commercial illustrators to perform this task. By the end of the nineteenth century the world of advertising had recruited some of Europe's most influential painters including John Everett Millais, Aubrey Beardsley and Toulouse Lautrec. Some artists, like Alphonse Mucha, were ultimately to become better known for their individual advertisements than for their art. Essentially the advertising industry itself remained in the hands of such talented individuals who used the medium as a successful way to develop both their style and the product's success. Into this category falls one of the most important poster artists of the century: Cassandre. His streamlined Modernist images remain some of the most enduring advertisements of the period.

In the twentieth century possibilities expanded rapidly and advertising was quick to exploit the potential of neon and electrical signs, radio, the cinema and television to the point where it has become an entertainment industry in its own right.

The advertising industry, with agencies and teams of marketing experts, was slowly beginning to develop, and in this America led the way. The 1920s saw the first development of professional advertising agencies in the USA, centred around New York's Madison Avenue, and these were imitated around the world.

BIRTH CONTROL

Many adverts in the 1920s exploited the new art of Cubism and Surrealism. The Surrealists sought to undermine bourgeois morals by unleashing the dangerous, erotic and disturbing world of the subconscious through their art. Initially launched as a literary group in 1924 by André Breton with his *Manifeste du Surréalisme*, the movement quickly gained the support of visual artists such as Salvador Dali, Marcel Duchamp, Max Ernst and Man Ray, all of whom influenced or were employed in advertising.

The surrealists experimented with ways of delving into their hidden desires and memories through chance operations, automatic writing and collaborative drawings. They also believed that the removal of objects from their context and the juxtaposition of unassociated objects would produce a momentary shock in the viewer that would facilitate the release of subconscious thoughts. Their approach could have been written as a plan for any successful advertising campaign and in this way their influence filtered into the mainstream world. Indeed for many people advertising was their first direct experience of the world of the avant-garde and this language of visual imagery still continues to be used in campaigns for products including cigarettes and drinks.

Advertising promises us much more than the commodity it seeks to sell. It suggests a fantasy lifestyle. It is an escape from reality. Advertising plays on our dreams and insecurities, but above all on our sexual desires. If you're not getting enough sex, it's because you don't drink a particular soft drink, don't wear the right perfume or don't drive the newest car. At the turn of the century, Alphonse Mucha and Jules Cheret injected their posters with an erotic charge without offending gentle sensibilities, by evoking the classical nude tradition of the fine arts.

As attitudes to sex have relaxed over the decades, sexual imagery in advertising has become ever more blatant, abandoning innuendo and coquettishness in favour of a direct assault on the libido. Now, the promise of sexual allure has been employed to promote goods as diverse as perfume, chocolate, shampoo, washing-up liquid and chewing gum. The 1970s saw the high point of obvious sexual manipulation in advertising. The

Be a good sport

"OLYMPICS" ANTI-AIDS CAMPAIGN

vulgarity and crassness of the sexual stereotypes of that period have now become unpopular as audiences have a more sophisticated attitude towards gender and sex. For example the recent commodification of the male body has added a new dimension to advertising seen in campaigns such as those for the fashion designer Calvin Klein. The man is no longer the simple macho figure of the 1970s – he is now a more complex entity, shifting between Michelangelo's David, the New Man and the New Lad. In this way advertising continues to reflect and direct important social trends and provides us with important readings of culture at the end of the century.

ANTI DRUGS

Salon des Cent Exhibition Poster

DATE: 1896

DESIGNER: Alphonse Mucha
(1860–1939)

Europe at the turn of the century
saw the birth of Art Nouveau. Mucha
was the first master of erotic
advertising. His skill as an artist
attracted many leading companies
who paid him royally to design
posters advertising products as
diverse as champagne and bicycles.
In most of his posters the products
advertised are upstaged by Mucha's
mysterious and beautiful women,
scantily clad in veils. Art Nouveau
was an inevitable reaction against
the repressive attitude to sexuality
that typified life in the nineteenth
century. In the world of art and
design these defining concerns
surfaced not only in the posters of
Alphonse Mucha but those of
Toulouse Lautrec and Aubrey
Beardsley. They produced unique
artistic forms that contained
exaggerated forms and naturalistic
shapes that almost invariably
focused on the female body and
cast the woman in the role of the
femme fatale.

AEG Poster

DATE: 1910

DESIGNER: Peter Behrens (1868–1941)

Although Peter Behrens began his career working influenced by the new *Jugendstil* movement, a restrained form of Art Nouveau, he is important in the history of advertising because he was one of the first poster designers to articulate a visual language for the new spirit of the twentieth century. When in 1907 he was invited by Emil Rathennau, director of the Allgemeine Elektricitäts-Gesellschaft (AEG), to become its artistic director he developed the first concept of company corporate identity. AEG occupied a considerable power in German industry and its output covered generators, electrical cable, light bulbs and electrical appliances not only for the domestic but the world market. From 1907 until 1914 Behrens was responsible for all aspects of the company's output from architecture to posters and products and he used his position to establish AEG as a model for the new German design. His influence was manifold. In 1907 he was a founder member of the Deutsche Werkbund, he designed typefaces and was responsible for one of Germany's earliest Modernist building the AEG's steel, glass and concrete turbine factory of 1909. In his position as art director he employed some of Europe's brightest young talents, including Le Corbusier, Mies van der Rohe and Walter Gropius.

Nord Express

DATE: 1927

DESIGNER: A.M. Cassandre (1901–68)

A.M. Cassandre is one of the best-known poster artists and type designers of the twentieth century. From the late 1920s to the early 1930s he produced a series of memorable advertisements whose influence continues to this day. Cassandre's achievement was to bring the creative experiments of avant-garde movements such as Cubism into the mainstream world of advertising. His technique employed a brilliant use of colour, powerful geometric forms and a brilliant integration of the company name with the image. Posters advertising trains like the classic Etoile du Nord and ships like the Normandie have now become some of the best-known advertisements in the world. The advertising agency that produced this work, and of which Cassandre was a founding partner, was the Alliance Graphique in Paris. They produced some of the most memorable poster images of the century and established a French style that evoked stylish, urban Parisian life. At the same time Cassandre also designed typefaces for the old-established Paris-based type supplier Deberny and Peignot. Cassandre typefaces balanced Modernism with a fresh approach to letterforms and this was to become a deeply influential tradition. He restricted letterforms on his posters to capitals, believing that they enhanced the effect of the poster and allowed the type to be used on a large scale without affecting legibility.

London Transport Poster

DATE: 1932

DESIGNER: Man Ray
(1870–1976)

CLIENT: London Transport,
London, England

Man Ray studied art in New York and participated in the city's famous Armoury Show of 1913, which introduced to America to the new spirit of European Modernism. Shortly after this date he became the friend and collaborator of the artist Marcel Duchamp and worked across many different media. Perhaps Man Ray's most original contribution was to photography, with his invention of images made directly onto film, which he called Rayographs. In the 1930s his work as a commercial photographer for a number of important fashion magazines disseminated his unique style to a wider audience and in 1939 he was invited to design a poster for London Transport. Man Ray actually produced two posters, one with the text, LT, the other with the copy "Keeps London Going", which were intended to be seen as a pair. Here the famous London Transport logo is transformed into a 3-D planet, which orbits around Saturn. London Transport therefore enters the firmament of the stars with its connections of speed, distance and the future. In this way Man Ray introduced to the British public the ideas of the Surrealist movement. The Surrealists experimented with ways of delving into hidden desires and memories through chance operations and automatic writing. The Man Ray poster is an example of the way the fine art imagery of Surrealism in the 1930s filtered through to the world of advertising and graphic design.

LONDON TRANSPORT –

London
Transport
Poster

DATE: 1949

DESIGNER: Edward McKnight
Kauffer (1890–1954)

CLIENT: London Transport,
London, England

Born and trained as a painter in
America, McKnight Kauffer became a
leading figure in British advertising
when he moved to London at the
age of twenty-five, although he
continued to paint for the rest of
his life. From 1913, as a young man,
he had seen at first hand the work
of the leading avant-garde
movements including Vorticism,
Futurism and Cubism. His talent was
to simplify the elements he
recognized in this new art to
produce a original advertising style
that was effective, popular and
successful. His first job was
designing posters for London
Transport whose publicity manager,
the legendary Frank Pick, was
scouting for young talent to create a
modern image for what was to
become the world's most extensive
city transport system. For over
twenty years, until the outbreak of
World War Two, when he emigrated
to America with his wife, the well-
known Modernist designer of
carpets and textiles, Marion Dorn,
McKnight Kauffer was considered to
be London Transport's leading
poster designer and completed over
one hundred advertisements.

Shell Mex Limited was the name under which the international Shell Group ran its British marketing operation and in 1932 they appointed a new Publicity Director, J.L. Beddington. His insight turned the British Shell advertisements of the 1930s into one of the classic campaigns of the twentieth century. Shell used the advertisements on the sides of their lorries and in the press. They were intended to appear in series, and to change every few weeks with the aim of striking a blow against the use of ugly hoardings that many felt were becoming a blight in the countryside. It was Beddington who decided to use a range of leading Modernist painters to provide strikingly original images for their product and the posters became works of art in their right. The idea of using leading artists to create advertising images was not new, there is a long tradition of such examples going back to the famous "Bubbles" painting by John Millais for Pears Soap. What made the Shell campaign so interesting, however, was that it was a clearly directed series that attracted attention for the product via its association with the new, and then daring, art of painters including McKnight Kauffer, Barnett Freedman and Graham Sutherland, who created this poster depicting the Great Globe at Swanage. The original paintings and artwork were hung throughout Shell Mex House and gathered together for special exhibitions including one at the London's National Gallery.

Everywhere You Go

DATE: 1932

DESIGNER: Graham Sutherland (1903–80)

CLIENT: Shell Mex Limited, London, England

DATE: 1940

CLIENT: HMSO, England;
printer J. Weiner Ltd,
London, England

In 1939 World War Two brought the careers of most designers to a close. The majority were called up for active duty, but the war effort did require certain design specialists and nowhere was this more urgently needed than in the field of propaganda. The British Ministry of Information needed the talents of graphic designers to spread public information, to increase morale and to use every weapon they could in the fight against the Nazis. A team of the best designers was therefore recruited to work for the Ministry, and subject to strict censorship, were allowed to develop the most effective design solutions to produce wartime propaganda. For many this meant going back to the most influential themes of the 1930s, including the impact of Surrealism, the introduction of photomontage and the bold use of type to create the strong visual images needed to bring home vital messages for the war effort.
The message in this poster was simple: save resources and grow your own food. "Dig For Victory" employed these avant-garde experiments to great effect, the bright orange colour, the scale and the bold use of large type enhance the dramatic image of the digging foot and spade.

Dutch Post Office

DATE: 1934

DESIGNER: Piet Zwart
(1885–1977)

During the twentieth century The Netherlands has always enjoyed a rich tradition of innovation in graphic and type design. From the 1920s Piet Zwart was the designer whose work helped to establish a particularly creative and fresh flavour to Dutch Modernist advertising. After World War One, Zwart became closely involved with the radical Dutch De Stijl movement working for one of its leading architects, Jan Wils. Through him Zwart met an important client, N.V. Nederlandsche Kabelfabriek, for whom he began designing posters. Zwart overturned the conventions of advertising by introducing the techniques of photomontage and random lettering. This work owes a debt to the experiments of Russian Constructivists whose work was published in the *De Stijl* magazine of the time. Although Zwart used the De Stijl preference for primary colours in his work his approach was freer and more exuberant than the formalist tradition of Dutch graphic design. He introduced the ideas of the Dada group and their exploitation of elements of humour and irony. The appeal and originality of Zwart's work attracted the attention of the Dutch Post Office (PTT) and from 1929 he began a long collaboration with them, working on the design of stamps and other material.

Air France

DATE: C.1965

DESIGNER: Roger Excoffon (1910–83)

Roger Excoffon is not well known outside his own country, but his work, more than any other graphic designer's, came to define a sense of postwar French style shown here in this powerful poster for Air France. Best known as the designer of freeform typefaces in the 1950s, in the 1960s Excoffon moved away from the flamboyance of his earlier work with the design for the typeface Antique Olive, now called Nord. It was a move he acknowledged as a commercial decision, prompted by the demand from French printers for a clean 1960s feel, in line with the success of the Helvetica and Univers sans serif faces.

Antique Olive started life in the late 1950s as a prototype upper case face for the Air France logo. With his assistant Gerard Blanchard, Excoffon embarked on a serious research programme reading all the literature and research they could find on legibility and the psychology and impact of reading. They came to the conclusion that the upper half of the letters are the most important in word recognition and Excoffon therefore emphasized that aspect of the new face's character. Antique Olive was hugely popular and is largely credited with revitalizing the sans serif letter forms. Key advertising projects included work for Bally shoes, French Railways and Christian Dior perfume. Typical hallmarks of the Excoffon style included the use of off-register or double printing, and interesting use of colour.

Olivetti

DATE: 1949

DESIGNER: Giovanni Pintori
(born 1912)

Olivetti have played a key role in the development of twentieth-century Italian design. This family firm applied key lessons learnt from America about production methods and marketing techniques and more importantly, the need for good design. Adriano Olivetti, the company founder's son employed Pintori along with another leading Italian designer, Marcello Nizzoli, the former given responsibility for advertising and graphics, the latter for industrial design. In the postwar period Olivetti's ambitions were to place the company at the leading edge of new technology and Pintori's brief was to reinforce this message via its advertisements. In 1947 he was responsible for the redesign of the company's logo and went onto develop a series of major advertising campaigns of which this poster was one of the most significant. In the 1940s Olivetti was justifiably proud of its technological achievement in the field of calculating machines most notably Nizzoli's Divisumma 14 adding machine. It was the spirit of such machines that Pintori's type design evoked with his use of chaotic, randomly sized and spaced numbers in bright colours. This image owes a debt to the Italian tradition of Futurist graphics but here given a contemporary modern feel with Pintori's Olivetti logo placed prominently in the centre.

Family Dog

DATE: 1967

DESIGNER: Rick Griffin
(1944–1991)

In the 1960s the arrival of Pop Design challenged the traditions of Modernism. Pop Design was instant, expendable, witty and ironic. In California, a number of people, often not trained as designers, created posters for bands, which were a conscious reaction to the "boring" Swiss-influenced design around them. Based in the Haight Ashbury district of San Francisco, and active participants in the emerging counter-culture movement, designers such as Stanley Mouse, Rick Griffin, Victor Moscoso and Alton Kelley, created posters with bright, clashing colours inspired by their experience of psychedelic drugs and Indian mysticism. Because they did not work for the mainstream, Madison Avenue world of advertising they were also free to break all the rules about legibility, clarity and communication. Influenced by the organic letter forms of Art Nouveau they created complex lettering, in which legibility took second place to the overall shape of the word. These posters were also intended to reflect the experience of the acid trip and targeted at the members of the counter culture who recognize the signs and codings of this group. Certain elements were picked up by the mainstream, such as hand-drawn type and colour, but the real impact and revival of these posters was to be seen in the 1980s and 1990s.

Volkswagen

DATE: 1960

DESIGNER: Doyle, Dane Bernbach, New York City, USA

CLIENT: Volkswagen, Germany

In the postwar period, when raw materials were scarce and petrol was rationed, the small economy car was of great significance to the European motor industry. However, no such constraints affected the USA and therefore, a more sophisticated marketing strategy was needed to win sales for the Volkswagen "Beetle" or "Bug" as it is known in the US. The company therefore decided to employ one of New York's most creative agencies, Doyle, Dane Bernbach (DDB), to devise an advertising campaign for the Beetle. Compared to American car design, the Beetle was quirky looking, to say the least. DDB were at the centre of a revolution in the advertising industry which was to give art directors equal roles with copywriters and which was to free up the creative possibilities of image, type and copy. These elements came together to create and award-winning campaign for the Beetle, which set new industry standards. Appealing to a new generation in the 1960s, the campaign was witty and amusing, here playing with the car's unusual shape and making a virtue, not a necessity of its engineering advantages.

© 1960 VOLKSWAGEN

Lemon.

This Volkswagen missed the boat.

The chrome strip on the glove compartment is blemished and must be replaced. Chances are you wouldn't have noticed it; Inspector Kurt Kroner did.

There are 3,389 men at our Wolfsburg factory with only one job: to inspect Volkswagens at each stage of production. (3000 Volkswagens are produced daily; there are more inspectors than cars.)

Every shock absorber is tested (spot checking won't do), every windshield is scanned. VWs have been rejected for surface scratches barely visible to the eye.

Final inspection is really something! VW inspectors run each car off the line onto the Funktionsprüfstand (car test stand), tote up 189 check points, gun ahead to the automatic brake stand, and say "no" to one VW out of fifty.

This preoccupation with detail means the VW lasts longer and requires less maintenance, by and large, than other cars. (It also means a used VW depreciates less than any other car.)

We pluck the lemons; you get the plums.

Benson and Hedges

DATE: 1978

DESIGNER: CDP, London, England

In the late 1970s the Hayward Gallery in London put on an important exhibition exploring Surrealism. The exhibition revived interest in the language of Surrealism and the way in which imagery could delve into hidden desires and memories through chance operations, automatic writing and collaborative drawings. The Surrealists believed that the removal of objects from their context and the juxtaposition of unassociated objects would produce a momentary shock in the viewer that would facilitate the release of subconscious thoughts. The potential to exploit these elements for advertising was recognized early on and during the 1930s these images filtered through to the wider world of film design, fashion and furniture as well as advertising and graphic design. Benson and Hedges were one of the first companies to exploit Surrealism for another agenda. In the 1970s the message that smoking kills began to reach a wider audience and governments began to restrict the kind of advertising manufacturers had used to promote their product in the past. No longer could smoking be shown as attractive to young people, as enjoyable and safe. Surrealism provided a visual medium to sell cigarettes which still continues to this day in campaigns for the Silk Cut and Marlboro brands. By using the Surrealist device of the unexpected, the consumer is drawn to the package and identity of the product but no claims are made, merely the association of the pack with wit, creativity and humour which the consumer has to learn to identify.

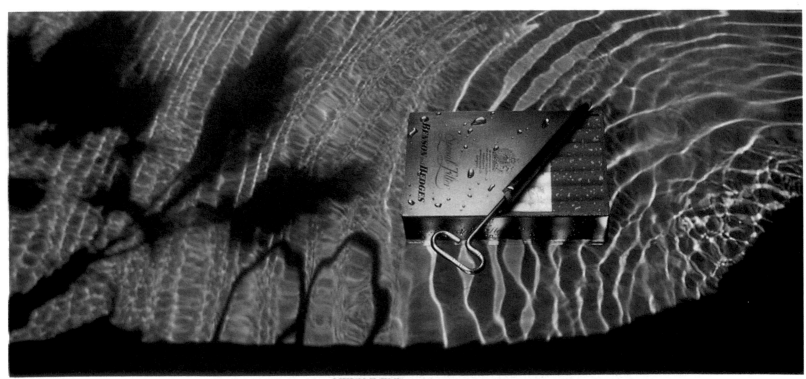

MIDDLE TAR As defined by H.M. Government
H.M. Government Health Departments' WARNING: CIGARETTES CAN SERIOUSLY DAMAGE YOUR HEALTH

Birth Control

DATE: 1970

DESIGNER: Saatchi and Saatchi, London, England

CLIENT: Health Education Council, England

This public health campaign also defined the trademarks of the new British advertising industry of the 1960s and 1970s. British agencies were now known for their use of humour, bold imagery and strong copy, taking on New York as the centre for creative advertising. For the generation born in the 1950s this poster promoting the use of contraception to prevent unwanted pregnancies remains an enduring image. The simple idea of faking an image of a male pregnancy made a simple and direct point that the responsibilities of a sexual relationship involved two people. By suggesting that men could get pregnant the campaign challenged the then widely held belief that unwanted babies were the problem and responsibility of the woman alone. In 1970 by emphasizing this obvious point the campaign touched upon the newly emerging ideas of the women's movement but gained widespread sympathy with its use of humour and Surrealist imagery.

Would you be more careful if it was you that got pregnant?

Anyone married or single can get advice on contraception from the Family Planning Association Margaret Pyke House, 27-35 Mortimer Street, London W1 N 8BQ. Tel. 01-636 9135.

The Health Education Council

Launderette

DATE: 1985

DESIGNER: Bartle Bogle Hegarty, London, England

CLIENT: Levi Strauss, USA

In the 1980s the world-famous Levi's Jeans company faced a financial crisis. Levi's had diversified into the wider clothing market, producing suits and accessories, but in doing so had lost its unique product focus. In the decade of the designer 1980s it looked to target its classic original denim jeans, the Levi's 501, and it needed a powerful advertising campaign to put across the message. When John Hegarty of Bartle Bogle Hegarty, one of London's best-known advertising agencies, created this sexy nostalgic theme an advertising legend was born.

Using a brilliant mix of the allure of the model Nick Kamen, references to 1950s youth culture and a touch of humour, the campaign was an instant success. Sales of Levi's 501s soared and the jeans became one of the most important fashion accessories of the decade. Bartle, Bogle and Hegarty followed this first advertisement with a series of eye-catching ads, usually based on a classic films and movie genres, which not only established a standard for Levi's but for the rest of the advertising industry.

These black and white advertisements created a sensation when they first appeared in 1991. The blatant sensual sell of these images was not unique, but the combination of product and association was. Ice cream was traditionally a seasonal market dominated in Britain by companies such as Walls and Lyons Maid. Campaigns were usually targeted at housewives and children or, exceptionally, a product aimed for the dinner party. Here the American company Häagen-Dazs targeted young affluent couples, using ice cream as a luxury up-market experience. The vogue for black and white erotic imagery originally came from the work of pioneer New York photographers including Herb Ritts and Robert Mapplethorpe and here, in an image taken by Jean Loup Sief the same explicit sensual allure is used to sell a product previously marketed as an ordinary commodity for the family.

Body Texture

DATE: 1991

DESIGNER: Bartle Bogle Hegarty, London, England

CLIENT: Häagen-Dazs, USA

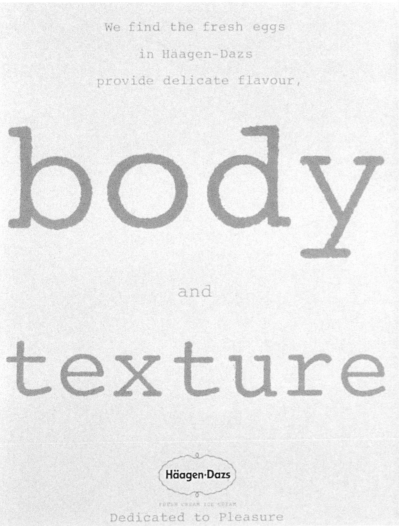

Olympics

DATE: 1992

DESIGNER: TBW,
Simons Palmer

CLIENT: Terence Higgins
Trust, London, England

The Terence Higgins Trust is a London-based charity that enjoys an international reputation for its pioneer work with Aids patients and their families. One of their first goals was to try and break down the massive public ignorance surrounding the disease and to try and ensure that Aids was not consigned to the gay community. Within this context, the publicity campaign the Trust commissioned reflects their overall strategy. The brief was not to present a terrifying message of death and despair but to target young heterosexual and gay couples using the same advertising techniques employed by fashionable and stylish companies such as Calvin Klein. The advertisments portrayed young and healthy people; they were not frightening images but friendly, informative and accessible. In this respect, they made an interesting contrast to the Government's public health campaign and they helped to inform a wide audience of young people at risk.

Be a good sport

The Terrence Higgins Trust ♡

For more information about safer sex call our helpline on 071-242 1010.

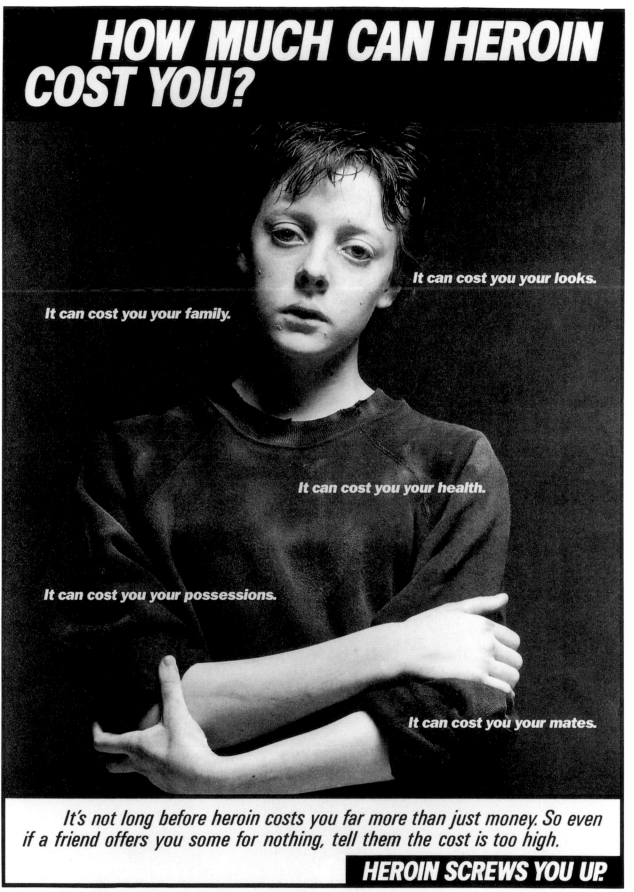

HOW MUCH CAN HEROIN COST YOU?

It can cost you your looks.

It can cost you your family.

It can cost you your health.

It can cost you your possessions.

It can cost you your mates.

It's not long before heroin costs you far more than just money. So even if a friend offers you some for nothing, tell them the cost is too high.

HEROIN SCREWS YOU UP.

DMP 5/86 PREPARED BY THE DEPARTMENT OF HEALTH AND SOCIAL SECURITY AND THE CENTRAL OFFICE OF INFORMATION PRINTED IN THE UK J0278NJ (HSSH) OCTOBER 86

How Much Can Heroin Cost You?

DATE: 1986

DESIGNER: TBWA, London, England

CLIENT: Department of Health and Social Security, UK

This campaign was launched in 1986 by the British Department of Health and Social Security. Its aim was to emphasize the terrible social consequences of heroin misuse among young people. The campaign used television commercials and press advertisements in the same series and its gritty, hard-hitting imagery made an immediate impact. The close-up black and white photographs spelled out in graphic detail the effect drug addiction had on teenagers' skin, hair, weight and general health. The message was simple: drugs are not only dangerous, they can ultimately kill. Although the style owes a great debt to the photographic style seen in influential British magazines such as *The Face* and *i-d*, there is no attempt to romanticize drugs. Within the advertising industry, this campaign was seen as an important shift in direction and ironically in the late 1980s its "style" was to be reworked as a marketing tool to promote rather different products, including ice cream and denim jeans.

Wolford Tights

DATE: 1994

DESIGNER: Helmut Newton
(born 1920)

In the 1970s Newton dominated the world of fashion photography with his images for French *Vogue* magazine, which were more often to do with the naked woman than the clothes they wore. He played up to decades of fashionable obsessions with themes of cross gender and chic gay and transvestite culture seen in the imagery of pop via David Bowie and Roxy Music. Newton's style became enormously influential and set the scene in the 1980s for the work of equally controversial photographs from Bruce Weber and Herb Ritts.

Helmut Newton was commissioned to take a series of startling black and white photographs to market Wolford tights. In his commission for Wolford, Newton used blatant sado-masochistic imagery, here in the use of leather ankle straps, black gloves, metal handcuffs and the leather riding crop. Wolford is a well-known hosiery company which produces top of the range tights and stockings much favoured by the fashion industry. In the 1980s it pioneered dense black tights using Lycra. Their products are expensive quality items aimed at a sophisticated market which Wolford felt could appreciate such controversial imagery.

What makes these images so extraordinary is the way the campaign played on references to lesbianism and sexual violence and combined them in such a blatant way to sell tights to women. Although tights and stockings both have a deeply fetishistic appeal, nonetheless this is a fascinating reflection of cultural values in the 1990s.

Tiger Savage is exceptional in the advertising world as a successful female art director. Her distinctive approach was expressed in a series of press advertisements and posters for Nike, a campaign that won several awards for its fresh and arresting use of images. The market for trainers is a huge and intensely competitive one which relies on advertising to create the right image. Savage felt that press advertisements and posters needed to be concise and to-the-point and that type and copy can often obscure the important selling message. If the image is strong enough, she argued, why detract from it? The Nike campaign in the United Kingdom proved to be something of an advertising milestone, as it was the first campaign to use advertisements with no copy. Instead it built its reputation on the dynamic interplay between image and headline. The first advertisement featured tennis champion Pete Sampras serving not a tennis ball but a grenade. This was followed soon after by a road symbol placed over a group of marathon runners. Tiger Savage's ability to achieve a strong, personal visual style for this client won her the award for best newcomer from the Creative Circle in 1984.

Gary Who?

DATE: 1996

DESIGNERS: Simons, Palmer Denton, Clemmow and Johnston, London, England

CLIENT: Nike

communication

THE COMMUNICATION INVENTIONS of the twentieth century have transformed the workplace and the ways in which business transactions are undertaken: they have revolutionized the pace and quality of domestic life in virtually every household in the industrialized world. The key inventions in the field of communications in the twentieth century are the radio, the television and the computer. But the twentieth century has also witnessed the massive development and refinement of essentially nineteenth-century inventions: the telegraph, the telephone, the camera and the typewriter.

CANDLESTICK

Of these, the camera gave individuals the possibility of documenting their own lives and society. However, the most significant inventions in terms of communications were the telegraph, the typewriter and the telephone. The Morse telegraph, established in 1844, enabled a telegraph message to be relayed thousands of kilometres in a matter of minutes. The telephone, invented in 1876 by Alexander Graham Bell, effected an even greater revolution, not only in the office, but in the home, becoming the most important means of communication between people in home to offices in cities all over the world. Typewriters were another invention that helped bring about the modern communication age. Invented in 1866 by Latham Sholes, and first manufactured by Remington and

ECKO

COLANI CANON

Son, typewriters transformed the old-style reliance on pen and ink. Typewriters also transformed the office. Frank Lloyd Wright's design for the Larkin Building in Buffalo, New York in 1904 was one of the first designs to accommodate the needs of the newly automated office. The Larkin Building housed 1,800 clerical staff processing mail-order enquiries. The development of the typewriter in the twentieth century followed the familiar pattern of modifications to increase speed and output as an expression of even greater efficiency. This saw the introduction of portable machines from the 1930s, the elimination of cumbersome levers with the invention of the IBM Golfball typewriter of the 1960s and the introduction of electronic machines in the 1970s. Nowadays the typewriter survives as the keyboard attached to a personal computer and its letter layout – the standard QWERTY sequence – remains virtually the same. With the introduction of scanning and voice technology however, the future of the keyboard looks increasingly uncertain.

Communications via public broadcasting, the cinema and television industries, and the ability to play music in the home, via record players, introduced other fundamental transformations to twentieth-century life. In 1896, Gugliemo Marconi patented a system that used "no wire" connection and the following year he registered his Wireless Telegraph and Signal Company. By the end of World War One, Marconi's system was used around the world as a means of linking ships at sea and by the 1920s this system was used for organized public broadcasting of entertainment programmes, leading in 1922 to the formation of the British Broadcasting Company in Britain. The earliest radio sets were either crystal sets or battery driven valve receivers, the former unreliable and the latter expensive. By the end of the 1920s, however, there was a radical change to the design of radios. With the electric components now housed internally, the manufacturer could concentrate on the design of the exterior casing and the radio was brought into the living room as a piece of furniture. Smaller and more personal products soon followed, notably the launch of the Sony transistor radio in the

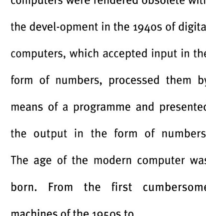
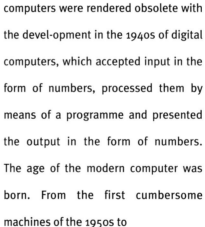

OLYMPUS TRIP

1950s. Such developments would lead to the manufacture of integrated sound systems including radios, record and compact disc players and personal stereos. Television design followed a similar pattern from the large wooden cabinets of the 1930s to hand-held models in the 1990s. Pioneered in 1925 by a British inventor, John Logie Baird, his 1930 Televisior was a neon lamp that flickered in response to the television signal from the owner's radio receiver. On November 2, 1935 the BBC began the world's first regular television transmission service at Alexandra Palace. The television revolution was in place.

Few technological advances, however, have had such a decisive effect on the twentieth century as the computer. The earliest types of computer were known as analog and analysed physical qualities such as electrical voltage and gave output in the form of other physical qualities. These computers offered extremely limited options and were designed to solve specific problems such as the point at which a bridge might collapse in high winds. Analog computers were rendered obsolete with the devel-opment in the 1940s of digital computers, which accepted input in the form of numbers, processed them by means of a programme and presented the output in the form of numbers. The age of the modern computer was born. From the first cumbersome machines of the 1950s to the invention of the silicon chip in the 1960s, which enabled cheap and portable computer technology, our industrialized way of life has been completely transformed. Before the computer, the story of industrial advancement was essentially the production of ever more specialized machines. Now the computer can be used for literally millions of different applications. It is hard to imagine how any modern business could operate without the service of modern information technology and telecommunications.

WALKMAN

APPLE EMATE 300

Candlestick Telephone GPO 150

DATE: 1924

MATERIAL: Bakelite

MANUFACTURER: General Post Office, London, England

The candlestick telephone was one of the most common designs in the early decades of the twentieth century and became the international standard table telephone. Although the version shown here is British, it was virtually indistinguishable from its American counterpart. One development that had a lasting impact on telephone design was the evolution of plastics. Telephone manufacturers looked for a material from which telephone components could be made easily and cheaply. In the 1920s improvement in chemical engineering and moulding techniques made Bakelite, from which the 150 is made. The major disadvantage of the candlestick was the fact that the mouthpiece was fixed onto the base, forcing the user either to crouch near to the telephone or hold both parts, one in each hand. Improvements in transmitter design, through electronic amplification, did not come until the late 1920s after research by engineers commissioned by the American Bell Company. Initially calls could only be made through the operator but the introduction of the dial, for which space was made on the base, enabled the caller to make connections automatically. The shape proved extremely popular and this standard table telephone lasted for many years. It is still marketed as a reproduction piece.

The Ericofon was conceived as a lightweight and compact version of the standard two-piece telephone. Its sculptural form was startlingly original, its shape incorporating the ear piece, speaker and dial into a single unit. This was made possible by the new technology of miniaturization. Over the course of the following fourteen years the Ericofon developed through new versions that saw successive improvements in its engineering and its form. The gradual evolution of the product was led by the Blomberg team of designers over a fifteen-year period. Its commercial success was established in 1954 when the Ericofon became available in a series of bright colours. Ericsson was the first company to manufacture telephones in Sweden and it remains the largest.

Ericofon

DATE: 1949

DESIGNERS: Hugo Blomberg (born 1897), Ralph Lysell (born 1907) and Gösta Thames (born 1916)

MATERIAL: plastic and rubber

MANUFACTURER: L. M. Ericsson, Sweden

Nokia 9000 Communicator

DATE: 1996

DESIGNER: Nokia in-house design team

MATERIAL: plastic

MANUFACTURER: Nokia Corporation, Finland

The Finnish Nokia company has developed the latest range of personal telephone communications, which represents an important step towards miniaturization. The Nokia 9000 Communicator allows the user to carry around a whole series of facilities. It combines digital voice, data services and personal organizer functions into a pocket-sized and easy-to-use unit. The Communicator features an impressive list of applications, including telephone, fax, e-mail, Internet browser, personal organizer, messaging terminal, calendar and calculator. It has an infra-red PC and printer connection and has an eight-megabyte memory.

Established in 1980, Hollington is a well-known British design consultancy with an international reputation for innovative products, ranging from furniture to pens and interactive design. Hollington was commissioned by a Dallas-based company, Camelot, specialists in Internet-related software, whose Digiphone Internet telephone package is a market-leader. To complement the Digiphone, Camelot wanted to develop a new class of telephone product. The Proficia is essentially a computer phone for making low-cost calls via the Internet; it is placed on the desktop along with the keyboard and mouse. The visual character of the handset has the quality of a small animal, with the back-wire resembling a tail; while the ergonomic balance requires the handset to be stable and comfortable to use wherever it is placed.

Proficia Internet Telephone Handset

DATE: 1997

DESIGNER: Geoff Hollington, Richard Arnott and Liz Ciokajlo

MATERIAL: injection-moulded ABS plastic

MANUFACTURER: Camelot Corporation, USA

Ekco AD 65 Radio

DATE: 1934

DESIGNER: Wells Coates (1895–1958)

MATERIALS: moulded brown phenolic Bakelite and chromium

MANUFACTURER: E.K. Cole Ltd, UK

Wells Coates was a Canadian-trained architect who came to London in the early 1920s and became one of the pioneers of British Modernism. He designed important buildings in the new architectural style and it was inevitable that he would attract the attention of manufacturers like E.K.Cole, who wanted to modernize their industry. Wells'

Wireless Receiving Set AD 65 was the result of a design competition held in 1932 by Eric K. Cole to produce the ideal plastic radio. Wells Coates' winning design was produced, with variations, from 1934 until 1946 and became a best-seller for the company. It was a radical departure from traditional forms and materials of radio cabinet

construction.The AD 65 had a distinctive circular cabinet of moulded brown Bakelite made to fit a circular speaker. The shape was reiterated in the controls and arc of the channel display and gave the radio an entirely novel form that also reduced tooling costs. A less expensive and more popular "walnut-look" version of the AD 65 was also available.

The Dutch company Philips was founded in 1891 to manufacture light bulbs and later diversified into the design and production of radio receivers, gramophone players and eventually televisions and other domestic goods. Philips was one of the first European companies to establish a design department – under the control of the architect Louis C. Kalff. Kalff was employed by Philips in 1925 and worked on the design of posters, exhibition stands and the interior of Philips showrooms. In 1929 his responsibilities were enlarged to include the aesthetic appearance of products. The design bureau employed technical draughtsmen and construction experts and the design of new products involved management, sales and technical staff. Surviving company records from this period suggest that product design at Philips was a result of such collaboration, and not the work of a single individual. The design of the 2514 Radio symbolizes Philips's approach to design. It incorporated new materials such as the synthetic Bakelite, available in different colour combinations. It also incorporated a distinctive circular speaker, described by the company in terms of its artistic quality, intended to adorn the modern living room. Kalff was to have an enduring influence on the design philosophy at Philips and he remained the company's design director until 1960, completing a remarkable thirty-five years of continuous service.

Philips 2514 Radio and Speaker

DATE: 1926

DESIGNER: Louis C. Kalff (1897–1976)

MATERIAL: metal, rexine and Bakelite

MANUFACTURER: Philips Ltd, Eindhoven, The Netherlands

RR126
Stereo
Hi-Fi

DATE: 1965–66

DESIGNER: Achille Castiglioni (born 1918) and Pier Castiglioni (1910–68)

MATERIAL: chrome, plastic and wood

MANUFACTURER: Brionvega, Milan, Italy

Originally radio manufacturers, Brionvega went on to produce televisions and hi-fi equipment. They employed a series of well-known Italian designers to transform their products.

The Castiglionis' stereo was a radical concept in the hi-fi market that fitted with the dominant style of the mid-1960s; its bold forms and colours lending a dynamic image to the product.

The RR 126 Stereo is a free-standing mobile unit which has speakers that can be stacked on top to form a box, or folded out into a horizontal arrangement.

VE 301 People's Radio

DATE: 1936

DESIGNER: Walter Maria Kersting (1889–1970)

MATERIAL: Bakelite

MANUFACTURER: Hagenuh, Kiel, Germany

Walter Maria Kersting designed, in a number of versions, the People's Radio (*Volksempfanger*), that was produced in enormous numbers in Nazi Germany. By 1939, it was estimated that twelve and a half million had been sold, thereby depositing in practically every German home a cheap, state-subsidized radio, an ideal medium through which to disseminate Nazi propaganda. The model number commemorated 30 January, 1933, the date when Hitler was made Chancellor of Germany. A political success for Hitler, the radio was powerful enough to receive home transmissions, but not the Allied broadcasts. The aesthetic was minimal and functional, a rectangular casing in dark brown, with simple dials and a large speaker: the only ornament being a Nazi swastika.

Phonosuper

DATE: 1956

DESIGNER: Hans Gugelot (1920–65) and Dieter Rams (born 1932)

MATERIAL: metal, wood and Perspex

MANUFACTURER: Braun, Frankfurt, Germany

This version of the Phonosuper transformed a product that had been manufactured since the 1930s. It also introduced the Perspex cover to hi-fi equipment. The original design featured a metal cover; this was replaced by Perspex in an effort to reduce vibration. The clean lines and strongly functional appearance were in keeping with the Braun design philosophy; however, its overly chaste and rather severe appearance earned it the nickname "Snow White's Coffin".

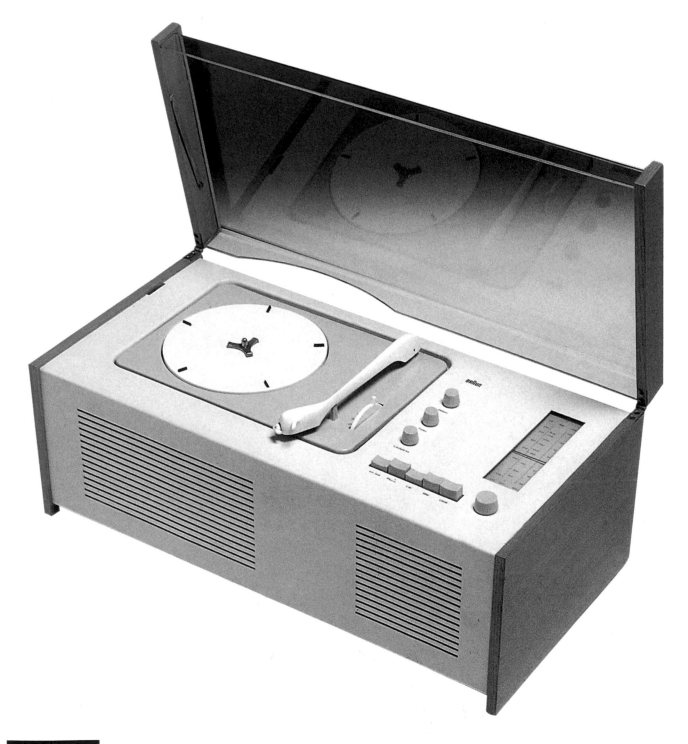

Brionvega was established as a radio manufacturer in 1945 and began producing television sets in the early 1960s. The design team of Marco Zanuso and his Bavarian-born design partner Richard Sapper worked regularly with Brionvega, as did Mario Bellini and Achille Castiglioni, other stars in the Italian design firmament. When closed, the TS 502 forms an anonymous box that conceals its function. It is a natural partner to the ST/201 television set, also designed by Zanuso and Sapper for Brionvega.

TS 502 Radio

DATE: 1964

DESIGNER: Marco Zanuso (born 1916) and Richard Sapper (born 1932)

MATERIAL: plastics and chromium

MANUFACTURER: Brionvega, Milan, Italy

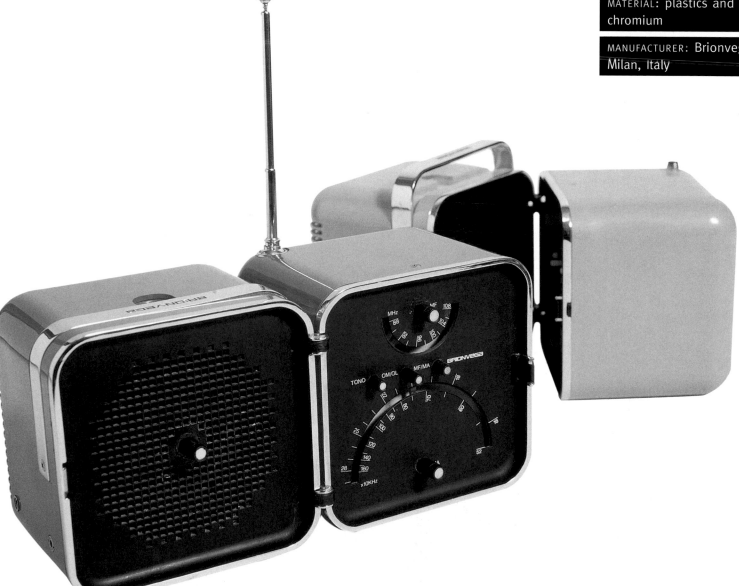

Beogram 4000 Turntable

In 1944 Bang and Olufsen launched the revolutionary Grand Prix 44 RG, a compact cabinet incorporating a record player and a radio. In 1968 the Danish designer, Jakob Jensen, was placed in charge of Bang and Olufsen's hi-fi design programme. His vision for the company was simplicity and elegance – timeless products notable for their logicality and technical precision. Jensen's anonymous and discreet styling for Bang and Olufsen has come to define the aesthetics of high-quality contemporary sound systems. Using state of the art technology with its precision components and electronic tangential arm, the Beogram was a rare example of a product from a European electronics company capable of holding its own in an industry dominated by the new Japanese companies. Bang and Olufsen continue to produce audio-visual equipment to high professional standards for the domestic market.

DATE: 1973

DESIGNER: Jakob Jensen (born 1926)

MATERIAL: wood and aluminium

MANUFACTURER: Bang and Olufsen A/S, Copenhagen, Denmark

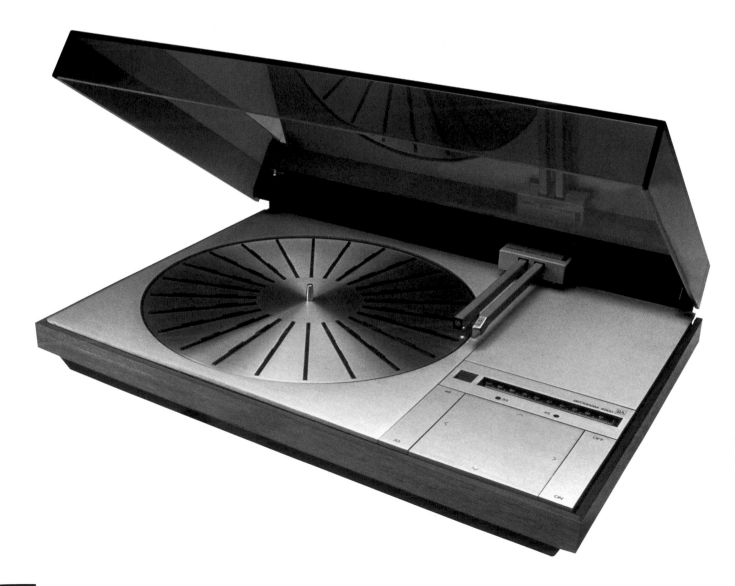

Totem Stereo

DATE: 1970

DESIGNER: Mario Bellini
(born 1935)

MATERIAL: plastic

MANUFACTURER: Brionvega,
Milan, Italy

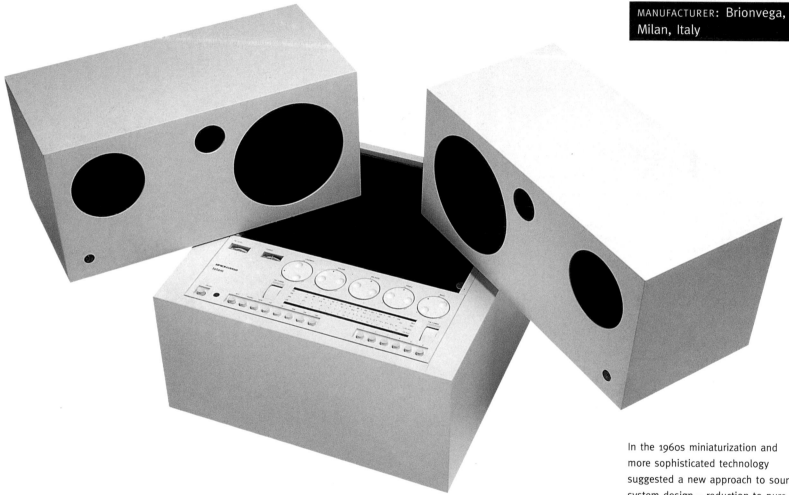

In the 1960s miniaturization and more sophisticated technology suggested a new approach to sound system design – reduction to pure geometric form. One of Italy's most innovative firms, Brionvega, combined minimalism with fun and playfulness, stressing the sculptural potential of the object. It maintained a close relationship with avant-garde Italian designers in the 1960s and 1970s, and commissioned Totem from Mario Bellini whose inventive electronic equipment includes work for Olivetti. Totem was a directional design with speakers rotating out on a pivot to reveal the hidden record deck. When closed it formed a simple white cube that conceals its function.

Sony Walkman

Sony chairman Akio Morita is said to have conceived this portable stereophonic cassette player whilst playing tennis, imagining a lightweight, easy-to-carry device for listening to music at any time. The Sony Walkman represents key changes in the 1970s and 1980s consumer markets. One of the first personalized products, both fashion accessory and functional object, the concept used existing technologies in an innovative and revolutionary way with new styling. With about fifty million sales, the Walkman has seen many versions, such as the model shown here. It continues to evolve in line with social and fashion trends and the need for individual customization.

DATE: 1978

DESIGNER: Sony Design Centre

MATERIAL: plastic

MANUFACTURER: Sony, Tokyo, Japan

Sony describes the PlayStation as its most important product since the Walkman. The company wanted something offering the sales potential of the Walkman, and invested $500 million in development, using teams of designers from around the world. The product entered a market dominated by Sega and Nintendo. Using 3D graphics, "real-time" on-screen action, and CD-quality sound, the PlayStation is powered by five processors computing half a billion instructions per second – over five hundred times more powerful than existing 16-bit consoles.

Sony PlayStation

DATE: 1996

DESIGNER: Ken Kutaragi

MATERIAL: plastic

MANUFACTURER: Sony Computer Entertainment, Tokyo, Japan

Sony Portable TV 80 301

DATE: 1959

DESIGNER: Sony Design Centre

MATERIAL: plastic and metal

MANUFACTURER: Sony, Tokyo, Japan

The postwar US occupation of Japan and subsequent Marshall Plan and package had a tremendous influence on the country's reconstruction. New Japanese industries concentrated on capital-intensive goods such as radios, television sets and cars. One of the best-known companies to represent this economic recovery was the Sony Corporation. In the 1950s the newly founded company bought the manufacturing rights to a new American invention, the transistor, and in 1955 produced its first radio. This was followed in 1959 by the world's first solid-state television receiver, which had an 46-centimetre (18-inch) screen and weighed only 6 kilograms (13 pounds). The television set in train the association of Japanese products with the latest technological advances, particularly miniaturization, and this television went on to win the Gold Medal at the Triennale di Milano in 1960. Sony's product development has been guided by technological innovation, supreme quality control and sound business management. It played a major role in establishing the profile of the Japanese electronics industry that would dominate global markets and transform the Japanese economy. Unlike Western companies, Japanese companies have tended to use in-house, anonymous design teams for product development rather than outside designers. The Sony team is responsible for all aspects of the company's products and their corporate identity, expressed through packaging and promotion.

Brionvega is an Italian company with a long tradition of commissioning leading designers to give a distinctive form to its products. In the 1960s it was also one of the few international companies whose products stood out in contrast to the prevailing simple white aesthetics of the German Braun company and their Japanese imitators. The black 201 television set was designed by Marco Zanuso and Richard Sapper in 1969, continuing a partnership established in the early 1960s to develop a new generation of television sets and radios. More than any other object, this television represents the most uncompromising movement towards minimalism in 1960s Italian design. It defined the idea of the mysterious black box, emphasized by making the screen only visible when the television was switched on. The positioning of the controls on top of the set contributes to the sleek lines, making the 201 a novel form for a familiar appliance. It quickly became a cult object.

Brionvega Black ST/201

DATE: 1969

DESIGNER: Marco Zanuso (born 1916) and Richard Sapper (born 1932)

MATERIAL: plastic and glass

MANUFACTURER: Brionvega, Milan, Italy

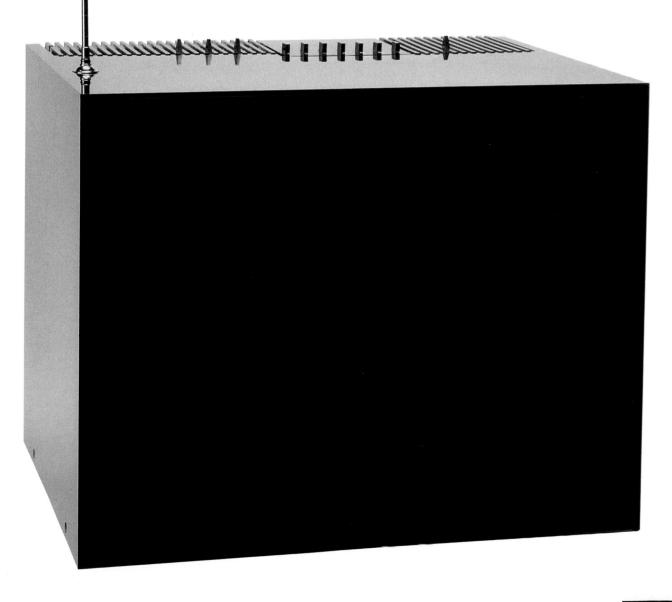

Sony Trinitron Television

DATE: 1968

DESIGNER: Sony
Design Centre

MATERIAL: plastic, chrome
and glass

MANUFACTURER: Sony, Tokyo,
Japan

Sony's innovative approach to research and development has led to many ground-breaking products. The Trinitron television set was the result of research focused entirely on the creation of a brighter, clearer and less distorted picture. This revolutionary product employed a new and highly sophisticated picture production device. The Trinitron television set also used a much flatter screen that enhanced picture quality. The Trinitron was the starting point in the quest for high-resolution television images, which has culminated most recently in the inception of digital television.

Now one of the world's best-known designers, Philippe Starck's output has been prolific. Not only has he produced important interiors, furniture and domestic products, he has also worked in the field of industrial products including this television, Jim Nature. Part of a more widespread move to challenge the dominance of the familiar Japanese techno box aesthetic, its sculptural case in some ways looks back to the spirit of 1960s Pop design, but significant here is Starck's use of multi-density wood or chipboard. This material raises the issues of ecologically sound materials in that the wood is essentially recycled. It also gives technology a more human and friendly face, a development that the consumer is beginning to find more appealing than the hard-edge black plastic used for most products in this field.

Jim Nature

DATE: 1994

DESIGNER: Philippe Starck (born 1949)

MATERIAL: high-density wood and plastic

MANUFACTURER: Saba (Thomson), France

Kodak Brownie 127

The Kodak Company was founded in 1881 by George Eastman Kodak. His products pioneered the simplification of photography, as suggested by Kodak's advertising slogan: "You press the button, we do the rest". Kodak is the world's largest photographic organization. It has designed and manufactured hundreds of cameras this century. This postwar model has the rounded contours that were popular in by Walter Dorwin Teague's series of popular cameras designed in the 1930s, the best-known of which was the Bantam special of 1936. This made it appear old-fashioned even when it was new. Several million were nonetheless sold.

DATE: 1959

DESIGNER: Kodak

MATERIAL: plastic

MANUFACTURER: Kodak, USA

Small, quiet and discreet, in the 1930s the Leica camera produced a revolution. It was the first compact camera that could produce professional quality work and it quickly became the most popular photojournalistic camera in the world. Its origins go back to 1911 when Oskar Barnack joined the German engineering company Leitz. Barnack was trained as an engineer and an enthusiastic amateur photographer who started to work on prototypes for a small camera based on a simple idea: small negatives but big pictures. He produced prototypes of this camera and after World War One his boss Ernst Leitz decided to put it into production as the Leica. Their first camera was shown at the Leipzig Fair in 1925 followed by the Leica1 in 1930 which was a new compact size and offered interchangeable lenses. These technological advances ensured that the Leica became the serious camera for professional photography in the 1930s.

Leica

DATE: 1930

DESIGNER: Oskar Barnack (1879–1936)

MATERIAL: plastic and metal

MANUFACTURER: Leitz, Germany

Nikon F

DATE: 1959

DESIGNER: Nikon Design Team

MATERIAL: plastic and metal

MANUFACTURER: Nikon, Japan

Initially called Nippon Kogaku K.K., Nikon was the first Japanese company to challenge the supremacy of Leica for professional quality cameras. In 1950 two photographers from the American magazine *Life* used Nikon lenses under extreme weather conditions; the quality of these photographs won two important prizes and brought Nikon international recognition. In 1959, Nikon introduced the Nikon F, its first 35mm SLR lens camera, which featured an instant return reflex mirror, linked reflex mirror and shutter, interchangeable finders and screens. The Nikon F was an immediate success, selling over a million cameras. It became more than an admired piece of professional equipment, as the Nikon F became bound up in the imagery and lifestyle of the Swinging Sixties. It was the Nikon that young, British fashion photographers like David Bailey used to stalk the leggy mini-skirted models of the period. In this context the Nikon was more than a camera: it was an accessory that helped to establish photographers as the new high-profile media stars of the decade.

The Nikon F series remains the professional standard today.

The Olympus Trip 35 was designed in 1968 and was in continuous production until 1988, selling over ten million units and making it one of the most successful cameras of the twentieth century. The camera was designed as a 35mm version of the Olympus range and combined high quality technical performance with a more affordable price. Aesthetically, the camera broke new ground, by wrapping the light meter cells ingeniously around the lens. It was simple and easy to use, compact in size so that it was easy to carry.

Olympus has continued its commitment to innovation. One of its more recent cameras, the 1993 Olympus Zoom, with distinctive sculptural contours, was the lightest 35mm camera on the market at that time.

Olympus Trip 35

DATE: 1968

DESIGNER: Olympus Design Team

MATERIAL: plastic and metal

MANUFACTURER: Olympus, Tokyo, Japan

Canon CB10

DATE: 1982–83

DESIGNER: Luigi Colani
(born 1928)

MATERIAL: plastic

MANUFACTURER: Canon
Cameras, Tokyo, Japan

This early biomorphic design marked a shift towards a more organic-looking product. The CB10 formed part of a special project commissioned by Canon. The brief to the designer, the Italian–Swiss Colani, was to think, in an entirely free and unfettered manner, about the future of camera designs. Colani, well-known for his highly individualistic design style, was to create a series of cameras that would serve as "pointers" to the future. The result was indeed radical: a series of biomorphic shapes that looked more like deep-sea fish than cameras. The series still appears revolutionary today. It is important to remember that at this time the black box ruled supreme – the marketing of such products was based largely on technical features and price. Colani introduced the radical idea that the simple, black rectangular shape was not the only way forward. Colani's excessive aerodynamic forms may have been extreme but they were a reaction against the functional aesthetic of the day and heralded an enormous shift in styling in the mass market for cameras.

Canon
Ixus

DATE: 1996

DESIGNER: Canon Design Centre

MANUFACTURER: Canon Cameras, Tokyo, Japan

The Canon Ixus was instantly hailed as a classic of design when it was launched in 1996. One of the smallest cameras on the market, the Ixus is the size of a packet of playing cards: it is only 9 centimetres (3½ inches) wide and six centimetres (2½ inches) high. Much of its appeal comes from the sleek, compact design of the metallic body. However, it is not just its appearance that places the Ixus at the forefront of design, it also represents the latest advance in camera technology, as it is loaded with the Advanced Photo System. This is a new type of film that requires no negatives and allows the user to select any of three different formats when shooting or printing images.

Valentine Portable Typewriter

DATE: **1969**

DESIGNER: **Ettore Sottsass** (born 1917) **and Perry King** (born 1938)

MATERIAL: **plastic**

MANUFACTURER: **Olivetti, Italy**

Inspired by American Pop Art, Ettore Sottsass wanted to humanize industrial design. The Valentine Portable Typewriter, which he designed with Perry King, was not the first portable; in the 1930s, the Swiss company Ernest Paillard had pioneered a model called the Hermes Baby. However, the Valentine signalled a new approach to office equipment, as it could so clearly be placed either in a domestic or office environment. Its brightly coloured plastic case, size and colour made it friendly, human and fun. The advertisements promoting the Valentine reinforced this image, often showing young couples reclining in fields alongside the typewriter or illustrated, as here, as giant works of Pop art.

Sottsass worked as a design consultant for Olivetti from 1957 and developed projects that range from typewriters to furniture and computers. Sottsass was concerned with ergonomics and new materials. A product that reflects the vitality of Olivetti and its informed approach to design, the Valentine proved a great commercial success.

the olivetti collection   1. Lettera 33   2. Lettera 31   3. Studio 45   4. Lettera 32   5. Valentine   6. A collector

Designed in 1963, IBM's golf ball typewriter revolutionized the 1960s office. For the first time a single machine offered interchangeable typefaces, carbon ribbon, electric drive, a small footprint and a weight of only 14 kilograms (31 pounds). Its success was due to a nickel-plated plastic type, positioned by a mechanism so that each stroke tilted and rotated to bring the required character to the front, before striking it against the ribbon and moving it on a space. Later variants gave an even greater quality of print. The International Business Machine Corporation (IBM) operated a clearly defined design policy in the 1950s under the direction of Eliot Noyes. With an eye on the work of Italian rivals Olivetti, in particular products designed by Nizzoli, the 72 represented not only a technical breakthrough but the expression of sophisticated sculptural form.

IBM Typewriter 72

DATE: 1963

DESIGNER: Eliot Noyes (1910–77)

MATERIAL: plastic

MANUFACTURER: IBM, Armonk, New York State, USA

IBM Computer System 360

DATE: 1964

DESIGNER: Eliot Noyes
(1910–77)

MANUFACTURER: IBM,
Armonk, New York State, USA

Eliot Noyes became director of design for International Business Machines (IBM) in 1956. He transformed the direction of the company by insisting on an integrated approach to design strategy and corporate identity governed by a set of published standards.

These design specifications covered all IBM products. Under Noyes, the company linked design to innovation and developed a number of revolutionary computer products. The System 360 is typical of Noyes' approach and epitomizes IBM design

characteristics. It is functional, and yet softened in places by avoiding the stark form so often associated with computers. It was designed to be easily operated and the controls were developed in conjunction with IBM's Human Engineering division.

Easy to use and housed in an off-white casing, the Apple Macintosh computer revolutionized the computer industry. Apple enjoyed a rather special corporate image – a reputation that it was a company managed by 1960s free-thinkers who believed that technology could empower the individual. Their choice of name evoked not big business but memories of the counter-culture and The Beatles' Apple Corps.

Based in California, Apple suggested the attitude of Haight Ashbury rather than Manhattan. In sharp contrast to their suit-wearing peers at IBM, Apple executives prided themselves on wearing jeans. Apple identified itself with the individual, not the corporate might of IBM. This profile was self-consciously exploited by Apple in their famous TV commercial for the Macintosh, directed by British film-maker Tony Scott and

broadcast during the Super Bowl. Playing on images from *Metropolis*, the ad showed people staring at a ranting "Big Brother" image only to be liberated by an Olympic athlete who smashed the screen to reveal the copy: "On January 24th, Apple Computer will introduce the Macintosh and you'll see why 1984 won't be like 1984". The Classic shown here was one of the popular early models.

Apple Macintosh

DATE: 1984

DESIGNER: Frogdesign/ Harmut Esslinger (born 1945)

MATERIAL: plastic housing

MANUFACTURER: Apple Computers, Cupertino, USA

Apple eMate 300

The Apple eMate 300 is the first of a new class of affordable mobile computers which works as a companion to Mac Operating Systems and Windows software-based computers in a distributed learning environment.

Developed by educators to meet the needs of students and educators, the eMate 300's unique industrial design is rugged enough to withstand the rigours of being carried, shared and used in a variety of environments. The eMate

weighs only 2 kilograms (4 pounds) so is easily portable and fits into a back pack. The eMate utilizes the Newton operating system, and so data can be entered using either a stylus or keyboard.

DATE: 1996

DESIGNER: Apple Design Team and Jonathon Ive

MATERIAL: plastic

MANUFACTURER: Apple Computers, Cupertino, California, USA

Founded in 1980, Psion is a successful UK company that currently enjoys thirty-three per cent of the worldwide market share in palm-top computers. The Series 3 includes an enhanced set of programmes that include an address book, diary and a facility that enables the user to transfer data via infra-red technology on to another Psion computer or indeed a printer.

Frazer Designers carried out all the industrial design and mechanical engineering design of the Psion Series 3 palm-top computer, overcoming a number of problems of size and pocketability. A separate elliptical spine, which gives the impression of holding the top and bottom of the machine together, houses two AA batteries. Pivoting on both the lid and the base, the spine folds down as the clam shell opens, jacking the keyboard up and out. The Psion Series 3 is a successful union of engineering and industrial design and is the culmination of the efforts of many design disciplines: software, electronic hardware, interface design and product design.

Psion Series 3c

DATE: 1996

DESIGNER: Frazer Designers

MATERIAL: plastic

MANUFACTURER: Psion, London, UK

futures

PART 13

THINGS TO COME

THE FUTURE IS NOTORIOUSLY difficult to predict. Yet visualizing the future is a recurring twentieth-century obsession – a project that has fascinated filmmakers, science-fiction writers, architects, designers and futurologists. Ironically, each decade seems to have predicted the future as a version of its present, and so many of the images shown in this section simply reinforce the cultural and design trends of their own time.

In some ways the use of future fantasy has become an industrial design aesthetic in its own right. One important source for futurist imagery is derived from science fiction, an essentially twentieth-century form of literature that has become an important genre. The most important figure in this context is the writer H.G. Wells, but later twentieth-century exponents whose work has influenced designers are Isaac Azimov, Arthur C. Clarke, and Philip K. Dick. Their written descriptions of fantasy scenarios have inspired countless illustrations, films and

METROPOLIS

video games and helped to construct the visual landscape of the future. Also important are the countless comic books and popular published sources that include visual representations of the future. These should not be discounted as merely ephemeral: there is a real relationship between the imagery produced for young adults and children and the design ideas of many futuristic clothes and objects.

Artists too have explored the future. Max Ernst's Surrealist collages, for example, explore the territory of prophetic dreams. With Ernst, as with other Dadaist and Surrealist artists, there is a fascination with elaborate mechanical machines and robots in their drawings and paintings.

At the beginning of the century, a number of architects attempted to produce realizable plans for the new city of the future. Inspired by the potential of the century's new technology, architects such as the Italian, Sant'Elia, and later Le Corbusier, laid out plans for the city that included towering skyscrapers, linked by walkways; although they remained unbuilt, these visions became important blueprints for city planners after 1945. Gradually in some of the world's largest cities, most notably New York or Brasilia, these visions began to take place. Providing people with a glimpse of the future became part of every major exhibition and industrial show of the twentieth century and the best-known example of this remains the 1939 New York World's Fair. The whole concept of the exhibition was to provide the viewer with a glimpse of the way technology was going to reshape the future.

The period after World War Two was the time when societies truly embraced the future. The promise of technology underpinned the whole political and philosophical credo of the 1960s and the British Prime Minister Harold Wilson referred to it as "the white heat of technology". At the same time important writers like Marshall McLuhan engaged in the theoretical implications such changes would have on the nature of society. These changes were seen in a positive light, but slowly a counter-movement gained a growing voice. Technology, the argument went, led to dangerous side effects. It produced ecological problems and was not the way forward. In response, future imagery demonstrated that it was not only about dark, overpowering visions of change, it also began to concern itself with low-tech self-sustaining technologies, projects that would involve recycling and the reuse of materials to build the future.

This division of feeling about the future has been thrown painfully into focus as we prepare to leave the twentieth century. The end of any century is an important moment, but the end of the millennium is historically charged with significance and portent. The millennium indicates the arrival of the future in which we look forward to building a better life while at the same time many fear that technology will overwhelm the individual. With this in mind designers and leading companies are asking themselves some basic questions. What will life be like in 2050? What will people want in

TOTALMEDIA MULTIMEDIA

terms of design in the future? What will interest them and make their lives more fulfilled?

CONCEPT HOME FACSIMILE

Traditionally, new products have been introduced mainly through technological innovation, but the rapid development and merging of technologies is making it increasingly difficult to predict the future. In order to stay in business large companies, such as Sony, Philips and IDEO, as well as smaller concerns, like Tangerine, have to try to predict the future. Their prototype products – or "future gazing" concepts – propose ways in which new developments in technology could improve the quality of people's lives. Companies have also been forced to recognize that technological innovation for its own sake is no longer acceptable. They recognize that products and services will have to come closer to meeting human needs and desires. Design will have to reflect the increasingly complex relationship between people and technology.

Until now the twentieth century's obsession with the future has focused on images of high tech and the power of the machine. The emergence of ethical and ecological concerns now challenge this vision. In the twenty-first century it will be interesting to see how the interplay between high-tech and sustainable low-tech shapes the next generation's predictions of the future.

PORTABLE SCANNER

MILLENNIUM TOWER

Une Cité Industrielle

DATE: 1904

DESIGNER: Tony Garnier
(1869–1948)

Tony Garnier received a traditional French Beaux Arts education, where he was a star pupil, winning the coveted Prix de Rome prize. In spite of his conventional training, he completed an extraordinary series of drawings at the beginning of the century that established a blueprint for twentieth-century town planning.

Garnier was the first architect to produce a plan for the industrialized city with *Une Cité Industrielle*, which was first published in 1917. More than any other designer, he established the idea that architects should direct their attention to the city as a whole, rather than the private house or the individual grand building. Garnier introduced the single and most influential precept in town planning, a method of organizing and regulating the industrial city – the idea of zoning. He divided his imaginary city of 35,000 inhabitants into distinct areas – industrial, residential, transport, sport and health. It was this categorization of the activities of modern life that proved so influential on architects such as Le Corbusier in the 1920s.

Garnier also recognized that the new technology of industrial materials could be used to create the modern city of the twentieth century – significantly, he chose reinforced concrete for all types of buildings. His two-storey residential houses are simple cubic shapes with classical forms which predated the look of Modernism. Garnier's aesthetics of simple cube houses, dramatically cantilevered public buildings and his use of reinforced concrete set a standard for subsequent city planning. His revolutionary urban vision remains with us to this day.

La Ville Radieuse

La Ville Radieuse (The Radiant City) is arguably among the most influential intellectual concepts of the twentieth century. It saw Le Corbusier draw on the ideas of early visionaries such as Tony Garnier and Sant'Elia to produce a model of the modern city and how it should be organized for maximum benefit of its inhabitants. It was a culmination of a series of city plans Le Corbusier had worked on in the 1920s. La Ville Radieuse was based around the use of zones for the key functions of modern life and work, arranged in a sequence of bands that could expand horizontally into the landscape. Particularly influential was his idea of layering the city – for example, placing the pedestrian above the car in walkways – which had an enormous impact on postwar planning. The reunion of man with nature was one of Le Corbusier's most important town planning principles. Consequently, his buildings were all raised above ground level on pilotis, releasing the land for use as "green" space.

There was one fundamental drawback to Corbusier's grand visions: to work properly, such cities had to be rebuilt from scratch. In practical terms this meant the imposition of zones – whether the inhabitants wanted them or not – the demolition of existing buildings, the wiping clean of history and the control of people's lives. While Le Corbusier did move away from this authoritarian position, many suffered as a result of huge postwar rebuilding programmes based on his town-planning schemes that are now seen as inhumane and brutal.

DATE: 1930

DESIGNER: Le Corbusier (1887–1966)

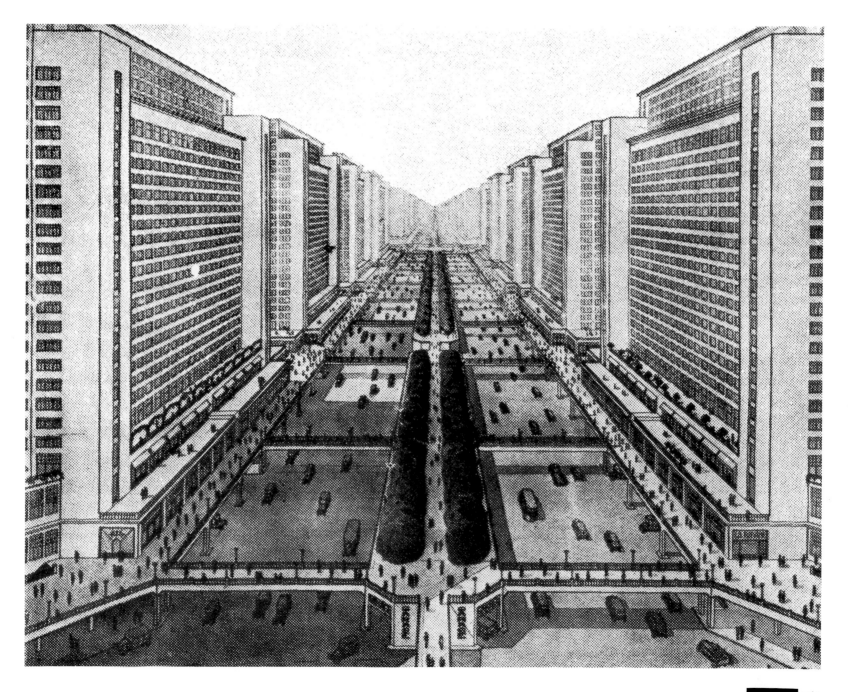

Monument to the 3rd International

DATE: 1919–20

DESIGNER: Vladimir Tatlin
(1885–1953)

Tatlin's monument is one of the most significant projects to be produced by an artist in the immediate aftermath of the 1917 Bolshevik Revolution. Its design was intended to symbolize the new Soviet society – the activities housed inside were meant to help foster the transition to this new way of life. In the first few years that followed the Revolution, artists were called upon by the State to provide new imagery and monuments to convey the new ideology to the ordinary people. Like many Russian artists after the Revolution, Tatlin rejected the bourgeois practice of art and pledged his skills to serving the Soviet State.

The tower was to have been 400 metres (1,300 feet) high and straddle the river Neva in Petrograd (St Petersburg). However, with few materials and even less money available, such a project was impossible in post-Revolution Russia and the tower was never built. The scheme comprised a massive framework – a double helix, with three transparent shapes inside: a cube housing Soviet legislative bodies; a pyramid housing administrators; and, at the top, a cylinder containing an information base. These offices were intended to rotate at different speeds to express the dynamism of the new society. Painted in red, the tower would symbolize the Revolution with its intersecting spire of the frame representing the dialectic of Marxist theory. It was, in Tatlin's words, "political sculpture".

La Città Nuova

DATE: 1914

DESIGNER: Antonio Sant'Elia
(1888–1916)

The Italian Futurists were obsessed with the notion of the New Age, the shocking, the chaotic and the radical. As the principal architect associated with the group, Sant'Elia was likewise captivated with scale, speed, technology and, above all, machines. In 1913 he began his plans for a new city which would be exhibited the following year along with a Futurist Manifesto on Architecture. Sant'Elia's city was not an exercise in town planning on the scale of Tony Garnier's earlier visions, but La Città Nuova presented an astonishingly original vision of what a twentieth-century industrialized city should look like. Sant'Elia viewed the new city as a gigantic machine. He insisted that the new mechanized way of life required a completely new form of architecture – an approach which, like other Futurist forms of expression, would break with the past and embody the speed and progress of the new century. Sant'Elia's telling description of architecture as a machine was later famously appropriated by Le Corbusier.

Sant'Elia's vision saw high-rise blocks built from reinforced concrete towering above the transportation level, standing on a network of power and communication. His drawings anticipated many details of contemporary architecture, such as the placing of lift shafts on the outside of buildings, and predate the work of modern architects such as Richard Rogers by seventy years.

Sadly, Sant'Elia's visionary ideas remained only as drawings – his life was cut tragically short when he was killed in action during World War One.

Things To Come

DATE: 1936

DIRECTOR: William Cameron Menzies (1896–1957)

More than any other writer, it was H. G. Wells who established the genre of science fiction writing in the twentieth century, and his visions of the future have exercised an extraordinary influence. In an early story, *The Sleeper Awakes*, Wells imagined the city of the future, a remarkable image of huge metal-framed buildings, and one which predicted the work of Modernist architects such as Le Corbusier. *Things To Come*, adapted from a later Wells novel, extended this theme and became one of the film sensations of the decade. The story covers a period of a hundred years of civilization. It begins in 1940, with a war that devastates the entire globe and exterminates most of mankind. The film ends with the Futurist utopia of 2040, in which human hardships have been eliminated and the population is assured of all its material as well as spiritual needs.

Directed by William Cameron Menzies, the film is noted both for the remarkable visions of the future created in its sets and for the extraordinary special effects by Ned Man (1893–1967). Using models and buildings to give the impression of lifesize dimensions, Man also created fantasy machines, including vision telephones and the delta-winged aeroplanes that attacked London. The English public laughed at the idea of an air attack on their capital city in 1936. Within five years, however, this fiction had become reality.

Produced in Germany in 1925, *Metropolis* was a hugely expensive film, with production costs reaching almost £2 million. Memorable for its futuristic sets and choreographed set-pieces which employed a cast of nearly forty thousand extras, it quickly established itself as the most significant science-fiction film of the silent era. *Metropolis* was both widely admired and highly influential – Hitler and Goebbels were both deeply impressed. Virtually every subsequent science fiction films owe a debt to its original vision of the future.

In the film's introductory sequences, Fritz Lang reveals a gigantic city of the future – a city of gleaming skyscrapers, connecting bridges and aeroplanes – where people live in comfort, devoted to intellectual and physical development. Although the film preaches a moral message about the threat technology represents to human spiritual life, the alternative to such progress is illustrated by the workers of the subterranean city who enjoy no individuality – a crowd from which personality rarely projects itself.

Using a refined cinematic language, *Metropolis* contained technical innovations which influenced Hollywood over the next two decades. The film made extensive use of uneven lines, the nameless crowd, contrasts of light and dark, half-shadows and silhouettes, much of which still serves to suggest mysterious and menacing actions or emotions. *Metropolis* established the potential for a film image to generate meaning – an example being the well-known scene in which the robot with its glittering female body, stylized breasts and inhuman mask makes its entry. Lang also shapes space with the help of human bodies and uses light so intensively that it takes the place of sound.

Metropolis

DATE: 1926

DIRECTOR: Fritz Lang
(1890–1976)

Perisphere and Trylon Structures

DATE: 1939–40

World of Tomorrow
Exhibition, New York City,
USA

DESIGNER: Henry Dreyfuss
(1904–72)

By the 1920s, the USA had established itself as the world's most powerful industrial nation. The country led the way in new methods of industrial production. For the Americans the machine was not only a reality but a potent symbol of the future. In 1939 this vision was realized in the World of Tomorrow Exhibition, which was held in New York. Here was an attempt to create the future in microcosm – a man-made future where visitors could enter Henry Dreyfuss' Democracity – the 60-metre (200-foot) diameter Perisphere and the 200 metre (700-foot) tall Trylon. These soaring white geometric shapes gave visitors the promise of a streamlined lifestyle and universe of the future. People could marvel at the universe of televisions, robots, transcontinental highways, the promise of space travel and a range of the latest electrical domestic products. The impact of the New York exhibition was, however, severely restricted by the outbreak of the World War Two. This was not the moment for Utopian dreams of the future, and more pressing concerns became the priority. The spirit of 1939 was held in abeyance until the political and economic stability of the postwar years returned.

City of
the Future

DATE: 1946

DESIGNER: Frank R. Paul
(1884—1963)

Throughout the twentieth century,
comics and science fiction
books have published visual
representations of imagined futures.
Far from being ephemeral or trivial
elements of popular culture, these
illustrated stories became an
important medium through which
we acquired ideas of the future.
Well-known science fiction
illustrators, such as Frank R. Paul,
visualized the future through the
present – effectively recording the
cultural aspirations of their own
time. There is also a real and potent
relationship between this kind of
popular imagery and design culture
– this creative visual language has
been borrowed time and time again
and appropriated for the visual
landscape of mainstream design.

Bicycle of the Future

DATE: 1946

DESIGNER: Ben Bowden
(born 1906)

In 1946, London's Victoria and Albert Museum reopened after the war with a design exhibition – "Britain Can Make It". Attracting thousands of visitors, one of its most successful features was Designs of the Future, a stand which included a futuristic kitchen, an air-conditioned bed and Ben Bowden's Bicycle of the Future.

Until the historian Paul Clarke researched his career, little was known of Bowden. Trained as an engineer, in the 1930s he was chief body engineer for Rootes, the British car manufacturer. After the war, he turned his attention to bicycles, the design of which had remained almost unchanged since the turn of the century. Bowden's bicycle abandoned tubular steel in favour of a hollow frame made from alloy, a technique that soon became the industry standard for mopeds and scooters. It was intended to be electrically assisted with a rechargeable battery shaft drive rather than a chain drive. When the bicycle was shown to the public in 1946 its new technology and radical shape – according to Bowden, inspired by the bows of the great ocean liner, the *Queen Mary* – created a sensation.

Bowden's bicycle was never put into production. He moved to the USA in the 1950s and in the following decade he produced small quantities of his design, renamed the Spacelander. The bike quickly became something of a legend, avidly sought by specialist collectors.

Skylon

DATE: 1951

DESIGNERS: Sir Philip Powell
(born 1921) and John Hidalgo
Moya (1920-1994)

In 1945 Britain's new Labour
Government supported plans laid
out by the new Council of Industrial
Design Industries, now known as
the Design Council, to use design
as a key strategy in the
regeneration of the postwar
economy. Their most ambitious plan
was a festival to mark the
centenary of the Great Exhibition of
1851. The Festival of Britain was
intended to show the British people
a new future and provide an
international forum to promote
British design. The festival's
organizers, headed by Hugh Casson,
were given 27 acres of bomb-
damaged land on London's South
Bank and a budget of £7 million.
The event caught the public
imagination. Opening in May 1951,
the Festival Of Britain had been
visited by over six million people
by the time it closed in September.

With an aim of creating some
memorable structures, the Festival
committee commissioned the
world's largest domed structure –
the Dome of Discovery – and the
world's tallest structure – the
Skylon. Designed by two young
architects, Powell and Moya, the
Skylon towered over the site, its
elegant and tensile structure
creating an aesthetic which left
a mark on a new generation of
designers.

Plug-In City

DATE: 1964

DESIGNER: Archigram–
Peter Cook (born 1936)

During the 1960s, the Archigram group produced some of the most Utopian and futuristic designs of the twentieth century. Archigram served as an umbrella for a group of young British architects which included Ron Herron, Warren Chalk, Dennis Crompton, Peter Cook, David Green and Michael Webb. They came together with a shared enthusiasm for the work of the Italian Futurists and the new Pop culture of science fiction, space age, throwaway consumerism, and the inspiration of

their guru, Buckminster Fuller. They believed that mainstream architecture was too bound up in history and tradition and wanted to replace this with an architecture more in tune with the period. They set up the magazine *Archigram* to show their projects and revitalize architecture. The group rejected the idea that architecture needed to be permanent, arguing that if society and peoples changed, then so too should their buildings.

The projects in the pages of

Archigram concentrated on an expendable architecture which drew its imagery from the new technology. Typical of this approach was Peter Cook's Plug-In City of 1964, which created a framework of basic utilities – such as water and power – onto which standardized living units could be attached. Although their work remained conceptual, it had an enormous impact on the major architects of the last twenty years, including Richard Rogers and Nicholas Grimshaw.

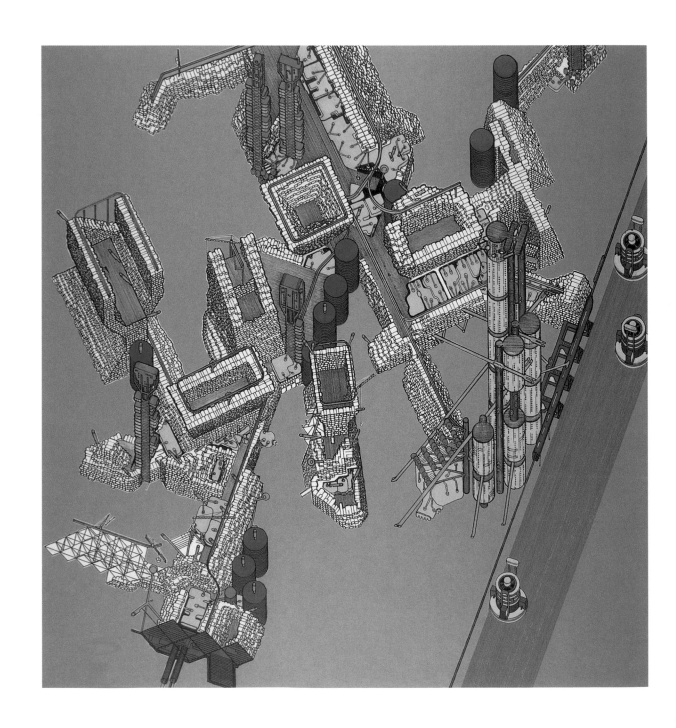

This husband-and-wife team was part of a young generation of postwar British architects inspired by the Modern Movement. Their interpretation of modernism, which used the new materials and construction methods developed in the 1930s, became known as New Brutalism because of its uncompromising forms using exposed steel beams and raw concrete. They were, however, interested in reworking the ideas of the Modern Movement to make it more relevant to their age and more in keeping with the consumer-orientated society of the 1950s. The Smithsons became some of the most important architectural thinkers in postwar Britain. The House of The Future represents their ideas of what the modern house should be in the new era. Built for the popular "Ideal Home" Exhibition, it expressed their ideas of the house as an appliance designed to facilitate everyday activities. It was moulded in plastic to form free-flowing internal walls that were easy to clean.

The lighting and fittings were all moulded into this wall surface. Visionary concepts included the kitchen, streamlined and fitted to produce not traditional food but prepackaged meals, and compartmentalized washing facilities with a sunken plastic bath and a pod-like shower unit. The Smithsons' idea that architecture could be consumable and disposable proved extremely influential and their moulded plastic furniture and fittings had a profound impact on 1960s design.

House of the Future

DATE: 1956

DESIGNER: Alison Smithson (1928—93) and Peter Smithson (born 1923)

Barbarella

DATE: 1967

DIRECTOR: Roger Vadim
(born 1927)

Barbarella provided a Pop-design vision of the future. It was not the stark streamlined vision found in such television programmes as *Star Trek*, but an image of the future as Pop culture. Interiors featured a satin bed, fur-lined walls, inflatable furniture and huge plastic membrane environments.

Barbarella appeared ahead of its time and inspired the architectural underground with its exploration of installation-type spaces – the curved, pliable and continuously adaptable areas echoed the experimental work of many designers of the 1960s, such as Verner Panton and Joe Columbo.

New materials, such as blown polyurethane foam and PVC, led to surprisingly sexual forms in furniture, with swelling shapes covered in tightly stretched, brightly coloured fabric. These witty Pop designs found a large audience through the styling of films such as *Dr No* and *Barbarella* and in this way cinema created some of the lasting future environments of the decade.

In the 1960s Paris couturiers recognized the style revolution that was affecting fashion from the street upwards. With the new independent boutiques setting the pace, it was not long before the great French fashion houses looked for ways to define the new modern woman of the period. In this context images of the future were particularly important. Their look for the new woman now included streamlined all-in-one cat suits, visor sunglasses and space age helmets such as Pierre Cardin's futuristic 1967 designs shown below. In 1964 Courrèges was the first couturier to include the mini-skirt in his collection and his theme, "the moon girl", used white plastic boots and beautifully cut body suits in black and white, inspired by the new geometry of Pop Art.

Another key fashion theme was new materials. Plastic, of course, was important, but Paco Rabanne extended this to include chain-mail minis, made from squares of brightly coloured perspex, metal and acrylic. With its tradition of superb cut and innovative fabrics, Paris soon re-established the lead in 1960s fashion.

Future Fashion

DATE: 1967

DESIGNER: Pierre Cardin
(born 1922)

Wichita House

DATE: 1946

DESIGNER: Richard Buckminster Fuller (1895–1983)

Despite the fact he never completed any formal architectural training, Buckminster Fuller remains a seminal influence in twentieth-century design and architecture. Using new technology, his original vision offered an alternative direction to what he and many others began to see as the more symbolic representation of modernity in the buildings of such architects as Mies van der Rohe and Le Corbusier.

In 1927 he invented a new house which he called Dymaxion, a word derived from the combination of the concepts of dynamism and efficiency. Using factory-built units, this startlingly futuristic house was Buckminster Fuller's model for technologically enhanced modern living. His approach was to have a profound influence on young architects in the postwar period. They admired this inventor maverick whose work never fully entered the mainstream.

The Wichita House, designed in 1946, is an extension of Buckminster Fuller's early ideas and provides a unique vision of his response to the machine aesthetic. Its use of factory components reflected the onset of the consumer age, the promise of the future and the potential of new technology. It was hardly surprising that Buckminster Fuller's experiments with geodesic dome structures and his extensive writings proved inspirational for a 1960s culture dedicated to the exploration of the future.

The Gutenberg Galaxy

DATE: 1962

AUTHOR: Herbert Marshall McLuhan (1911–80)

PUBLISHER: Routledge and Kegan Paul, London, England

In 1951 Marshall McLuhan, a Canadian academic, published *The Mechanical Bride*, a unique analysis of American advertisements. In 1962 he identified key changes prompted by the new electronic age in a study called *The Gutenberg Galaxy*. These writings made Marshall McLuhan the most important futures guru of his age and his work made more conventional academics look hopelessly outdated and anachronistic. McLuhan's main point was that new electronic media would restore a sense of community and collectivity to a fragmented society, uniting humanity in a "global village". McLuhan argued that new communication technologies would bring new ways of perceiving reality, changing the individual's understanding of time, space and self. His theories were dense and complex but his popularity was reinforced by two strengths. The first was that his writing always included a spiritual, almost mystical, dimension, which had tremendous appeal to the counter culture of the 1960s. The second was a unique talent for creating "sound bites" with his memorable book titles and quotes: "The medium is the message" became the cliché of the 1960s. In the 1970s technology did not develop as quickly as McLuhan had predicted and his ideas fell out of favour. Recently, however, his work has been favourably reassessed and his status as a guru is ensured.

Blade Runner

DATE: 1982

DIRECTOR: Ridley Scott
(born 1929)

More than any other film of the 1980s, *Blade Runner* established a visual landscape of the futuristic city which continues to dominate the popular imagination. Adapted from Philip K. Dick's novel *Do Androids Dream Of Electric Sheep?*, the film stars Harrison Ford as a cynical hero whose job is to retire "replicants" – androids with a human instinct for survival – in an overcrowded Los Angeles of 2019. The famous opening sequences show a city of the future, dominated by advertisements projected onto skyscrapers, "cars" that can fly, and an oppressive, dark, chaotic urban vision.

Art-directed by Douglas Trumbull, who worked on the influential *2001: A Space Odyssey* (1969), *Blade Runner* continues to influence films, advertising and fashion design. The effects were created by a kind of add-on architecture constructed from buildings and sky-scrapers which extend onto existing structures. To create this darkly oppressive city, layers of texture were built up so that visual information is densely packed on to the screen. Details proliferate throughout, which leads to the view that, as a movie, *Blade Runner* was designed rather than filmed.

In the 1980s the Eve Machina design was part of a widespread attempt to humanize the industrial aesthetics of the machine. The choice of name was no accident – the Eve in the title is the woman of forbidden fruit fame, and GK Dynamics described the bike as a "love toy". This startling prototype design, by the largest industrial design group in the world, suggests nothing less than a woman and machine joined in the sexual act and in doing so reinforces the strong connections between motorbikes and male sexual power. Strongly reminiscent of the sculptures created by Allen Jones in the 1960s, the concept has aroused strong criticism for its submissive portrayal of the female form.

Eve Machina

DATE: 1980s

DESIGNER: GK Dynamics Incorporated, Tokyo, Japan

Concept Home Facsimile

DATE: 1996

DESIGNERS: Tangerine –
Martin Darbyshire and
Peter Phillips

MATERIAL: plastics

The Tangerine product design consultancy was formed in 1989. Tangerine's designers have aimed to stretch the potential of the products that they design, the manufacturers who make them, and the users who buy them. They are a rare example of a young British design company which has already acquired an international reputation for innovative computers, telephones and fax machines for clients including Apple, Hitachi and LG Electronics.

The Home Facsimile was designed for the needs of the home user. This function led Tangerine to challenge the internal format of existing fax machines to create a thought-provoking "niche" product. This concept fax machine occupies a minimum amount of space whilst providing a decorative function to complement the domestic interior. It is also intended to send any format of printed material whether it is a book, photograph, diary or personal handwritten greeting.

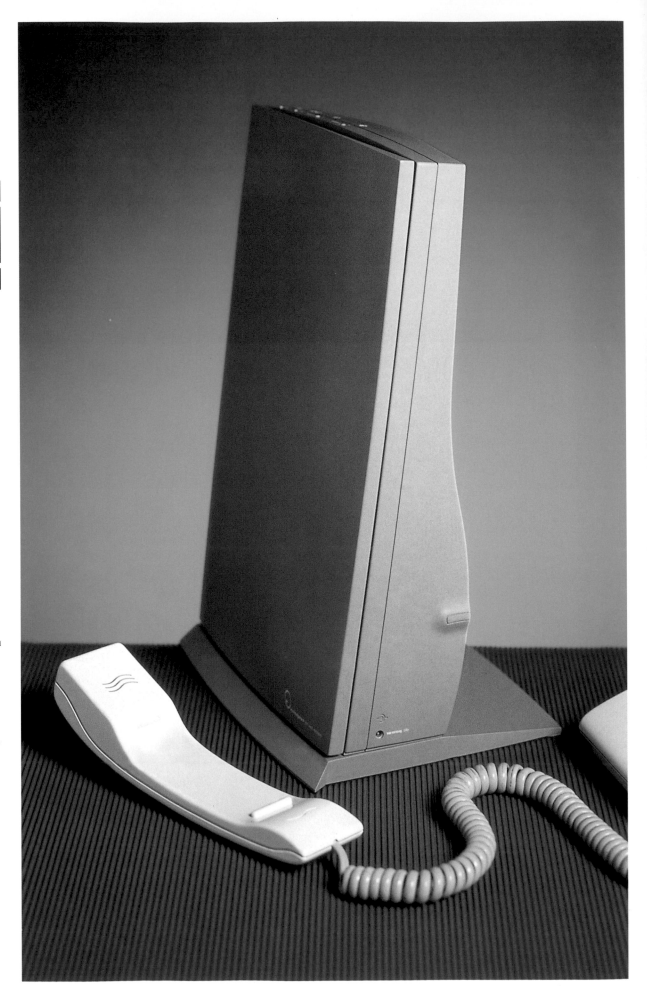

The Concept Microwave Oven asks one simple question – why do all microwave ovens look the same? The cylindrical format microwave provides a basis for unique styling, serving to differentiate the product in a generic market. The product's main innovation is a cylindrical door which revolves back into the casing. Accessibility is improved and the need for a door swinging out across the work surface in front of the oven – a hazardous and inconvenient feature of existing models – is eliminated. Because the cylindrical oven cavity follows the circular turntable, the overall dimensions are smaller.

The outer casing of the microwave is manufactured in plastic allowing big, soft forms to replace the hard unfriendly lines of folded sheet metal. Plastic provides the freedom to explore less technical and softer forms. Fixings are integral, making assembly quick and simple, also making disassembly for recycling straightforward. The keypad is laid out "intuitively" in a linear format so that programming starts on the left and progresses to the right. The concept heralds a clear move away from totally fitted kitchens toward the original and stylish free-standing appliances of the 1990s.

Concept Microwave Oven

DATE: 1996

DESIGNER: Frazer Designers, London, England

MATERIAL: moulded plastic

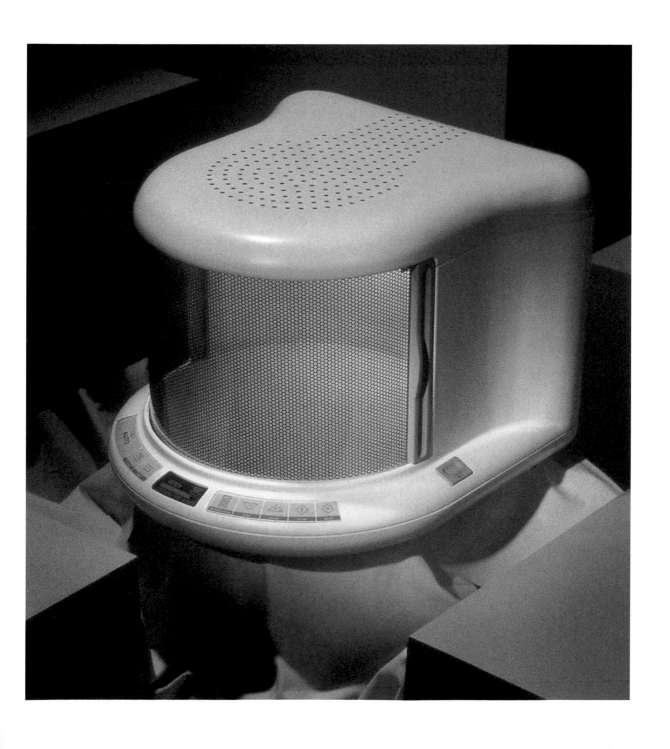

Crystal Mu MDV Information Display System

DATE: 1996

DESIGNERS: TKO –
Anne Gardener (born 1961)
and Andy Davey (born 1962)

MATERIAL: LCD, plastics
and metal

MANUFACTURER: NEC Design
Ltd, Japan

Designers TKO were commissioned to produce a new computer display unit that would feature NEC's state-of-the-art transparent liquid crystal display (LCD) technology, driven by a lap-top computer system. NEC envisages the unit being used in museums and galleries. Other applications include showrooms and shops, where the information screen can be used to inform consumers about products.

Crystal Mu can present 3-D objects and computer data at the same time. The window is a transparent LCD, on which graphics, text, multimedia or interactive programmes can be viewed in full colour. 3-D objects can be displayed behind the window and seen through it.

NEC and TKO wanted to create a new form, different from traditional products – one that could in itself be a decorative display object. The concept of "transparency" was central to blurring the boundaries between art and technology, between the appearance of physical objects and electronic data display.

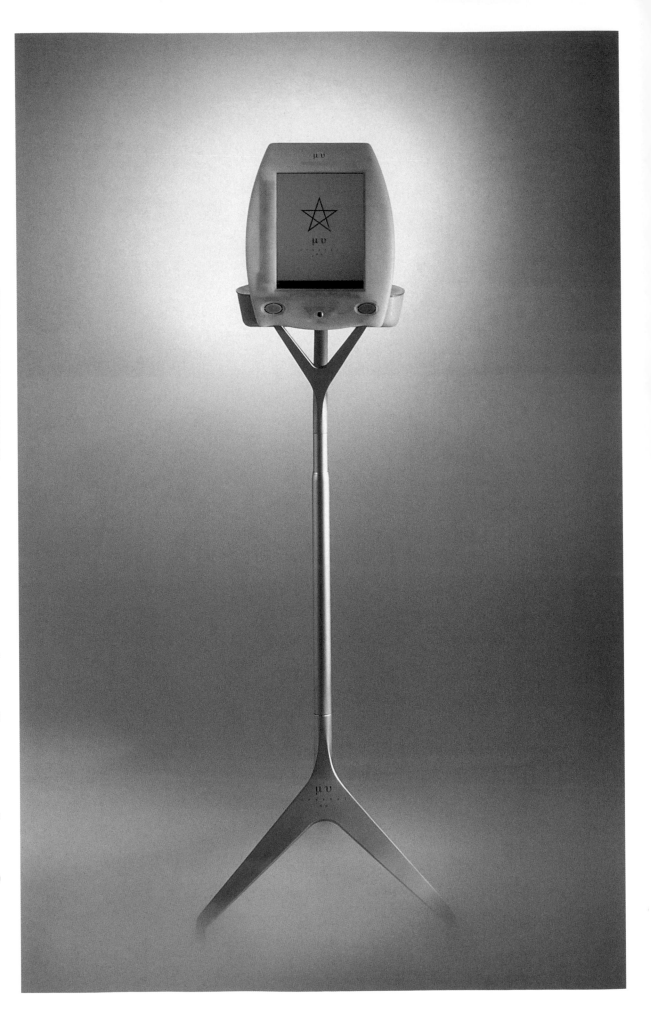

The TotalMedia computer is a concept which was never intended to go into production. It is the result of a collaborative exercise with Samsung to design a computer which would "push the limits of in-the-house multimedia technology". Samsung and IDEO's California office, led by Jochen Backs, designed TotalMedia as an easy-to-use multimedia device for the home and home-office environments. It is a hybrid of computer, audio system, television, video system and games unit. Current technologies have been integrated to incorporate an internal adjustable video camera and microphone. A remote control telephone device allows users to access the screen from a distance as well as receive or make telephone calls. IDEO is an international product design consultancy, founded in 1969, with offices in London, Boston, Chicago, San Francisco and Tokyo. The company now employs a team of three hundred people worldwide. Clients include Apple, Black and Decker, British Telecom, Hoover, Nike, Samsung and Whirlpool.

TotalMedia Multimedia Computer

DATE: 1997

DESIGNER: IDEO, San Francisco, California, USA

Vision Project

DATE: 1997

DESIGNER: IDEO, San Francisco, California, USA

IDEO is a product design consultancy which concentrates on the development of products and environments which employ future technologies, state-of-the-art computing and ergonomic design. The Refreshment Wall is part of the Vision Project undertaken by the San Francisco office of IDEO. It is a new look at reception areas and an example of a search for imaginative, ground-breaking and theoretical solutions to everyday consumer issues. The starting point for this exploration is an awareness that the transitional spaces that separate "outside" from "inside" are a critical part of the client/company relationship.

The design comprises three environments with IDEO's corporate wit very much in evidence. The Vision Project reception is an unmanned complex of built-in devices: the Information Wall, the Refreshment Wall and the Communication Wall. Visitors are free to choose their level of involvement. On a practical level, they can take a magazine from the interactive Information Wall, have a glass of water from the Refreshment Wall or ask advice from the Communication Wall. But it is the designer-meets-inventor aspect of the experience and the essential element of discovery and surprise that expresses the real IDEO personality and attitude to design. The Refreshment Wall presents a combined experience of ceremony, technology and function.

The early computer games were developed in the 1970s for television sets. They were basic and simple "bat and ball" games, but provided some, albeit limited, interaction with the viewer. Technology improved and almost inevitably the games dealt with increasingly graphic violence and popular themes for children. This, combined with the amount of time that children spent on the toys, attracted a great deal of concern from parent groups and educationalists. Nonetheless, via these experiences, children came

into contact with fantasy worlds of the future, in the same way that their parents and grandparents had read "Superman" comics and seen early television programmes featuring Batman and Robin. Final Fantasy is a Sony video game designed to be played on the PlayStation, which was launched in 1996.

The new technology of the PlayStation represents a further advance in the sophistication of the video-game experience for children. Cutting-edge technology maximizes the use of 3-D

graphics for game play, animation, vivid battle scenes, aerial views and hundreds of computer generated images. These games provide children with what Sony describe as "an immersive experience", and an opportunity to visit a variety of "unique worlds" created by one of the industry's most famous designers, Hironobu Sakaguchi, whose company, Squaresoft, is one of the world's premiere game developers.

When Final Fantasy was launched in Japan in 1997, it sold an incredible two million copies in the first three days.

Final Fantasy V11

DATE: 1997

DESIGNER: Hironbu Sakaguchi

MANUFACTURER: Sony Computer Entertainment Europe

Nurse Work Station

DATE: 1997

DESIGNER: Philips Future Project, Eindhoven, The Netherlands

This prototype product was developed as part of the Philips' "Vision of the Future" project. The broad aim of the project was to explore what people will perceive as useful, desirable and beneficial in the future – to create a technological roadmap of people's needs and aspirations and, in particular, of what qualities they would value in future products and services.

Within hospitals there is a real need for a variety of portable information devices, and this need will continue. These devices could be used by doctors and nurses on the move, but also in work areas where portable products could be recharged and used. The Work Station work tablets offer video communication and information access, replacing the clipboard charts used today.

They can bring together all patient information such as scans, notes and medication details, with up-to-the-minute monitoring. Hygienically enclosed in transparent plastic, they are touch screen displays which can be used either at the Work Station as a general information access point, or by the patient's bedside for monitoring, conferencing and reference during examination.

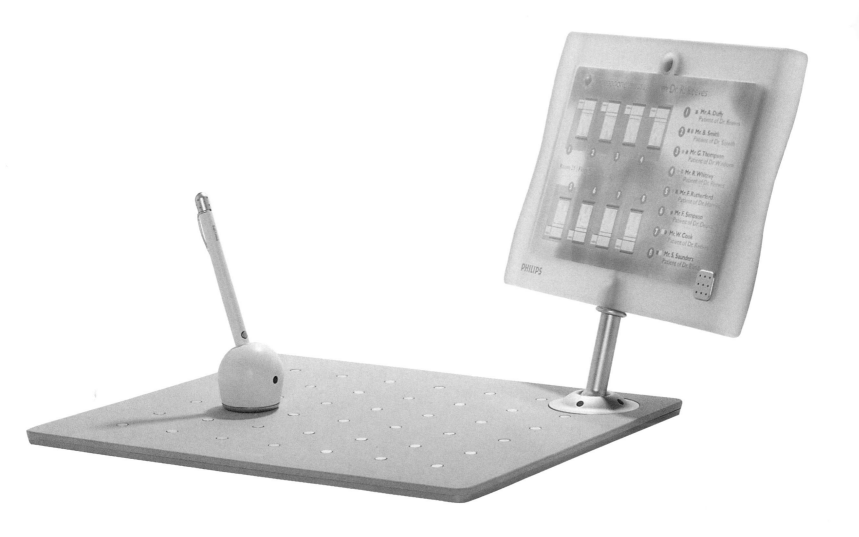

Tangerine chose to design a prototype digital camera that is simple to use and allows even the most inexperienced photographer to create successful pictures. The camera viewfinder is a large LCD display which allows the photographer to focus on the exact image without having to bring the camera up to the face. Once taken, the pictures are stored digitally on a removable cartridge which is sealed, making it impossible to expose photographs and unnecessary to process film in the traditional manner. The cartridge simply slides out of the camera and into the electronic photo album where it displays the slightly larger images on a flat screen. This provides the user with a medium through which to view photographs as well as offering an opportunity to manipulate images to optimum effect.

Blink Concept Digital Camera and Electronic Photo Album

DATE: 1997

DESIGNER: Tangerine – Martin Darbyshire and Peter Phillips

Philips Portable Scanner

DATE: 1997

DESIGNER: Philips,
Eindhoven, The Netherlands

This product was developed as a portable scanner and communication terminal for mobile medical staff. As vital diagnostic equipment such as magnetic resonance scanners becomes smaller, it will be made as portable units. This will allow diagnosis and treatment of patients in the field or in the ambulance, saving valuable time. This system provides a network link between ambulance paramedics or mobile hospital staff and their base, giving direct access to experts and medical data. The mobile units may also be able to treat and release some patients on the spot, relieving pressure on hospital facilities and cutting the costs of unnecessary hospitalization. "Mobile hospitals" such as these can also act as self-sufficient units travelling to remote places to provide assistance in emergencies or periodic screening facilities.

Technological research was carried out both within the Philips organization and with reference to global forecasting conducted in Japan and Germany. In order to gain an insight into how people will live in the near future, information was gathered from trend-forecasting institutes such as the Research Institute for Social Change (RISC). Philips identified what they called "sensitivities" – new attitudes, preoccupations and concerns within society.

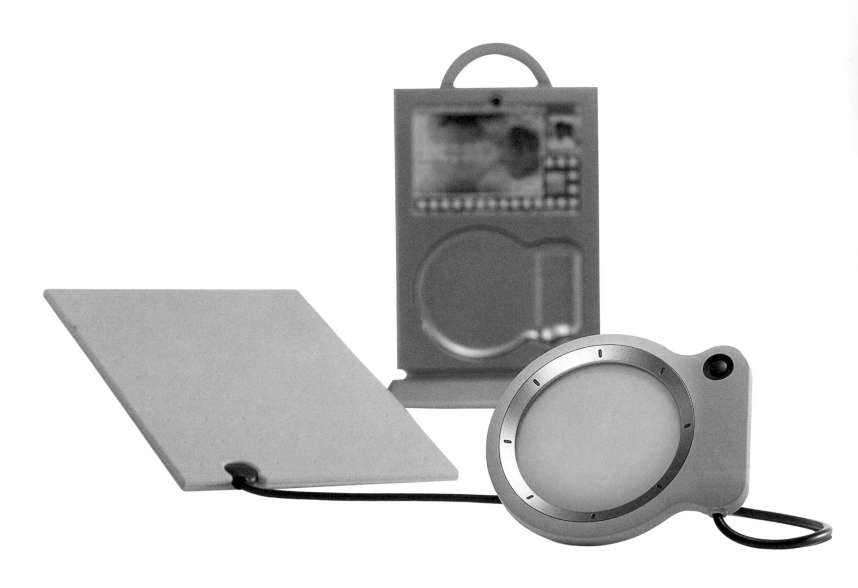

This prototype multimedia kiosk is an updated public telephone booth, allowing the user access to tele-services and videophone. Phone booths could easily be replaced with enhanced Multimedia Kiosks within the existing telephone cable infrastructure. The kiosks could be offered as a public service and will have a new identity, which would make them recognizable as a place for communication and information access. The concept allows the user to perform various tasks simultaneously in a private and secure environment. Time spent in the kiosk and services used would be charged and directly debited from users' bank accounts. Via a large-screen videophone it would be possible, for example, to book a holiday through a travel agent, arrange to make payments or obtain foreign currency from a bank, and make a doctor's appointment for injections. Relevant information could also be printed out and taken away.

Philips Multimedia Kiosk

DATE: 1997

DESIGNER: Philips, Eindhoven, The Netherlands

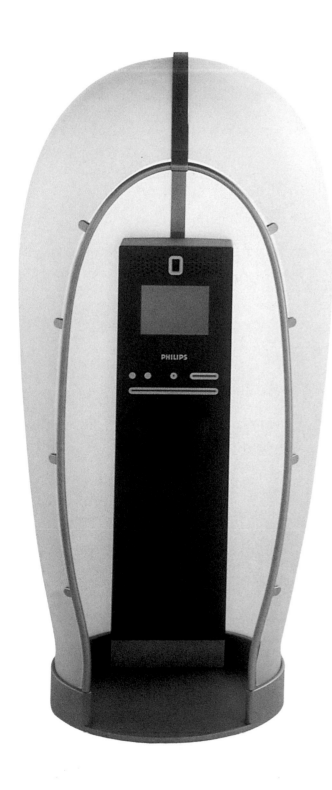

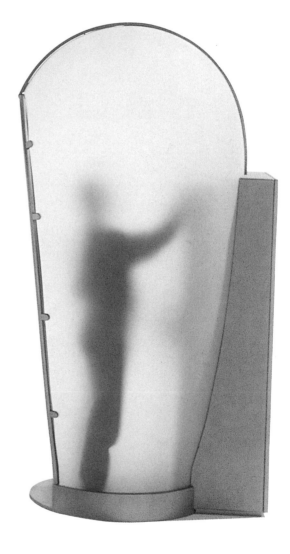

Millennium Tower

DATE: 1995–97

DESIGNER: Foster Associates, London, England

The proposed London Millennium Tower will provide offices, dealing floors, shops, restaurants, cafés, sky gardens and a public viewing gallery with panoramic views of London from its 300-metre (1,000-foot) glass atrium. Trafalgar House Property Ltd, which commissioned the project, submitted a planning application to the Corporation of London to construct the tower in 1996. Planning permission was originally rejected, so the architects started working on a revised scheme. Designed by Sir Norman Foster to be Europe's tallest building, the tower is a 95-storey building for the site of the Baltic Exchange, which was badly damaged by an IRA bomb in 1992. The Millennium Tower will be taller than the 250-metre (800-foot) main tower at Canary Wharf – at present the tallest building in Britain – and the 300-metre (984-foot) Commerz-Bank in Frankfurt.

The tower is a continuous series of curves in different kinds of glass which will respond to changing sunlight throughout the year, so giving an ever-changing appearance. The top divides into two elegant tail fins of different heights, ensuring that every view of the building is unique. Views through the glazed double-height lobby and an open plaza in front of the tower create a feeling of spaciousness and light at ground level. Energy efficiency strategies will ensure an ecologically sound building.

Eden

With funding from the UK Millennium Commission, the Eden project brings together a team of highly acclaimed architects, engineers, surveyors and project managers to create an environmental centre for the new millennium.

Based in Cornwall, the centre will consist of a group of individual glass houses called biomes. Each of these will recreate a different aspect of the Earth's environment: for example, the rainforest, the desert and the Mediterranean. The intention is that visitors will become immersed within these buildings, unaware of the external structure that encloses it. Each of the biomes will be built according to the necessities of the environment it represents and will optimize access to light, depending on the needs of the plants within.

The biomes will also be built to adapt to their particular climate; the framework is such that it can be shifted and changed as necessary. As such, the structure needs to be light and flexible. Supporting rods will be made from steel and the envelope will be constructed from a transparent film, underneath which will lie pneumatic pillows, with sensors that react to weather changes.

COMPLETION DATE: 2000

St Austell, Cornwall, England

ARCHITECT: Nicholas Grimshaw and Partners, London, England

The author would like to thank the following people for their help on this project: All the staff at the Design Museum especially Christine Atha, Gerard Ford, Karen Mann and Angela Summerfield. Special thanks are due to Elizabeth Darling for her help on the architecture and interiors section and Jeff Dale for his help on packaging.

picture credits

Architectural Association Picture Library/W. Arets 87, John Chilton 71, Lewis Gasson 79, Dennis Wheatley 60, FR Yerbury 57
AEG 217
The Advertising Archive Ltd. 14, 215, 232, 239, 318, 360
AKG London 80, 343/Erik Bohr 51, 55
Alessi s.p.a. 188, 190, 191
©1960 Allegra Fuller Snyder Courtesy, Buckminster Fuller Institute, Santa Barbara 382
Alvar Aalto-Museo 56, 176/M.Kapanen 175
Courtesy of Apple Computer Inc. 363
Ron Arad Associates Ltd. 137
Aram Designs Ltd, London 117
Arcaid 101/R Bryant 48, 49, 66, 68, 77, 92, 94, 96, 97, 100, 109, 111 /Michael 52/Dennis Gilbert 67/Ken Kirkwood 76, Ezra Stoller, Esto 61
Archigram Archives/©Peter Cook 1964, 378
Archivio Gio Ponti ©Salvatore Licitra 211, 222
Archivio Storico of Olivetti, Ivrea, Italy 323
Giorgio Armani 31
Artemide GB Ltd./Aldo Ballo 152
BFI 257, 372, 373
Bang and Olufsen Holding A/S, Denmark 346
Jonathan Barnbrook 277
Barneys, New York 95
Bauhaus-Archiv, Museum fur Gestaltung, Berlin/Gunter Lepkowski 146, 172
Tim Benton 54
Bibliotheque Nationale 375
Bite Communications Limited 364
Braun, Germany 214
British Architectural Library Photographs Collection, RIBA, London 176, 368, 369, 371
Neville Brody 271
Bulthaup BmbH & Co. 224
CDP, London 326
Canon 358, 359
Cassina S.p.A./Aldo Ballo 131, 132,

Andrea Zani 122
Catalytico 160, 161
Jean-Loup Charmet 78
Prunella Clough/Irongate Studios 53, 81
Branson Coates Architecture Ltd./Fred Rotkopf 98, Phil Sayer 385
©Nick Cobbing 73
Coop Himmelblau/Gerald Zugmann 70
Corbis UK Ltd. 43, 44, 45, 46, 47, 58, 62, 63, 64, 65, 69, 115/Bettmann 16, 50, 374/Bettmann/UPI 10, 25, 236, 383/Dave G. Houser 240/Museum of Flight 242
Department of Health 331
Design Council Archive, University of Brighton 180, 183, 216, 220, 379
Design Museum, London 6–7, 34, 42, 84, 118, 119, 130, 140, 150, 156-8, 162, 166, 170, 173, 181, 182, 187, 193, 194, 199, 202, 206, 213, 238, 252, 254, 263, 274, 314, 315, 321, 394, 395
Dissing & Weitling 88
Dyson Appliances Ltd. 200
E.T. Archive 212/Museum Fur Gestaltung, Zurich 316
©FSI GmbH, Fuse 276
Fiat Auto SpA 85
Flos Ltd. 153, 159
Sir Norman Foster and Partners Limited 134/Tom Miller/Hayes Davidson 396
Frazer Design Consultants Ltd. 387
GCI Group 219
Abram Games 260
Ken Garland 259
Gebruder Thonet GmbH 108, 113
Geffrye Museum 121
© J Paul Getty Trust & Richard Meier & Partners/Tom Bonner 72
©Peter Gidal 91
Ronald Grant Archive 241
The Graphic Unit 255
Kenneth Green Associates Ltd. 305
Sally & Richard Greenhill 27
Nicholas Grimshaw & Partners Ltd. 397
Haagen-Dazs/Bartle Bogle Hegarty/Jean Loup-Sieff, Maconochie Photography, London 329
Habitat UK Ltd. 89
Robert Harding Picture Library 59
Heal & Son Ltd. 110

Hollington 339
Hulton Getty 17, 18, 19, 21, 28, 376, 377
IBM UK Ltd. Photographic Services, Hursley 258, 362
Ideal-Standard Ltd. 223
IDEO SF 390
Imagination Ltd. 93
Imperial War Museum, London 320
Infoplan Limited, London 208
©Ilttala Glass, Finland 174
Jam, London 225
Ben Kelly 99
Keramiskt Centrum Gustavsberg Porslin 173
David King Collection 169
Photo: Nick Knight. Sarah Wingate for Yohji Yamamoto. Paris 1986, 30
Knoll, New York 139
The Kobal Collection 22/The Ladd Company, Warner Brothers 1982, 384
Levi Strauss/Bartle Bogle Hegarty (Artist:Nick Kamen/Rick Cunningham) 328
Leica 355
London Features International Ltd./Frank Griffin 32
London Transport Museum 233, 253, 317
McDonald's Restaurants Ltd. 301
Manx National Heritage 167, 250
Enzo Mari/Aldo Ballo 184
Michael Marriott 141
Mash & Air 103
David Mellor 189
Metadesign plus GmbH, Berlin 266
The Montreal Museum of Decorative Arts/Richard P. Goodbody 178/The Chateau Dufresne, The Liliane & David M.Stewart Collection 154, 155
Moto Cinelli 237
Photo: Musee des Arts Decoratifs, Paris, collection Albert Levy, tous droits reserve 82
© 1997 The Museum of Modern Art, New York 278/Le Corbusier, Grand Confort, petit modele armchair (1928) Gift of Phyllis B. Lambert 116
The National Trust Photographic Library/Dennis Gilbert 83
NEC Design Ltd. 388
Collection New York Central System Historical Society Inc., Ohio 231

Nikon UK Limited 356
Nokia 338
The Robert Opie Collection 262, 283-289, 291-295, 297, 298, 300, 302, 304, 307, 308, 310, 319
Osterreichisches Museum Fur Angewandte Kunst 168
N. du Pasquien 192
Pernette Perriand 114
Philips Corporate Design 163
Philips Electronics 392
Pictorial Press Ltd. 235/Rankin 38
Pira Ltd. 195
Politecnico di Torino, Sistema Bibliotecario, Biblioteca centrale di Architettura, archivio "Carlo Mollino" 86
Popperfoto 230/Reuters 39
Porsche design GMBH, Zell am See 201
Priestman Goode 221
Psion 365
Quadrant Picture Library 229/Paul Sherwood 243
Resure Har 209
Retna Pictures Ltd./Frank Micelotta 33
Rex Features Ltd. 37, 144, 380/Lynn Goldsmith/LGI 29, Sipa Press/Barthelemy 36, Sipa/Rolf Neeser 218
Rowenta 207
SCP Limited 138
Saatchi & Saatchi Advertising 327
Saba Personal Electronics 353
Sainsbury Centre for Visual Arts, UEA, Norwich 147
Samsung TotalMedia 389
Schopenhauer Gruppo Fontana Arte 135
Science & Society Picture Library 234, 361/Science Museum 198
Science Photo Library/Martin Bond 247/NASA 244, 245
©1993 Jon Sievert 265, 324
Dave Carr Smith 104
Sony UK Ltd. 348, 349, 350, 352
Sony Computer Entertainment Europe 391
Sotheby's 145, 171
Space Studio Ltd./Mario Testino 136
Specialized 246
Stedelijk Museum Amsterdam 112
Studio Castiglioni 151
SuperStock Ltd. 228
Svenskt Tenn AB Stockholm 186
TBWA Simons Palmer/Lewis

Mulatero 330/Tim O'Sullivan 333
TKO Product Design/Ian McKinnell 343
Tangerine Product Design Consultants 386, 393
Theatre Arts, Harry Ransom Humanities Research Center, The University of Texas at Austin/Mrs Edith L. Bel Geddes 205
Thirst 272
Topham Picturepoint 12, 13, 20, 23, 24, 26, 381
©Tupperware Corporation 185
Ty Nant Spring Water Ltd. 306
©Visual Arts Library/Stockholm, Modern. Tatlin, Monument a la 3e Internationale 370
Vitra Design Museum Collection, Weil am Rhein, Germany 120, 123-128, 133
Vitra Museum, Basle 149
Volkswagen 325
Jon Wealleans 90
The Trustees of The Wedgwood Museum Trust Limited 177, 179
Wolfgang Weingart 264
Paul Straker Welds 345
Westminster City Archives 15/Liberty's 11
Elizabeth Whiting & Associates 102
©Wolford Tights, photo: Helmut Newton 332
Zanotta spa/Marino Ramazzotti 129
Zanussi Ltd. 203

ADDITIONAL PHOTOGRAPHY
Matthew Ward

PICTURE RESEARCHER
Charlotte Bush

ADDITIONAL PICTURE RESEARCH
Elizabeth Walsh, Richard Philpott, Irene Lynch, Antony Moore